KILIMANJARO
& EAST AFRICA

A CLIMBING AND TREKKING GUIDE

KILIMANJARO
& EAST AFRICA

A CLIMBING AND TREKKING GUIDE

INCLUDES MOUNT KENYA, MOUNT MERU, AND THE RWENZORIS

CAMERON M. BURNS

SECOND EDITION

THE MOUNTAINEERS BOOKS

This book is dedicated to my two
wonderful sisters, Penelope and
Gillian, who never let me forget
I was their little brother.

THE MOUNTAINEERS BOOKS
is the nonprofit publishing arm of The Mountaineers Club,
an organization founded in 1906 and dedicated to the exploration,
preservation, and enjoyment of outdoor and wilderness areas.

1001 SW Klickitat Way, Suite 201, Seattle, WA 98134

First edition, 1998. Second edition, 2006.

Published simultaneously in Great Britain by Cordee, 3a DeMonfort Street, Leicester, England, Le1 7HD

Manufactured in the United States of America

Acquiring Editor: Deb Easter
Project Editor: Julie Van Pelt
Copy Editor: Julie Van Pelt
Cover and Book Design: The Mountaineers Books
Layout: Jennifer Shontz, Red Shoe Design
Cartographer: Kerry L. Burns and Jennifer Shontz
Photographer: Cameron M. Burns unless otherwise noted

Cover photographs: Front, *Elephants walking single file* © Tim Davis/Corbis;
  Back, *Ann Burns at Kibo Hut, Kilimanjaro, with Mawenzi behind*
Frontispiece: *Charlie French on Margherita, Mount Stanley, Rwenzoris, with
  Alexandra behind*

Library of Congress Cataloging-in-Publication Data
Burns, Cameron.
  Kilimanjaro and East Africa : a climbing and trekking guide / by Cameron—M.
Burns. —2nd ed.
    p.   cm.
  Rev. ed. of: Kilimanjaro & Mount Kenya. 1998.
  Includes bibliographical references and index.
  ISBN 0-89886-604-9 (pbk.)
1.—Mountaineering—Tanzania—Kilimanjaro, Mount—Guidebooks. 2.—Moun-
taineering—Africa, Eastern—Guidebooks. 3.—Hiking—Tanzania—Kilimanjaro,
Mount--Guidebooks. 4.—Hiking—Africa, Eastern—Guidebooks. 5.—Kilimanjaro,
Mount (Tanzania)—Guidebooks. 6.—Africa, East—Guidebooks.—I. Burns, Cameron.
Kilimanjaro & Mount Kenya. II. Title.
  GV199.44.T342K553 2006
  796.52'20967826—dc22

                                                              2006013161

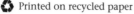 Printed on recycled paper

CONTENTS

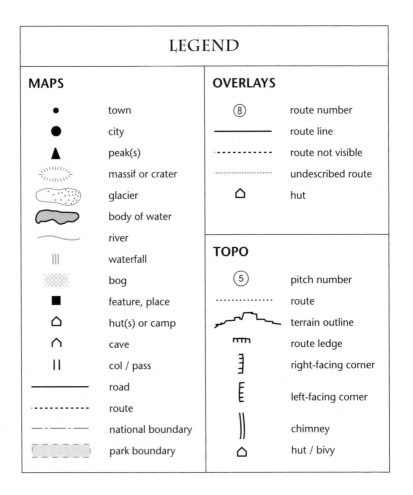

LEGEND

MAPS

- •   town
- ●   city
- ▲   peak(s)
-     massif or crater
-     glacier
-     body of water
-     river
-     waterfall
-     bog
- ■   feature, place
- ⌂   hut(s) or camp
- ⌃   cave
- || col / pass
- ——   road
- - - - - -   route
- — · — · —   national boundary
-     park boundary

OVERLAYS

- ⑧   route number
- ——   route line
- - - - - -   route not visible
- · · · · · · · ·   undescribed route
- ⌂   hut

TOPO

- ⑤   pitch number
- · · · · · · · ·   route
-     terrain outline
-     route ledge
-     right-facing corner
-     left-facing corner
-     chimney
- ⌂   hut / bivy

PREFACE TO THE SECOND EDITION

Finally, the second edition! It's been eight long years since I first pulled to-gether as much useful information as I could gather and compiled it for this book. Since that time, half a dozen new guidebooks to Kilimanjaro have been produced (see Appendix F), and the Internet has vastly changed how people gather information before a climbing trip.

But there are bigger changes afoot in East Africa as the region looks more and more to tourism and less to its traditional agricultural economy. Just driv-ing the road between Kilimanjaro International Airport and Moshi during a recent trip to northern Tanzania, I was astonished at the amount of building that has taken place. I was also surprised at how popular slugging up Kili has become. A decade ago there were about 14,000 people per year doing it; now, that number is up to (nearly) 30,000 a year.[1]

The worst things to see were the changes brought about by global warm-ing. Comparing my 1997 and 2005 photos of Kili's glaciers showed that they had retreated considerably. Sadly, it's the airplanes and cars we use to get to the mountain that cause the greatest damage, and even when we're on it, we burn fossil fuels in the now-required stoves, further warming the planet.[2] This guidebook has changed substantially since the first modest edition. First of all, it's got a new title reflecting the addition of new content (I've added a chapter on the three highest summits of the Rwenzoris—Ptolemy's exotic "Mountains of the Moon"—as well as Mount Meru, Kili's 4,566-meter [14,976-foot] little sister). Second, the references and suggestions on where to get additional information have been greatly expanded, helped by the fact that these days everything has a website URL (uniform resource locator) attached to it.

And thirdly, I've used endnotes to accommodate commentary about issues discussed in the text. I've always found authors' personal impressions and ideas useful, and sometimes—in the name of objectivity and clarity—editors remove such notation. My notes are included simply to give you a better idea of how to prepare, what to expect, and why I'm suggesting something in the main text. And yes, they are often opinions (which are part of every book).

Also, for future editions I plan on relying more on you, the reader, to help keep the material up to date, so I've included my email address (*mountaincam@yahoo.com*). You can also contact me via the publisher, whose address is listed at the back of the book. All comments, criticisms, and suggestions are welcome.

Cam Burns, June 2006

Stream below the Machame Huts, Machame Route, Kilimanjaro

INTRODUCTION

Africa is a land of contrasts.

It's a land where some of the driest deserts butt up against the wettest jungles; a place where the strongest creatures in the world can be seen tearing the flesh off the most beautiful; and a continent where the imported European view of things rubs hard up against the indigenous understanding of the world.

Similarly, Kilimanjaro, the highest peak on the African continent, is a mountain of contrasts.

Few peaks on the planet have the distinction of being a continental high point and an exotic destination: Kilimanjaro is both. At 5,895 meters (19,341 feet), Kilimanjaro is a must-climb on every world adventurer's list of mountaineering objectives, as well as a colorful backdrop for dozens of famous literary works and films.

Perhaps more than anything, Kilimanjaro—and its sister peak, Mount Kenya—are contrasts in complexity.

From a distance, Kilimanjaro, and her little sister, Mount Meru, look like little more than big rounded hills, large volcanic cones sawed off at the stump and left with few features of interest to technical climbers. Likewise, from many vantage points, Mount Kenya looks like a single lopsided spire sitting above the Kenyan jungle. And, at first blush, the Rwenzoris look like one long geographically-straightforward ridge.

Closer examination reveals that both Kili and Mount Kenya are not single-summited mountains, but multispired massifs. Indeed, rising thousands of meters above the surrounding jungles and plains, both mountains boast their own ecosystems and create their own weather.

Specifically, Kilimanjaro is dominated by two major summits, Kibo (5,895 meters/19,341 feet) and Mawenzi (5,149 meters/16,893 feet), which are separated by an 11-kilometer-wide saddle. The rounded snow-covered summit of Kibo contrasts easily with the craggy rock spire of Mawenzi. And while many sides of the mountain offer gentle slopes to wander up, massive cliff bands like the fabulous Breach Wall present technical climbers with alpine testpieces. Some climbing routes on Kilimanjaro are mere strolls at high altitude. Others are long, serious, and very difficult undertakings, as challenging as anything in the world and requiring all a mountaineer's skill.

Like Kilimanjaro, the lopsided spire of Mount Kenya is actually two major summits—the higher, more westerly summit of Batian (5,199 meters/17,058 feet) and the only slightly lower Nelion (5,188 meters/17,022 feet)—separated by a gap of 140 meters. There are also numerous other spires on the Mount Kenya massif, each with its own distinct characteristics.

Mount Meru (4,566 meters/14,976 feet), Kilimanjaro's generally-overlooked little neighbor, in Arusha National Park, is also a classic volcano, perhaps more volcano-like than Kilimanjaro and Mount Kenya themselves. While most people who climb Kili don't visit Meru, climbing Meru is one of the most exciting mountain trips you can ever experience—you walk through open forest whose diverse fauna includes baboons, buffaloes, elephants, hyenas, and other wildlife.

The Rwenzoris, meanwhile, are quite unlike the solitary volcanic masses of Kilimanjaro and Mounts Meru and Kenya. They're what geologists refer to as a block-fault range, a real mountain range, with dozens of high peaks, big walls, and fingerlike spires. The three highest peaks in the Rwenzoris—Mounts Stanley, Speke, and Baker—are like Kilimanjaro and Mount Kenya in that they boast multiple summits. Their high points are, respectively, Margherita (5,109 meters/16,763 feet) on Stanley, the third-highest mountain massif (though not the third-highest summit) in East Africa; Vittorio Emanuele (4,890 meters/16,039 feet) on Speke; and Edward (4,843 meters/15,885 feet) on Baker.

There are some sweeping generalizations about East Africa's mountains that aren't wholly correct. First, when people refer to Kilimanjaro as a "walk-up," they're talking about the trekking routes on the mountain. There are many difficult technical rock and ice climbs, as well as scrambles, on Kili, and likely the hardest alpine route in all Africa, the Breach Wall, climbed in 1978 by Reinhold Messner.[3] Likewise, there are easy trekking routes on Mount Kenya's third-highest summit (Point Lenana), as well as several routes that go to its highest points (Batian and Nelion) that require only minimal rock-climbing skills. Indeed, there are over a hundred documented routes of all difficulties on both Kilimanjaro and Mount Kenya.

Meanwhile, the standard route on Mount Meru, described in this book, is a straightforward hike (what climbers would refer to as a Class 2 route)—yet it's a grueling one.[4]

Likewise, the Rwenzoris offer the entire range of climbing experiences. Although you might read elsewhere that technical mountaineering skills are required, the Rwenzoris' three high points described herein require only the most minimal glacier travel skills, and every year trekkers with no prior experience with glacier travel don crampons and easily tromp to the summits of Mounts Stanley, Speke, and Baker.[5] There are also some outstanding, and harder, technical climbs as well.

This book covers all the major forest and moorland routes that lead to the main peaks on Kilimanjaro and Mount Kenya. Specifically, I describe the most popular routes to the summits of Kibo and Mawenzi on Kilimanjaro, and to Batian, Nelion, Point Lenana, and other summits on Mount Kenya.

The standard trekking circuit around the high peaks of the Rwenzoris, as well as summit climbs, is described, as is the standard trekking route up Mount Meru. Greatest attention is given to the most popular routes, with decreasing amounts of information on less popular, more obscure ones. Not every route on these mountains is covered; some are rarely climbed and are of little interest to the majority of visiting climbers and/or trekkers.

A selection of maps shows the areas around Kilimanjaro, Mount Meru, Mount Kenya, and the main Rwenzori peaks, as well as the forest and moorland approach routes to the main peaks. Technical mountaineering routes are covered both in verbal descriptions and with photographs and route overlays.

Because my aim is to help North American and European mountaineers understand the various requirements for entering Tanzania, Kenya, and Uganda, as well as those of the national parks in which the mountains lie, I have also included preliminary chapters on these topics. And since the crux of climbing in East Africa is getting to the mountains and dealing with everyday East African problems, there are sections on trip planning, transportation (to and within East Africa), visa requirements, currency, health, and details important to the traveler. Useful addresses, a glossary of local languages, a suggested reading list, and other resources are given in appendixes at the end of the book.

Finally, this book is an attempt to persuade you, the visiting mountaineer, to both keep these popular mountains clean and to consider the incredible destruction being wrought by our modern, fossil-fueled ways. The high points of continents—the "seven summits," as they're commonly known—are being hammered. Trash is commonplace on all these peaks, local economies have been skewed (a simultaneously good and bad thing), and the ice caps are disappearing. Kilimanjaro already has a limit of sixty nonresident visitors per day on the Marangu Route. The more garbage and human waste that park rangers have to pick up after us, the lower the quotas are likely to be.

East Africa's peaks are wild mountains, in a beautiful part of the world. And they all offer a wide range of climbing experiences. Better yet, by going to East Africa you get to meet some of the world's friendliest people, experience fascinating cultures, travel through striking landscapes, and come face to face with some of the world's grandest creatures. Go, enjoy, climb, and learn what it's like to be in awe.

A NOTE ABOUT SAFETY

Safety is an important concern in all outdoor activities. No guidebook can alert you to every hazard or anticipate the limitations of every reader. Therefore, the descriptions of roads, trails, routes, and natural features in this book are not representations that a particular place or excursion will be safe for your party. When you follow any of the routes described in this book, you assume responsibility for your own safety. Under normal conditions, such excursions require the usual attention to traffic, road and trail conditions, weather, terrain, the capabilities of your party, and other factors. Keeping informed on current conditions and exercising common sense are the keys to a safe, enjoyable outing.

Political conditions may add to the risks of travel in East Africa in ways that this book cannot predict. When you travel, you assume this risk, and should keep informed of political developments that may make safe travel difficult or impossible.

The Mountaineers Books

On the Umbwe Route with Kibo behind

Chapter 1

HISTORY

...a vast mountain of gold and silver in the far interior, the approach to which was guarded by evil spirits.
— Johann Rebmann, after sighting Kilimanjaro on May 11, 1848

For more than two thousand years, the mountains (and lakes and rivers) of East Africa were a great big puzzle that geographers struggled to understand.

In the ancient world, centered around Europe and North Africa's "inland sea" (the Mediterranean[6]) sailors, traders, and scholars were obviously well aware of the Nile's existence, but its massive output of freshwater originating in the desert was a paradox. Where did it come from? Why was it so big? And if there was that much water coming from its source, what the heck else was up there?

According to many accounts, the first geographer to assemble a notion of mountains as the river's source was the Greek-born Claudius Ptolemy (ca. AD 90–168) of Alexandria, who in about AD 150 wrote of the "Mountains of the Moon," or Lunae Montes in his *Guide to Geography*. But Ptolemy had many predecessors, starting with Aeschylus, who in 500 BC wrote of "Egypt nurtured by the snows." Aeschylus was followed by Heredotus,[7] who in 440 BC described a spring fed by the waters of a bottomless lake located between two steep peaks, Crophi and Mophi, and then by Aristotle, who in 350 BC wrote of a "Silver Mountain" as the source of the Nile.[8] Where the ancients got their information is also speculation, but East Africa has been investigated from Egypt and sailed past by Arab and Indian traders for millennia, so it's little surprise the region's high mountains were reported by these early travelers.

According to some historians, Ptolemy based much of his geographical work on that of the Greek geographer Eratosthenes (276 BC–194 BC) and Marinus of Tyre (ca. AD 70–130).[9] Both men were "mathematical" geographers, meaning that they assigned latitudes and longitudes to locations.[10] One of the more remarkable tales Marinus recorded was a circa AD 110 journey of a Greek merchant, Diogenes, who reportedly traveled inland from the East African coast for 25 days to the "two great lakes and the snowy range of mountains where the Nile draws its twin sources."

Although many historical accounts of East Africa's tall mountains claim that between the time of the ancients and the nineteenth century nothing was written about these mountains, there are numerous references to high peaks throughout this long period.

In the ninth and tenth centuries, respectively, references to high peaks were contained in the writings of the geographer and traveler Ibn Khordadbeh and in the reports of Al-Masudi (ca. 888–957).[11]

In 953, Captain Buzurg ibn Shahriyar of Ramhormuz, a shipmaster from the Persian province of Khuzistan, compiled the stories and accounts of Arab sailors in *Agaib al Hind* (*Book of the Wonders of India*).[12] In it, there is a reference to what historians believe is Kilimanjaro; more significantly, we get one of the first references to Kilimanjaro's specific topography. In a story by Jazid of Oman, a Zeng boat captain, Jazid describes two tall mountains in Zanj, a coastal region of Kenya north of Zanzibar: "I have seen two great mountains in that country, and between them is a valley which has traces of fire, calcined bones and burnt skins."

In the mid-fourteenth century the Syrian geographer Abulfida mentions the Mountains of the Moon in his description of Melinde, quoted by Kilimanjaro historian Harald Lange: "To the west of Melinde extends a large bay, into which flows a river from the Mountains of the Moon." Lange asserts that Abulfida is referring to the Tana River and that the mountains he describes are surely the peaks of Mount Kenya. Moreover, Lange notes, Abulfida is obviously confused by what appears as snow at the equator when the Syrian geographer mentions, "in his Tadkira, Al-Nasir of Tus says that some people have seen the Mountain of the Moon from afar, and it was white with the snow that lay upon it...when at eleven degrees latitude north, such a heat already prevails as that in Aden, how can there be mountains with snow at eleven degrees south?"[13]

In 1519 the Spanish scholar Fernandez de Encisco, wrote, "West of [Mombasa] stands the Ethiopian Mountain Olympus, which is very high, and beyond it are the Mountains of the Moon, which are the sources of the Nile."[14]

Were the mountains feeding the great river the same peaks that the Greek geographers and Arab traders knew so well? Or were the high peaks along the eastern edge of the continent unrelated to the river, which was fed by some other water source?

"There has been much dispute among geographers as to whether these early references applied to the Rwenzoris, the Virunga Mountains, the country of Banyamwenzi [the "people of the moon"], Mount Kenya and Kilimanjaro, or Ethiopia," wrote British mountaineers Henry Osmaston and David Pasteur in their 1972 guidebook to the Rwenzoris.

Reports of tall mountains west of Mombasa continued to be made throughout the first millennium, then well into the early part of the second, most of them originating with Arab colonists and traders—but these too were likely based, at least in part, on Ptolemy's *Geographica*.

While there are many references to East Africa's high peaks throughout history, there is little recorded exploration, which occurred, for the most part, in the nineteenth century. Between the 1830s and the end of the nineteenth century, a procession of British and German missionaries, explorers, and empire builders plied the savanna between the coast and the Rift Valley in search of souls to convert, the Nile's headwaters, and new territories to call their own.

The references to the moon for all East African mountains—and Mountains of the Moon as the alternate name for the Rwenzoris—might seem puzzling until you consider the origin of all this moon-influenced nomenclature. Ptolemy used the term Lunae Montes back in AD 150, but where did he get it?

Filippo de Filippi, chronicler of the Duke of Abruzzi's 1906 expedition to the Rwenzoris, suggests the title came from the Africans themselves. In *Rwenzori*, de Filippi describes the activities of the Austrian explorer Oscar Baumann in the 1890s. Baumann was likely the first European to explore the Kagera, a river thought to be the biggest watercourse feeding Lake Victoria. It flowed from the mountains of *Missossi ya Mwesi*, which are situated "to the northeast of Lake Tanganyika."

"These, he [Baumann] considered to be the mountains mentioned by Ptolemy," de Filippi wrote. "*Missossi ya Mwesi* does, as a matter of fact, mean literally Mountains of the Moon. The surrounding country is called *Charo cha Mwesi*, which means 'Land of the Moon.' At the same time, the Kagera, which had been called by Henry Morton Stanley [the explorer] the Alexandra Nile, may certainly be counted as the southernmost and one of the principal sources of the Eastern Nile." Certainly, it's possible that a simple historical hiccough caused the Rwenzoris—not other ranges or regions—to get the colorful appellation.

The mysterious mountains of East Africa—and the existence of snow near the equator—were a point of curiosity and controversy for years, but in the nineteenth century, European explorers began to make sense of this vast and varied wilderness.

KILIMANJARO

The mid-nineteenth century saw exploration of East Africa by European colonial powers eager for raw materials, agricultural lands, and slaves. While many sought wealth, a few—like London-based Church Missionary Society representatives Johann Rebmann and Dr. Ludwig Krapf—sought souls in need of saving.

In 1846, Rebmann and Krapf landed on the east coast of Africa and established a mission near Mombasa, where they heard tales of an enormous mountain lying in the interior. On May 11, 1848, while on a journey inland, Rebmann caught sight of Kilimanjaro from a point about a day's travel from Taveta. In his diary he wrote:

> This morning, at ten o'clock, we obtained a clearer view of the mountains of Jagga, the summit of one of which was covered by what looked like a beautiful white cloud. When I inquired as to the dazzling whiteness, the guide merely called it "cold," and at once I knew it could be neither more nor less than snow.... I immediately understood how to interpret the marvelous tales Dr. Krapf and I had heard at the coast, of a vast mountain of gold and silver in the far interior, the approach to which was guarded by evil spirits.

On a second expedition in November, Rebmann reached the village of Majamé (Machame), a point closer to Kilimanjaro than any other European had ever traveled, and was able to accurately describe the shape of the enormous mountain:

> There are two main peaks, which arise from a common base measuring some twenty-five miles long by as many broad. They are separated by a saddle-shaped depression, running east and west for a distance of about eight or ten miles. The eastern peak is the lower of the two, and is conical in shape.

The western and higher presents the appearance of a magnificent dome, and is covered with snow throughout the year, unlike its eastern neighbor which loses its snowy mantle during the hot season. By the Swahili at the coast, the mountain is known as Kilimanjaro (Mountain of Greatness) but the Wa-Jagga call it Kibo, from the snow with which it is perpetually capped.

On a third expedition in early 1849, Rebmann again reached Majamé and, venturing toward Kilimanjaro, got "so close to the snowline that, supposing no impassable abyss to intervene, I could have reached it in three or four hours." Unfortunately he was too ill to continue the ascent.

In November 1849, Krapf made his own inland expedition. First visiting the Ukamba district, east of Kilimanjaro, he obtained "a magnificent view of the snow-mountain Kilimanjaro in Jagga, which loomed up from behind the ranges of Ndara and Bura.... Even at this distance I could make out that the white substance crowning the summit was certainly snow." Krapf estimated Kilimanjaro's height at 3,810 meters (12,500 feet). He then continued on to Kitui, in what is today central Kenya, to make the first definitive recorded sighting of Mount Kenya by a European.

The Great Debate

"The reality of snow on these twin equatorial mountains, Kilimanjaro and Mount Kenya, was not at first accepted in London, and learned discussions took place on the subject before the Royal Geographical Society," wrote Halford John Mackinder, the explorer to make the first ascent of Mount Kenya.[15] The argument was not over whether snow-clad peaks could exist at the equator, as scholars were already well aware of the high peaks of the Andes. The issue was whether these particular mountains in East Africa were tall enough to have snow.

In August 1861, German explorer Baron Karl Von der Decken and English geologist R. Thornton attempted to climb Kilimanjaro and spent 3 days trying to penetrate the forest zone on the mountain's lower slopes. They were eventually forced back by bad weather, having reached only 2,500 meters.

In 1862, Von der Decken returned with Dr. Otto Kersten. Starting from Moji (Moshi) in December, the two became the first white men to climb beyond the forest zone, reaching a height of 4,300 meters. "During the night it snowed heavily," Von der Decken recorded in his journal, "and next morning the ground lay white all around us."

Von der Decken and Kersten estimated the height of Kibo at 5,700 meters (18,680 feet), its snow line at 4,998 meters, and its vegetation line at 3,657 meters. They estimated Mawenzi at a height of 4,953 meters (16,250 feet). Their findings ended, for the most part, the intense debate.

First Attempts

The flood of Kilimanjaro exploration and first-ascent attempts that followed Von der Decken and Kersten came partially as a result of the struggle between the East African colonial powers to turn the findings of the continent's explorers into material gain.

By the early 1880s, a railroad was under construction across the central portion of Tanzania from Dar es Salaam to Ujiji on Lake Tanganyika, and to travelers on the completed portions of this line, Kilimanjaro had become a familiar sight to the north.

Lying close to the coast and to overland routes to Lake Tanganyika, Kilimanjaro saw several attempts at ascent in the early 1880s, mostly by missionaries and government officials.

By the late 1880s, ascents to the saddle between Kibo and Mawenzi were commonplace, and the village of Marangu was generally accepted as the best starting place for attempts on Kilimanjaro, as it was the highest point on the mountain that could easily be reached.

First Ascent: Hans Meyer

Following advice from the Austro-Hungarian team of Count Samuel Teleki and Lieutenant Ludwig von Holnel, who had reached 4,815 meters on the mountain, Hans Meyer, a leading German geographer of the day, and his companion, Herr von Eberstein, began an ascent of Kilimanjaro in August 1887. Climbing to the Saddle, they reached an altitude of 5,486 meters on Kibo, probably the highest any European had ascended to date. "Here, further progress was checked by the precipitous face of the ice cap, and we were compelled to turn back," Meyer later wrote.[16]

In the fall of 1888, Otto Ehlers, a representative of the German East Africa Company, attempted the peak with a Dr. Abbott, an American naturalist. Ehlers would be the first European to assert he had reached Kibo's summit—a claim he later rescinded. After pitching camp at 2,987 meters, Ehlers set off alone for Mawenzi, reaching an altitude of 4,998 meters. He and Abbott then shifted camp to the foot of Kibo. The next morning they began an ascent of Kibo, but at around 5,181 meters, Abbott became ill and returned to camp.

At around 10:00 AM, Ehlers reached "the wall of ice which encircles the entire summit." After a few more hours spent searching for a way through the ice, Ehlers wrote, he "succeeded in reaching the northwestern side of the summit and gained a tolerably extensive view of the surroundings."

Ehlers's ascent was widely questioned, and he later admitted that there was a point on the crater rim south of the spot he reached that appeared to be 60 meters higher, and that he had probably been mistaken that the point he had reached was the summit.

With Europeans wandering all over Kilimanjaro, Meyer knew the prize of the first ascent wouldn't last long, and in the northern summer of 1889, he put together a second expedition to Kilimanjaro with Ludwig Purtscheller. From Mombasa, the expedition—which included sixty-five porters—traveled to Marangu. There, Meyer assembled a smaller team of porters that would attempt the mountain and also made arrangements for an intermediate camp between Marangu and the saddle area, to be restocked with food by Marangu porters every few days.

Meyer's team departed Marangu on September 28 with nine porters, two headmen, two guides, and several cooks. On October 2, after several days' travel through the forest, they reached 4,328 meters, camping about 2.4 kilometers from the foot of Kibo. As they examined the peak that evening, Meyer and Purtscheller decided to attempt a route that climbed a prominent ravine, then ascended the Ratzel Glacier.

Leaving camp at 2:30 AM, they toiled for several hours on the gravelly lower slopes of Kibo and by 7:00 AM reached an altitude of 4,998 meters and "the first flakes of snow."

"Every ten minutes we had to pause a few seconds to give heart and lungs a rest, for we were now far above the height of Mount Blanc," Meyer later wrote, "and the increasing rarity of the atmosphere made itself more and more painfully felt."

At the base of the Ratzel Glacier, Purtscheller donned his crampons. Meyer, who had none, had to trust his hobnailed boots. Chopping steps up the glacier was a formidable task, and every step took "some twenty strokes of the axe."

In all, they took about 3 hours to climb the glacier and by 2:00 PM had reached the crater rim. "A few more steps in eager anticipation and the secret of Kibo lay unveiled before us—at our feet yawned a gigantic crater, with precipitous walls, occupying the entire summit of the mountain," Meyer wrote.

They decided against continuing on to the true summit, which appeared to be at least an hour and a half away, and descended the route by which they had come, rechopping steps in the glacier and struggling into camp just before 7:00 PM.

The next day, Meyer moved camp closer to the base of Kibo, and after a night's rest he and Purtscheller began another ascent on October 5. "At a quarter to nine, we reached our old point on the crater rim at an altitude of 19,200 feet [5,852 meters]," he wrote, "but almost immediately pushed on again, all eager to reach our little outstanding pinnacle on the southern side, on which our hearts were set."

The pair walked around the crater rim, scaling three small "rocky pinnacles" in a "leisurely and systematic fashion" before Meyer took an aneroid reading and found the central pinnacle "attained an altitude of 19,700 feet [6,004 meters], overtopping the others by some forty or fifty feet." The happy climbers congratulated each other, and Meyer planted a small German flag in the volcanic debris of Kibo's summit, which they named Kaiser Wilhelm Spitze (Kaiser Wilhelm Peak) in honor of their king.

They made several sketches of the crater, then returned by way of the Ratzel Glacier to their high camp.

On October 13, Meyer and Purtscheller made a bold attempt to climb Mawenzi (also known then as Kibwezi) but were defeated by loose rock and difficult routefinding. On October 15, they attempted the mountain again but accidentally climbed Klute Peak (5,095 meters / 16,716 feet), one of Mawenzi's many subsidiary summits. On October 21, they made a third attempt on Mawenzi but were again thwarted in reaching the main summit (5,149 meters / 16,893 feet).

The remainder of Meyer's now famous "ten days above fifteen thousand feet"— the title of a chapter in his book describing the first ascent of Kilimanjaro—were spent attempting Kibo from the north. Several more attempts resulted in their reaching Kibo's crater, which they wandered around inside, but they did not, however, regain the summit.

Meyer's original name for the highest point of Kibo, Kaiser Wilhelm Spitze, still appears on some maps of Kilimanjaro.

Kilimanjaro, 1890–1970s
It was a decade before Kibo was climbed again. In 1898, Meyer returned with E. Platz and climbed Kibo to the crater rim. In October of the same year, Captain Johannes Korner climbed a route close to today's Normal Route, as far as Gillman's Point. Like many people who made ascents to the crater rim in the following years, Korner did not continue on to the true summit.

In July 1909, a surveyor, M. Lange, and his assistant, a man named Weigele, climbed the Normal Route to the crater rim via Johannes Notch, then continued to the summit of Kibo, making what is generally accepted as the second ascent of the mountain and the first ascent of the Normal Route.

In 1912, the summit of Mawenzi was claimed for the first time—like Kibo, by German climbers. On June 29, Fritz Klute and Edward Oehler made the first ascent of Hans Meyer Peak (5,149 meters/16,893 feet), the tallest point on Mawenzi. They then climbed Kibo from the west, via the Upper Drygalski Glacier, and descended via the Great Western Arch (the Western Breach Route).

Klute and Oehler were followed a few months later by German climbers Walter Furtwangler and Ziegfried Koenig, who reached the summit of Kibo (on skis) for its fourth ascent, and that of Hans Meyer Peak for Mawenzi's second ascent. Two more ascents of Kibo were made before World War I, as well as the first ascent of Gillman's Point by a woman, Frau von Ruckteschell, a German.

After World War I, Mawenzi became a focus for many climbers, mostly because so little was known about the impressive peak.

In 1924, George Londt of the Mountain Club of South Africa and a local guide named Offoro attempted to climb Hans Meyer Peak but miscalculated and made the first ascent of South Peak (4,958 meters/16,266 feet; now Londt Peak).

On July 28, 1927, English climbers William West, Otho Brown, and the first woman to climb Mawenzi, Sheila MacDonald, made the third ascent of Hans Meyer Peak, by a variation of the original route. A few days later, MacDonald went on to become the first woman to climb Kibo to Kaiser Wilhelm Spitze.

Also of note during these early years was an ascent of Mawenzi in March 1930 by the talented British team of Eric Shipton and Bill Tilman. After climbing Kibo, the pair made an ascent of a couloir running northwest of the west face, which Shipton correctly believed to be the Oehler Gully. At the top of the gully, Shipton and Tilman went left, instead of right, and climbed Nordecke Peak (5,140 meters/16,863 feet). "I think the mistake gave us a first ascent," Shipton later wrote. They then descended and climbed Hans Meyer Peak.

In 1932, Kibo Hut was built, and hotels in Marangu began operating guided ascents of Kilimanjaro for tourists.

By the early 1960s, climbing Kilimanjaro had become a "popular busi-ness...one must expect competition from all ages and sexes, from middle aged ladies to 12-year-old boys," observed F. R. Brooke in the *Alpine Journal*. The journal also recorded that in 1959 more than seven hundred people attempted Kilimanjaro, but only about half that number reached Gillman's Point.

The first half of the twentieth century also saw the beginning of explora-tion of the southern glaciers, with the first ascent of the Decken Glacier by E. Eisenmann and T. Schnackig on January 12, 1938. First ascents of the Kersten and Heim Glaciers followed in the 1950s.

The 1970s saw, perhaps, the greatest number of new routes established in Kilimanjaro's history, when climbers like Iain Allan, Ian Howell, Mark Savage, Bill O'Connor, John Cleare, Dave Cheesmond, and John Temple explored new lines and variations on the existing glacier routes.

By the late 1970s, the one prize that still awaited climbers was the Breach Wall, a 1,400-meter precipice containing two steep glaciers separated by hun-dreds of meters of rock and vertical ice. In 1977 and 1978, two teams—one British, the other American—attempted the wall unsuccessfully.

In January 1978, Reinhold Messner and Konrad Renzler attempted "the Breach," and, following two prominent icefalls directly up the wall, climbed the route in an astonishing 12 hours. Messner later called it "the most dangerous wall I have ever climbed."

MOUNT MERU

Being a smaller mountain and farther from the coast, the history of Mount Meru is not as well recorded as that of her bigger sister, Kilimanjaro. Most histories of Meru state that the first recorded sighting of Meru was by Von der Decken and Thornton in 1862.

However, in the early 1850s the missionaries Rebmann and J. Erhardt un-dertook a serious effort to map large sections of East Africa, and they eventually produced something called the Slug Map (so called because the huge lake in the center of the map looks like a slug).

Many mountains are depicted on the map, including Oldonyo Lengai, "Kignea" (Kenya) and Kilimanjaro, as well as "Meru Mt." According to some accounts, the map was never published, and the only copy was given by Erhardt to the Royal Geographical Society on November 10, 1855.[17] According to other sources, it was published in Germany in the mid-1850s.[18]

Regardless of where it first appeared, the Slug Map, as one historian has noted, includes a "reference to the fact, particularly noticeable around Mount Meru, that a high flourine [sic] content in the drinking water, does cause a brown stain to the teeth which cannot be removed"—clearly predating most histories' suggestion that Meru's first recorded sighting was in 1862.

In 1862, Von der Decken, again accompanied by the young geologist Thorn-ton, explored the areas around Kilimanjaro, visiting Lake Jipé and areas east of Kili, eventually producing their own map of the region, which Scottish explorer Joseph Thomson lauded for its "approach to scientific accuracy."[19]

In a second expedition that year, the two men (Von der Decken and

Thornton), with Dr. Kersten, furthered their knowledge of the areas around Kili, refined their map, climbed to 4,268 meters on Kili and "triangulated Mount Meru."[20] In Thomson's own 1885 map of East Africa, Meru appears as an insignificant wart next to a sprawling and impressive Kilimanjaro.

The first ascent of Meru was likely made by the scientist Carl Uhlig in 1901 or by Fritz Jaeger in 1904, who made the first recorded ascent of Kenya's Oldonyo Lengai the same year, although records are inconclusive.

Like Kilimanjaro, Meru became a popular climb (from various directions) rather quickly, and by the early twentieth century, local European residents were making the ascent regularly. David Read, a European who attended the Arusha School in the 1930s, reported that there existed an annual Meru climb and, more significantly, a "Conquered Meru Board" in the school, which listed students who'd climbed the peak, garnering them considerable respect from those who had not made the ascent.

In his 2000 book, *Beating About the Bush*, Read wrote, "Boys over the age of fifteen were, with their parents' consent, allowed to make the attempt. I had taken part in the previous year's [1937] climb from the west, but at 13,500 feet [4,116 meters] many of the boys had dropped back, unable to make it, and the exercise was aborted. This year there was to be no repetition of that and the mountain would be attempted from the south."

Although Mount Meru is a popular ascent these days, you are unlikely to see anything like the crowds that jam onto Kili, hence it makes for a wonderful, semiwild experience.

MOUNT KENYA

Although by the early 1880s, Kilimanjaro was the subject of much exploration, the existence of Mount Kenya was still being questioned by many explorers and geographers.

In 1883, the Geographical Society sent Joseph Thomson to investigate. Beginning at the coast and traveling inland, Thomson passed Kilimanjaro, found the elusive Mount Kenya, and even made an attempt on the peak that reached 2,743 meters (8,997 feet). In his 1885 report of the trip, he suggested that the mountain was an extinct volcano.

First Ascent: Halford John Mackinder

After unsuccessfully attempting Kilimanjaro in 1887, the Hungarian explorer, Count Samuel Teleki von Szek, attempted to climb Mount Kenya from the southwest. However, although he managed to reach the upper portion of the mountain and a height of 4,350 meters, the summit eluded him.

Several years later, a group of British East Africa Company officials under the command of Captain F. G. Dundas attempted the mountain from the south but failed to even penetrate the forest surrounding the main peaks.

In 1893, John W. Gregory, a British geologist, managed to climb to 4,730 meters—remarkably, since he had no climbing equipment and was suffering from fever.

Gregory was followed in 1894 and 1896 by George Kolb, a German physician

Climber on the Point John couloir, Mount Kenya (Photo © Benny Bach)

who pioneered a route through the forests on the east side of the mountain but failed to reach the main peaks. Ironically, Kolb's badly supplied expeditions became a model of "what not to do" for Halford Mackinder, the first person to summit Mount Kenya.

Born in 1861 in Lincolnshire, England, Halford John Mackinder was a scholar whose life revolved primarily around academia and science. He was familiar with the exploration of East Africa during the latter half of the century, as well as the various reports of a great mountain mass in the central part of the British East African Protectorate, as Kenya was then known, and in 1899 he put together an expedition to attempt an ascent of the mysterious mountain.

In June 1899, Mackinder set sail for Africa with Campbell Hausberg, Douglas Saunders, César Ollier, and Joseph Brocherel. Riding the newly built inland train from Mombasa, they arrived in Nairobi on July 15. After some negotiations and the hiring of porters and guides, the party struck out across the Kapoti Plains north of Nairobi on July 28.

"All told, we were 170 strong," Mackinder wrote in the *Geographical Journal*. "Six Europeans, 66 Swahilis, two tall Masai guides, and the remainder were naked Kikuyu."

It is remarkable that Mackinder's expedition ever made it to Mount Kenya, let alone managed to climb the mountain. Throughout the month-long approach march, the guides and porters regularly became ill, they took food and women from the local villages through which they passed (angering the local people), they stole provisions from the expedition itself, and they deserted Mackinder at every turn. Additionally, the local chiefs were at times extremely hostile and killed dozens of Mackinder's men.

Amazingly, by August 18, Mackinder had reached the foot of the mountain and set up a base camp in the forest east of the main peaks. From this point, the climbing party was trimmed down to twelve "volunteers" who would stay on the mountain with Mackinder, and forty-two porters and Kikuyus who would carry loads to a high camp.

Mackinder approached the mountain following the Hohnel Valley, and made his high camp, Camp XXII, at around 3,140 meters in the upper Teleki Valley.

On August 30, Mackinder, Ollier, and Brocherel attempted an ascent of the peak via the south face of Nelion. They came very close to making the first ascent of Nelion but—after a cold night out just below the summit—retreated in the morning.

On September 5, Hausberg, Ollier, and Brocherel made a circuit of the main peaks, climbing Point Lenana (4,985 meters/16,355 feet) in the process.

On September 11, Ollier and Brocherel attempted to climb the peak via the Darwin Glacier but were turned back by bad weather.

Finally, on September 12, Mackinder, Ollier, and Brocherel started up the mountain yet again, climbing the south face of Nelion to the crest of the south ridge. After spending the night in a Mummery tent (an oversized bivouac sack that used ice axes as poles) among the rocks on the ridge crest, the trio descended to the Upper Darwin Glacier, then traversed Nelion and crossed the top of the Diamond Glacier into the Gate of the Mists—the gap between Batian and Nelion.

"It took three hours to cut our way across the hanging glacier to the further side of the gap between the two summits," Mackinder later wrote. "The glacier was steep, so that our shoulders were close to it. Had we fallen, we should have gone over an ice cliff onto the [Lower] Darwin Glacier several hundred feet below."

A short scramble led to the summit of Batian (5,199 meters/17,058 feet), where the climbers celebrated and took photographs. They retraced their route to the Lewis Glacier, then to Camp XXII, which they reached at 10:30 PM, "hungry and weary, but triumphant."

Mount Kenya, 1900–1930

After Mackinder's successful ascent, there were many exploratory expeditions to Mount Kenya in the first two decades of the twentieth century, but none of these was successful in reaching the summit.

Then, at the end of the 1920s, famed British mountaineer Eric Shipton teamed up with various partners to climb several new routes on both the main peaks and made first ascents of many of the subsidiary summits.

On January 3, 1929, Shipton and fellow Briton Percy Wyn Harris made the first ascent of Nelion via the modern Normal Route. Descending into the Gate of the Mists, they then climbed Batian, making the second overall ascent of the mountain. The climb was repeated on January 8 by Shipton, Harris, and Norwegian climber Gustav Sommerfelt.

The Normal Route was repeated a third time in December 1929 by Shipton and Pat Russell; the pair then went on to make the first ascent of Point John (4,883 meters / 16,020 feet).

In July 1930, Shipton returned to Mount Kenya with Bill Tilman. The two began an extensive reconnaissance of Batian and Nelion, during which they made the first ascents of Point Dutton (4,885 meters / 16,207 feet—then known as Dutton Peak) and Point Peter (4,757 meters / 15,607 feet).

On August 1, Shipton and Tilman made the first ascent of the west ridge of Batian, climbing the route in one long day from Firmin Col. This ascent was also the first traverse of the mountain, as the descent was made down the Normal Route. On August 5, the pair climbed Sendeyo (4,704 meters / 15,433 feet), and the next day made the first ascent of Point Pigott (4,957 meters / 16,263 feet), via the northwest face. On August 9, they made the first ascent of Midget Peak (4,700 meters / 15,420 feet), climbing the south gully.

The few years before World War II saw relatively little activity. The highlights of the period included the first ascents of both Nelion and Batian by women. In February 1938, Miss C. Carol reached the summit of Nelion with Mtu Muthara, the first African to climb that peak. And in March of 1938, Miss Una Cameron became the first woman to climb Batian.

The North Face

By the early 1940s, ascents of Batian and Nelion via the Normal Route were becoming commonplace, and all serious mountaineers had their eyes on the north face of Batian.

"The war and postwar periods brought to Kenya a large number of Europeans, amongst whom were some keen mountaineers," observed Mount Kenya historian John W. Howard in a 1953 issue of the *Alpine Journal*.

The leading pioneer of this period was undoubtedly Arthur Firmin, who succeeded on several new, important routes and in the period between 1943 and 1950 climbed Batian five times, by every existing route except the west face.

In early 1944, Firmin and two fellow Brits reached a height of 4,907 meters on the north face. In July, Firmin returned and with fellow Briton P. H. Hicks managed to climb the North Face Route in just a morning, reaching the summit of Batian at 1:30 PM.

In January 1946, Firmin and John W. Howard climbed the southwest ridge, calling it "one of the shortest and most direct routes to the top of Batian." And, finally, in 1950, Firmin and John S. Bagenal climbed the Darwin and Diamond Glaciers, thus creating the South Face Route. It was the second time—after Mackinder—that the Diamond Glacier had been traversed.

In 1952, two French climbers, Maurice Martin and Roger Rangaux, climbed a route on the northeast face, 100 meters left of the Firmin-Hicks (North Face Standard) Route.

In January 1955, R. A. Caukwell and G. W. Rose made the first ascent of the west face of Batian, joining the west ridge not far below the summit of Batian. Unfortunately, Rose was badly injured and knocked unconscious while the pair were descending the Normal Route on Nelion. Upon reaching the Lewis Glacier, Caukwell ran 32 kilometers down the mountain to summon help, but by the time he returned with a rescue party, Rose was dead. Because of the hazards that might occur while lowering the body, Rose was left—for a time—on Nelion's southeast face.

Shortly after Rose and Caukwell's climb, Howard calculated that by January 1955, Batian had been climbed nineteen times and Nelion thirty.

In January 1959, Kisoi Munyao became the first African to climb Batian, making the ascent with Howard and Peter Fullerton. During the same month, John Graham, a sixty-three-year-old American from California, climbed Batian with two Zermatt guides.

In February 1959, the Northey Glacier Route was climbed by W. M. Adams and Robert Chambers of the Mountain Club of Kenya. The pair took 9.5 hours to reach the summit of Batian from a bivouac at the foot of the Northey Glacier. Adams returned in August and climbed the north chimney variation of the French Route with A. Bennett.

In October 1959, the Mountain Club of Kenya produced its first guidebook to Kilimanjaro and Mount Kenya, under the editorial direction of Ian Reid.

In January 1961, a "strong" party from the University of Cape Town visited Mount Kenya and climbed several new routes. On January 4, Robert "Rusty" Baillie and R. M. Kamke made the first ascent of the Southern Slabs Route, left of the Diamond Couloir, in 10 hours. Next, Baillie and Chris Rhys-Jones climbed a variation of the South Face Route. Instead of finishing by ascending Batian, the pair then climbed the south face of Nelion.

The East Face
By the early 1960s, interest had shifted to the east face of Mount Kenya.

In 1953, John W. Howard observed:

> The only face of the mountain that has not yet been climbed is the east or northeast face which looks towards Simba Col. It is a tremendous jumble of precipices, buttresses and organ pipe columns; if Shipton and Wyn Harris could not find a gap in these defenses, then anybody who succeeds without the use of ironmongery (and probably with it, too) will have something to be proud of.

Kenyan climber Barry Cliff was the pioneer in east-face routes. In August 1963, Cliff and Denis Rutowitz decided to try the northeast face. First, the pair made the second ascent of the 1952 French Route so they could examine the pillar left of the route. Then, on August 2, they began climbing "the last great problem on Mount Kenya." "Unexpectedly, the rock was firm, much better than on any other part of the mountain," Cliff later wrote in the *Alpine Journal*, "and here also there were odd little alpine flowers growing in the eastern facing corners." After two bivouacs on the wall (one below the Grey Pillar, the second above), the two men summited on August 4, at about 1:30 PM, then rappeled their route. The climb is now known as the Northeast Pillar of Nelion.

A few days later, Cliff was at it again, this time with Austrian climbers Heinrich Klier and Siegfried Aeberli. On August 7, the trio climbed the East Face Route, a series of cracks that runs from the summit all the way to the Krapf Glacier.

In March 1964, Baillie returned to Mount Kenya and with Tom Phillips made the first "Grand Traverse" of the mountain, climbing the south ridge of Point Pigott, descending to Firmin Col, making the third ascent of the west ridge to Batian, then crossing the Gate of the Mists to Nelion before descending the entire south ridge of Nelion to Point John. The pair made two bivouacs. Baillie and Phillips also climbed a new route on Point John, then hauled up the materials to construct "Baillie's Bivy" near Mackinder's Gendarme on Nelion's Normal Route.

The 1970s saw something of a new-route explosion on Mount Kenya, as not only the hardest rock routes were established, but nearly all the major ice routes were climbed for the first time.

Nairobi-based climbers Ian Howell and Iain Allan undoubtedly led the pack, but many other climbers were involved during this period, including Roger Higgins, Phil Snyder, Mark Savage, John Temple, T. Mathenge, Y. Laulan, and B. LeDain. The massive record of new routes produced during the 1970s is too long to list here; suffice to say that all the major lines on Mount Kenya were climbed by the end of the decade.

The first ascent of the Diamond Couloir is noteworthy, because it was accomplished over a five-year period as various parties climbed portions of the route. In 1971, Howell and Snyder climbed the couloir to the bottom of the Diamond Glacier, at which point "the climb was virtually over" before the lateness of the day prompted the pair to rappel down the couloir to camp. In 1973, Snyder returned with Mathenge and climbed the entire route. Then, in 1975, Yvon Chouinard and Michael Covington climbed the steepest portion of the headwall below the Diamond Glacier, the route many parties now take. In 1977, Hillary Collins became the first woman to make the ascent of the Diamond Couloir.

By the early 1980s, all the major lines on Mount Kenya had been climbed, and ascents of new routes had slowed to a trickle. In 1989, Polish climbers Krzysztof Gwozdz and Zbyszek Wach added a new route on the Diamond Buttress, called Diamond Natasha, which crosses Southern Slabs before ascending a series of cracks between Southern Slabs and the Diamond Buttress Original

Route. In 1992, British climbers Andrew Wielochowski and Chris Mockett pioneered a route on the north side of Nelion's south ridge, while Brits Pat Littlejohn and John Mothersele climbed a new route on Point John's overhanging west face.

Future climbers to the mountain are likely to find little in the way of new wholly independent routes to be done, and, as in other mountaineering arenas of the world, will likely focus on speed ascents and variations.

THE RWENZORIS

The travails of British explorers searching for the headwaters of the Nile in the mid- to late nineteenth century are the stuff of legend. The many attempts to find a solitary source for the river by adventurers like Francis Burton, John Hanning Speke, Samuel Baker, and others eventually drew them to the western edge of the Nile basin and the lakes that formed there (Albert, Edward, etc.) and, finally, to some mysterious shining mountains that appeared to be as tall as anything else they had seen in East Africa.

There are various accounts as to which European explorer saw the high, shimmering form of the Rwenzoris—and first comprehended them to be mountains. The reason no one saw them until well into the nineteenth century is simply because the mountains are nearly permanently shrouded in mist and cloud. Samuel Baker ("Baker of the Nile"), who searched for the source of the Nile in the early 1860s, saw a range of mountains south of the huge Lake Albert. He called them the "Blue Mountains." Whether he had seen the Rwenzoris, or was referring to the mountains west of the lake—today often called the Blue Mountains—is unclear; it was probably the latter. In 1876, Ramolo Gessi, who explored the western edge of Lake Albert, wrote several letters mentioning visions of snow-covered mountains in the sky, which were reportedly attributed to hallucinations.

Most historians give credit to Henry Morton Stanley for recognizing the Rwenzoris as mountains.[21] In May 1888, he was on his final journey into Africa to attempt to rescue Emin Pasha, the governor of Equatoria, in the southern Sudan.

"When about five miles from Nsabé camp, while looking to the southeast and meditating upon the events of the last month, my eyes were attracted by a boy to a mountain, said to be covered with salt, and I saw a peculiar shaped cloud of a most beautiful silver color which assumed the proportions and appearances of a vast mountain covered with snow," Stanley later wrote in *In Darkest Africa* (1890). "Following its form downward, I became struck with the deep blue-black color of its base, and wondered if it portended another tornado; then as the sight descended to the gap between the eastern and western plateaux, I became for the first time conscious that what I gazed upon was not the image or semblance of a vast mountain, but the substance of a real one, with its summit covered with snow."

Stanley didn't venture into the Rwenzoris in 1888. The following year, however, he traveled along the entire western edge of the mountains. He then traveled to Lake Edward and up the eastern edge of the Rwenzoris. "He thus

spent more than three months, from April to July, in the immediate neighbor-
hood of the range, and saw the snowy peaks again and again," wrote de Filippi
in *Ruwenzori*. Wanting more information about the strange, high mountains,
Stanley sent his second-in-command, Lieutenant William G. Stairs, into the
range in early June. He entered the mountains via one of its northwestern valleys and spent days struggling through the bush, aiming, more or less, at a pair
of conical-shaped peaks ("Twin Cones").

On June 7, 1889, Stairs reached an elevation of 3,253 meters on one of the
peaks, however, he could clearly see more and higher mountains. One snowy
peak he estimated at 5,060 meters (16,600 feet), and he could plainly see that
was not the highest mountain in the range. Stairs was the first European to
venture into the Rwenzoris, and he is commemorated in the name of one of
the peaks in the southern part of the range.

In 1891, the German doctor, explorer, and administrator who went by the
name Emin Pasha, led a German expedition into the equatorial lakes region,
and by June the outfit was camped at Karevia, on the western edge of the
mountains, at an elevation of 1,330 meters. From here, one of the expedition's
members, Dr. Franz Stuhlmann, spent 5 days exploring the Butawa Valley, one
of the larger western valleys in the chain, and reached an altitude he measured
as 4,063 meters. Stuhlmann, an excellent naturalist and observer, noted at least
four major massifs and named them Kraepelin, Moebius, Semper, and Weisman.
He also noted that the range was not volcanic in origin, as Stairs had presumed,
but was instead a real mountain range.

In 1894–1895, the naturalist G. F. Scott Elliot made five separate journeys
in the range, via the Yeria, Rwimi, and Nyawamba Valleys on the east, and the
Butawa Valley on the west, reaching an altitude of 3,963 meters in the Butawa
Valley.

In early 1900, J. E. S. Moore led an expedition to study the fauna of the
mountains and traveled up the Mobuku Valley to its head, reaching a point of
4,543 meters on the main ridge of Mount Baker.[22] Moore was the first explorer
to ascertain that the vast white areas were actual glaciers, not just snowfields,
as Stairs and Stuhlmann had assumed.

A few weeks later, M. Fergusson, a member of Moore's expedition, repeated
the journey up the Mobuku Valley and reached 4,451 meters. A short time
later, Fergusson traveled again up the Mobuku, this time in the company of S.
Bagge, who had a rough trail cut—something that would prove invaluable to
subsequent explorers.

In September 1900, Sir Harry Johnston, special commissioner of the protectorate of Uganda, repeated the journey up the Mobuku Valley and reached an
altitude of 4,520 meters. Johnston also renamed the major peaks he saw—replacing both the local African names and those given to the high peaks described
by Stuhlmann from the west. "Thus, in the year 1900 alone, the Mobuku Valley
had been explored by four separate parties," noted de Filippi.

Between 1901 and 1904, there were three other excursions up the Mobuku
Valley, and one from the west, in which Dr. J. J. David traveled up the Bugawa
Valley and reached an altitude of 5,000 meters. From this point, which de Filippi

postulates was between the Savoia and Elena peaks of Mount Stanley, David described the valleys descending to the east, into Uganda.

In 1905, a railroad was completed between Mombasa and Port Florence, on the eastern edge of Lake Victoria, making the Rwenzoris a more accessible mountaineering objective for curious Europeans, and a subsequent flurry of expeditions to the fabled Mountains of the Moon ensued.

In November 1905, the first expedition with mountaineering as a primary objective entered the range. Comprised of Douglas Freshfield, A. L. Mumm, and the Geneva mountain guide Moritz Inderbinnen, the expedition traveled up the Mobuku Valley but—besides reaching an elevation below Moore's high point of 1900—was stymied by incessant bad weather. Also in 1905, the first ascent of one of the range's tall peaks was achieved when Austrian mountaineer R. Grauer and the English missionaries H. E. Maddox and the Reverend R. W. Tegart ascended a small rocky peak at the head of the Mobuku Valley. They estimated its height at 4,573 meters (15,000 feet) and named it in honor of King Edward (the peak is now called Grauer Rock).

In October 1905, the British Museum sent an expedition to study the flora and fauna of the range. Its members included H. B. Woosnam, G. Legge, R. E. Dent, M. Carruthers, and A. F. R. Wollaston, who was an experienced mountaineer. This capable team traveled up the Mobuku Valley and made several noteworthy ascents, including repeat ascents of Grauer Rock as well as of another subsidiary summit on the south ridge of Edward.

All the historically and nationally focused exploration of the nineteenth century led, in 1906, to perhaps one of the most significant expeditions in mountaineering history. The Duke of Abruzzi, an Italian nobleman who in 1878 had made the first ascent of Mount St. Elias in Alaska, who in 1899 had

Skull Cave's skull, Rwenzoris

come close to being the first man to reach the North Pole, and who in 1909 would attempt the first ascent of K2, set his sights on exploring Ptolemy's Lunae Montes and surveying and climbing the major peaks.

The duke's expedition was devised like none before it and ultimately included more than four hundred individuals.[23] This was more than just a climbing trip. And, with several months at his disposal, the duke and his friends were able to make the first ascents of all the range's major peaks—peaks that he diplomatically named in honor of British and Italian monarchs and explorers.[24]

People rate climbs, they don't tend to rate expeditions. The duke's expedition, however, was deemed by many subsequent mountaineering journalists as one of the most skillfully assembled up to that time. In his classic 1942 book, *High Conquest*, James Ramsay Ullman noted:

> *The Duke's expedition was put together on a grand scale. In addition to a group of mountaineers and sportsmen he took with him a small army of scientists and technicians, writers, photographers, physicians, alpine guides and porters.... What gave the expedition its unique character, however, was not so much the individual talents of its members as the fact that it was organized in a manner new to mountaineering. Theretofore the typical climbing party had been simply a group of friends, with or without professional guides, casually bound together in a common purpose. The Abruzzi venture, on the other hand, was a planned, integrated organism in which every member has specialized functions and responsibilities. As such it was to set the style for more than the conquest of an individual peak. It was to set the style for virtually all ambitious mountaineering expeditions in the future.*

And the duke's approach would persevere well into the 1970s, as mountaineers of the twentieth century sent team after team to the Himalayas in the Abruzzi style. What the duke was able to achieve was not remarkable in terms of climbing, but it was remarkable in terms of putting up with the Rwenzoris themselves.

By early June 1906, the duke and his team were at the base of Grauer Rock, a subsidiary summit of the Mount Baker massif. They had spent the previous weeks in total cloud cover and had seen nothing of the mountains that surrounded them. That morning dawned clear, however, and they were able to see the main peaks of the range and to ascertain their characters. Just seeing the mountains was a significant achievement. As Osmaston and Pasteur wrote in their 1972 guide to the Rwenzoris, "All previous explorers from the east had been...confused, for none except Wollaston had obtained even a partial view of them from Baker owing to bad weather."

The duke and his men wasted no time, and that day traversed Semper (another subsidiary peak on Baker) to the highpoint: Edward. They then descended into the Kitandara Valley and camped, and in the subsequent days made first and repeat ascents of Alexandra, Margherita, Elena, and Savoia (the major summits of Stanley). Moving camp over Stuhlmann Pass and the Col Georges, southeast and northeast of Mount Speke, respectively, they climbed Vittorio Emanuele (the summit of Speke) and a few days later, Umberto. Moving camp again, they climbed a raft of minor peaks, including Iolanda, Bottego, Moebius, Sella, Cagni, Stairs—all the while repeating ascents of the main peaks they had already climbed. By mid-July, after a period of 40 days they had made more than thirty ascents of peaks, an amazing achievement for any expedition, let alone the first real expedition to the Rwenzoris.

There were many more expeditions to the Rwenzoris through the following years—and many of the subsidiary and small peaks were first climbed, as were many new routes on the peaks that had already been ascended. Most of these dozens and dozens of expeditions aren't worth recounting here, with the exception of those undertaken by G. N. Humphreys, who began exploring and climbing in the Rwenzoris in 1926, when he made the second ascent of Margherita with E. H. Armitage, R. T. Wickham, and G. Oliver. On that trip, they also climbed a dozen other peaks by new routes and variations. Humphreys returned to the mountains repeatedly, and as Osmaston and Pasteur noted, "In the course of seven expeditions, Humphreys climbed fourteen major and four lesser peaks, explored many new routes, and was able to make substantial additions to the map, especially to the north and south of the central peaks."

Women were active in the early history of Rwenzori mountaineering, traveling and exploring the range from the beginning. In 1935, Frau and Fraulein Geilinger made the first female ascent of Edward on Mount Baker, and in 1938, Miss Una Cameron climbed Semper and Edward, with guides, then went on to climb Alexandra and Sella. The first ascent of the range's highpoint by a woman didn't come until 1954, when June Slinger climbed the east ridge of Margherita with R. F. Davies and I. Keith.

In the mid-1960s, political unrest in the Congo and fighting between the local Bakonjo and Batoro people would hamper access to the range. According to Osmaston and Pasteur, between 1964 and 1967 the range averaged 11 visitors per year, compared with the previous average of 50 and the 101 who would visit in 1967.

During the 1990s, however, rebels destabilized much of western Uganda by attacking the Ugandan army from hideouts in the Rwenzoris and other mountains (the town of Kasese at the foot of the range went from 70,000 people to 30,000 within a few years). Because of the fighting, Rwenzori National Park was closed in 1997 (then experiencing 1,600 foreign visitors per year). Aware of the lost tourism dollars to all the parks in western and southwestern Uganda, the government moved quickly to bring stability to the region in the late 1990s, and by 2001 Rwenzori National Park had reopened (to 400 foreign visitors per year).[25]

Although rebels' landmines are still commonly found in the southwestern part of the range, the Bujuku–Mubuku Circuit (described in this book) and the routes on Stanley, Speke, and Baker, are very safe in terms of human-created dangers.

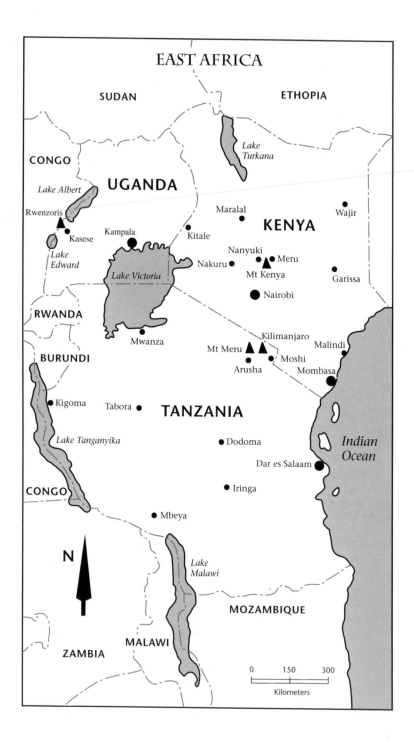

Chapter 2

ABOUT EAST AFRICA

GETTING THERE

General travel in East Africa is a topic far too broad to be covered in this guidebook. However, when it comes to getting to East Africa's mountains, the information you need to know is fairly brief.

Kilimanjaro and Mount Meru lie in northern Tanzania; Mount Kenya is smack dab in the middle of Kenya; and the Rwenzoris are in the southwestern corner of Uganda. Each of the three countries' capital cities (Dar es Salaam, Nairobi, and Kampala, respectively) are good starting places, but they are not the only options. There are smaller towns near the mountains themselves that offer most services (but not the gear) you'll need for mountain climbing.

For trekkers/climbers heading straight to Kilimanjaro or Mount Meru, it's very easy. Just an hour's drive from the main towns at the base of Kili (Moshi and Arusha), is Kilimanjaro International Airport (KIA), a tiny airport that sprang up as a result of the Kilimanjaro trade. You can fly direct from Europe to KIA. The Dutch airline KLM offers daily service from Amsterdam, and the plane does a loop from Amsterdam to KIA to Dar es Salaam, then back to Amsterdam.

Another option for climbers heading for Kilimanjaro is Dar es Salaam. Dar, as it's more commonly known, is also served by the big-three airlines (Lufthansa, KLM, and British Airways), plus many African and Middle Eastern airlines. It also has a port, so you can sail there, if you really want to make your trip a life (and long) experience.[26]

For climbers and trekkers heading to East Africa and wanting to do it all from a centralized base, Nairobi is an excellent option. As with any other big African city, though, don't go out after dark unless it's in a taxi! Getting to Nairobi by air from most parts of the globe is fairly simple. There are no North or South American, and few Asian, airlines that fly to Africa directly or indirectly; however, several European airlines fly there several times per week.

The most reliable and frequent services from Europe are offered by Lufthansa, KLM, and British Airways because of obvious historical ties. Lufthansa offers Nairobi service from Europe and North America via a connection in Frankfurt; KLM offers Kilimanjaro and Nairobi service via Amsterdam; and British Airways offers Nairobi and Kampala service via London. Also, it's worth checking out some of the Middle Eastern airlines, some of which fly direct from Europe to East Africa and which are often cheaper than their better known Western cousins—expect, however, a stopover in the Middle East.

African Safari Airways also flies between the United Kingdom and several other European cities (including Vienna, Basel, Frankfurt, and Milan [Malpensa]) to and from Mombasa several times a week. For climbers heading to the Rwen-zoris, the best way to get there is via Uganda's main airport, in Entebbe (near Kampala). There are daily flights to and from other East African cities and several European cities (British Airways flies direct from London).

When it comes to price, getting to East Africa will be the single most expensive part of your trip. From North America, you can expect to pay anywhere between US$1,200 and US$2,000 round trip, depending on the length of your stay and the season. From Europe, tickets range from about US$400 to (generally no more than) US$1,000.

When you get to your international carrier, ask for one of their huge plastic bags designed to protect backpacks in the airport's luggage system. The bags distributed by domestic airlines in North America are very thin and basically worthless. The European airlines (Lufthansa, KLM) make great plastic bags—so good, in fact, that I keep my pack in one the entire time I'm in East Africa. At night on the mountains, the bag is excellent for keeping out dew.

Nairobi

Nairobi is a large, modern city of about two million inhabitants sitting on the Kenyan plain at about 1,660 meters (5,400 feet). The downtown area is fairly compact, though, and it's easy to get around on foot. Nairobi has all the services you could ever want or need, from five-star hotels to YMCAs, and from the latest big-screen films to upscale boutiques.

Upon your arrival at the airport, you'll be besieged by eager taxi drivers. Since there are no hotels anywhere near the airport and most international flights arrive late at night, you'll need to take a cab into town to a hotel. The ride should cost Ksh1,770 (1,770 Kenyan shillings), or about US$25. (For more on Tanzanian, Kenyan, and Ugandan currency, see Currency.)

During daylight hours, there is bus service from the airport into Nairobi, leaving from between Unit 1 and Unit 2 in the departures area. The ride costs about Ksh35 (US$0.50). However, I can't recommend the bus, even for budget travelers—many tourists get their pockets picked on it. I did.[27]

Many travelers on their first visit to Nairobi take a taxi straight to one of the various hotels on Harry Thuku Road in the university district. The hotels here are quiet, high-quality, and, most important, just a short walk from the Davanu shuttle depot. (For more on the Davanu shuttle, see Getting to the Mountains in Chapter 3.) There are many low-budget hotels in Nairobi, but if it's your first trip to Africa, staying in a nice place on your first night is a good idea.

Most of the cheaper hotels are located on the east side of town, between Tom Mboya Street and River Road. The YMCA is on State House Road, and the YWCA is on Mamlaka Road. You can stay at these places for around Ksh710 (US$10) per night. (For more on Nairobi hotels, see Appendix E.)

Most hotels in Nairobi will store baggage for free, or a small fee. Faxing or emailing a reservation from the United States or Europe is highly recommended for your first night.

As far as restaurants go, there are hundreds of good places to dine, and you'll soon find that Nairobi has exceptional Indian and Middle Eastern food.

Kibo from the Shira Plateau

One place that many climbers head for to celebrate a successful trip is Carnivore. At this unique restaurant, meat of all sorts—including zebra, crocodile, waterbuck, hartebeest, giraffe, and various gazelles—are grilled over an open pit on Masai spears. Waiters wander around the place with huge *pangas* (machetes), carving off as much meat as you want. Dinner is about Ksh2,485 (US$35), but the taxi ride will cost you another Ksh1,065 (US$15) or so each way. An even better experience—if you like to mix with the locals—is a *nyama choma*, or barbecue place. There are many, and they are much cheaper than Carnivore, but you'll most likely be eating domestic meat rather than game.

Dar es Salaam

Dar es Salaam, Tanzania—at about 2.5 million—is the largest city in East Africa, yet it has the flavor of a seaside town. Sitting on the Indian Ocean, Dar's history is reflected in its culture—a mix of Indian, Arab, and of course, African languages, cuisines, and attire. Built over a century and a half, Dar's architecture reflects its colonial past, and the city is something of a rabbit warren of alleys, paths, and stone buildings. Weirdly, though, Dar is not the capital of Tanzania. That job was given to a city called Dodoma, in the middle of the country, in the 1970s.

Geographically, Dar is centered around its huge, bustling port (Mzizima Bay), and the central business district sprawls out from there in a confusing jumble of streets. A few hours around the port can be some of the most interesting, as you'll see traditionally rigged dhows skimming along the water under the looming bulks of twenty-first-century cruise liners and cargo ships. On the peninsula north of Mzizima Bay is the city's main fish market, where the dhows unload their catch every morning. It's a fascinating place to watch the local economy in action.

Nicknamed the "Haven of Peace," Dar still has the ubiquitous East African crime problem, and walking around after dark is not recommended, especially around the port; the beaches north of the city, around Kunduchi, are reportedly quite dangerous too.

Kampala

Like, Dar and Nairobi, Kampala, Uganda (1,120 meters/3,740 feet), is a large city, although much more compact than the others. With a population of 1.2 million, Kampala is remarkably lush, and the trees and green spaces make it very appealing. Kampala boasts a big hill on its northern side (Kampala Hill), which was the historic site of rulers and today houses many of the city's embassies, nicer hotels, and government institutions. It's a great place to wander around.

Perhaps most interesting are the huge Maribou storks that seem to inhabit this part of the city, atop the many trees. In the 1950s and '60s, Kampala was regarded by many as a showpiece East African city, but the rise of Idi Amin and the subsequent wars Uganda experienced reduced its glory. That said, as the new millennium dawns, Kampala (and all Uganda, really) is coming back, and it's starting to see tourism, and the refined infrastructure that goes with it, blossom.

Kampala doesn't have the endless restaurants of Nairobi or Dar, but there are still dozens of good places to eat and cuisines for every palate. There are many hotels for every budget, and transportation services of every kind. (For more on Kampala hotels, see Appendix E.) The best places to stay are arguably on Kampala Hill, historically the center of town (where various rulers' forts were located). In addition to the best hotels,[28] the hill boasts parks, gardens, and historical buildings, and it's where the bus and taxi depots are located.

Kampala doesn't have its own airport, and getting to the city requires traveling through Entebbe, about an hour's drive away. A taxi ride costs about Ush54,600–72,800 (54,600–72,800 Ugandan shillings; about US$30–40).

Moshi and Arusha

Moshi (812 meters/2,663 feet) and Arusha (1,387 meters/4,549 feet) are small towns in northern Tanzania, just a few kilometers from Kilimanjaro and Mount Meru, respectively, and are the best places to base yourself when climbing these peaks. Both towns can be easily reached by air (via Kilimanjaro International Airport, which lies nearly midway between them); buses and shuttles run from Nairobi and Dar; and taxis are plentiful.

Both towns are heavily geared toward the tourism trade, and most of the services of Nairobi and Dar are offered. The upscale hotels here aren't as lavish as you find in the bigger cities, although Arusha has a Novotel, partly because Arusha is the base for many high-level government and international conferences. Also, there's a fabulous little local guidebook to Moshi, *The Moshi Guide*, that is generally available. It's updated every few years and is tremendously helpful in finding businesses and services.

Kasese

Kasese (1,000 meters/3,280 feet), Uganda, is a small town on the southeastern edge of the Rwenzoris and it is where most climbers base themselves when doing Rwenzoris climbs and treks. There are several hotels, several banks, a Western Union office, many restaurants, and dozens of grocery/dry-goods stores, even an Internet cafe—run by a famously friendly guy named Kabau, who goes by the nickname Kabau Chucknorris.[29]

Kasese is hot, dry, and dusty, and sandals are recommended. One of the more surprising things about Kasese—that you might never notice unless you snoop around a bit—is that there's a huge market in the center of town. Dozens of individual stores are in it, selling household goods, shoes, clothing—you name it. It's just off Margherita Road (and it's best to ask a local for directions).

Airport Departure Tax and Value Added Tax

Kenya, Tanzania, and Uganda formerly required an airport departure tax each time a visitor left the country, payable either in local currency or U.S. dollars. That has recently been done away with but it could return—and probably will—at any time.[30]

Also, East African nations tack on an extra 15 percent government tax—the value added tax (VAT)—to most goods and services. This tax will be included in most of your bills, but occasionally you will see "VAT" at the bottom of a bill, with the actual shilling or dollar amount of the tax.

GETTING ALONG

Whereas most European mountaineers and trekkers are generally familiar with East African society because historical ties are strong and the area is relatively close, North Americans tend to be a bit more naive about life in East Africa.

Kenya, Tanzania, and Uganda are developing nations, and travelers must be prepared to deal with all the problems such countries experience. Many things we take for granted in Western nations simply don't apply in Africa. Vehicles break down with alarming regularity. The telephone system is old (but is getting much better with the advent of cellular technology).[31] People drive like maniacs. Appointments can occur days late. And the water can be bad.

But for all those problems, East Africa is a magical place, and the people who live there are incredibly friendly. Often, traveling throughout the region, you might be taken aback by the serious stares you'll get from the local people. They're just checking you out, trying to figure out what you're all about. Crack a smile, and instantly an East African's face will go from serious to smiling.

Also, if you're going to climb East African peaks, you'll notice a difference between Tanzanians, Kenyans, and Ugandans. Tanzanians tend to be much more outgoing; Kenyans are more serious and more reserved; the current generation of Ugandans, who've not been exposed to the tourism the other two nations have seen as a result of several turbulent decades, are extremely friendly. Of course, as with anywhere, this is all dependent on where you meet them—in the big cities, people are more reserved; in the country they are generally very cheery.

Wages and Tips

Some of the richest and poorest people in the world live in East Africa. However, by North American and European standards, the average person is dirt poor.

The average monthly wage of a gardener or laborer in Tanzania is about Tsh70,680 (US$60); a car or truck driver makes about Tsh47,120 (US$40); a security guard, around Tsh70,680 (US$60). Wages in Kenya are comparable. The average monthly wage of a waiter in a small town is about Ksh1,200 (about US$17), excluding tips.

East Africans work incredibly hard. The waiter who makes Ksh1,200 (US$17) a month may work from 7:00 AM to midnight every day. Because of their low wages, people who serve you hope that good service will be rewarded with a tip. In the past, I have tended toward overtipping (sometimes as much as 30 percent for really good, cheerful service), but 10–15 percent is the standard and it's important that travelers attempt to maintain some kind of standard. Workers in regions such as East Africa who are becoming used to the tourist trade are also becoming extremely used to tips, and tips skew the economic balance.[32] Stick with the standard 10–15 percent and you'll do the locals, yourself, and your fellow travelers a huge favor.

Language

The predominant languages in East Africa are Kiswahili, more commonly known in the West as Swahili, and English. Most East Africans grow up learning their tribal "mother tongue" first. English and Swahili come later. Fortunately for travelers, nearly everyone in Kenya, Tanzania, and Uganda has some working knowledge of English, and most speak and write English exceptionally well.[33] Beyond English, the more common European languages (French, German, Spanish) are not as well known.

While Swahili is commonly understood throughout the region, English is, remarkably, probably better known. In specific mountain areas, however, many locals still prefer to speak in their tribal languages (e.g., Wachagga on Kili, Meru on the east side of Mount Kenya, and Bakonjo in the Rwenzoris, for example). In Appendix G are Swahili, Kikuyu, Meru, Chagga (Marangu), and Bakonjo translations for words commonly used in mountaineering.

Food

For the gourmet, East Africa will be something of a disappointment, but that's not to say you won't be well fed with healthy, fresh meals. Certainly, many meat dishes are fried or deep-fried, but the majority tend to be very well boiled—mostly containing, in addition to some kind of meat, a starchy food like potatoes or rice thrown in to soak up the grease. Even on Kili, where your meals are prepared by local cooks, most of the food is boiled.

One staple you'll run into in Kenya and Tanzania is *ugali*, a type of cornmeal often served with meat. On its own it's extremely bland, but soaking up the juice from a stew, it's delicious. In Uganda, expect to eat at least some *matoke* (a starchy meal made from plantain bananas).

The uncooked fruits and vegetables are also superb, especially the fruit. Just be sure to peel all fruits and vegetables before eating them raw. If you're a vegetarian, good luck. I went on a camel safari in Kenya where the vegetarians were fed plain white rice and plain cabbage.[34]

Alcohol

There are numerous brands of excellent local beers in Kenya, Tanzania, and Uganda. They come in 500-milliliter bottles, so if you normally like a couple of beers after climbing a mountain, you might need only one of these. In Kenya, Tusker and Pilsner are the most prevalent brands. Kenbrew, Citizen, and Castle (from South Africa) are also common. In Tanzania, the most common beer is Safari Lager. In Uganda, you might enjoy a Nile, brewed at the headwaters of said watercourse, or a Bell lager.

Besides beers, there are several locally made spirits that are worth a try. Kenya Cane (in Kenya) and 70-proof Konyagi (in Tanzania) are distilled from sugarcane and actually taste fairly good.[35] In Uganda, try some famed Uganda Waragi, a liquor fermented from bananas; it's really good, especially with cola or tonic water (and ice).[36]

Wines are available throughout the region, though you're most likely to be served something from South Africa when you request a bottle. Prices for beer, liquor, and wine are all extremely reasonable.

If you want to go totally native after coming down from Kilimanjaro, ask your driver to stop for some banana beer. This stuff is served in 2-liter plastic buckets and is made of ground-up, half-fermented bananas—or at least that's what it looks like. It costs about Tsh50 a bucket—just a few pennies in U.S. currency! In Kenya, you might be offered some *changaa*. This pungent liquor is distilled from maize.[37] A liter is only Ksh100 (about US$1.50), but it's so foul you'll want to skip it altogether.

One thing to watch out for: East African beer bottles splinter easily. When you or your waiter pops the top, keep an eye out for slivers cracking off around the rim. If it happens, don't drink the beer! Ask for another. Also, if your wine has gone to vinegar, request a new bottle; East Africans hardly drink wine, so if you're buying it in an out of the way place, you might get an "old-to-really-old-to-really-really-old" bottle.[38]

Currency

The currency in Tanzania, Kenya, and Uganda is the shilling.[39] Amounts are written with prefixes "Tsh" (Tanzanian shillings), "Ksh" (Kenyan shillings), or "Ush" (Uganda shillings). As of early 2006, the exchange rate was about Tsh1,178, Ksh72, and Ush1,820 to the U.S. dollar.

Traveler's checks and foreign currency can be exchanged at most banks or at Forex Bureaus, government-approved currency exchanges that can be found in most towns throughout Tanzania, Kenya, and Uganda.

If you use traveler's checks, VISA traveler's checks seem to be more widely accepted in East Africa than any other type. I've seen people with American Express traveler's checks turned down when trying to cash them. Also, a few picky Forex Bureaus won't cash traveler's checks unless you have the receipts showing that you purchased them. Those are the same receipts you normally keep separate from the checks themselves in case you are robbed, so make an extra set. Most banks will cash your traveler's checks without any problems.

In Kenya, credit cards are widely accepted. VISA cards are the most commonly accepted ones. Make sure that when you go to Africa your credit card is new and that the magnetic strip is in good condition. A few East African business owners/operators are still somewhat naive about credit card charging, and if their card reader can't read your magnetic strip, they won't let you charge anything.

When you get to Tanzania, you can put your credit card away. Almost no one accepts them. Some Tanzanian banks won't let you draw cash on a credit card as they do in Kenya, and ones that do charge about 30 percent commission. Businesses that accept credit cards of any kind are few and far between.

Kenya is starting to see ATMs (cash machines) go up everywhere. As in the rest of the world, these machines accept credit cards and are a good way to buy the local currency. There is an ATM in the arrivals building at Jomo Kenyatta International Airport in Nairobi that dispenses Kenyan currency. There's also one in Meru, at the Barclays Bank. There is still no ATM at Kilimanjaro International Airport; there is, however, a National Bank of Commerce money exchange open until the last flight each night arrives and I recommend you immediately exchange money there (even if only US$20–30 for tips and incidentals).

In Uganda, be prepared. Virtually no businesses in the country towns take U.S. dollars of any denomination or traveler's checks (and lines at banks can last many hours). There are, however, banks in Kampala that will take ATM cards, as long as you persist. In Kasese, at the foot of the Rwenzoris, banks (or, bank tellers, at least) are extremely wary of U.S. currency and traveler's checks.[40]

When you go out into the country (to Moshi and Arusha for Kilimanjaro and Mount Meru, or to any of the small towns surrounding Mount Kenya and the Rwenzoris), bring lots of small change. Many hoteliers, restaurateurs, shop owners, and taxi drivers will claim they have no change when you hand them the equivalent of a US$20 bill for a US$5 product or service.[41] In Uganda, new to the current tourism boom, U.S. dollars are accepted more and more places, but I recommend relying on the local currency as much as possible—and bring small bills.

Besides money for park fees and guides or porters while climbing the mountains and transportation around Tanzania, Kenya, and Uganda, I always try to bring the equivalent of US$500 for emergencies, souvenir shopping, and general fun, although US$200–300 is plenty if you're on a budget.

In Tanzania, I never bring notes bigger than Tsh10,000, and I try to get the majority of my cash converted into Tsh1,000 notes. In Kenya, I never bring notes bigger than Ksh1,000, and usually I try to get the majority of my cash converted into Ksh500 or Ksh200 notes. In Uganda, notes of Ush1,000, Ush5,000, and Ush10,000 are most useful.

If for some reason you forget to get your money exchanged before heading off to the mountains in Kenya or Tanzania, don't worry. U.S. currency is widely accepted in these countries, especially Tanzania, where U.S. dollars are often preferred over Tanzanian shillings.

Bank hours are generally 8:30 AM to 3:30 PM Monday through Friday, and some even close at 12:30 PM. There is no banking done on weekends, and be prepared: if you go to a bank for anything, you could be waiting for several hours or days.

Telephones

Making a phone call using a land line can be one of the more frustrating things you might attempt in East Africa. Although many hotels have telephones you can use, the charge is enormous, partly because the tax on private phones is high. Expect to pay about US$10–20 for a 3-minute call to the United States, slightly less for Europe.

There are many telecommunications centers in East African towns that offer far more reasonable rates, sometimes as low as US$6 for a 3-minute call. You can also fax from most telecommunications centers for about the same price.

Calling to East Africa is fairly simple. The country code for Tanzania is 255; for Kenya, 254; for Uganda, 256. To dial direct from North America, Europe, Australia, Asia, and other African countries, it's necessary to first dial for an international line (your local carrier should be able to help you, but check www.countrycallingcodes.com if they can't), then the country code (a + symbol before a number signifies a country code), followed by the phone number. See Appendix A for an explanation of phone and fax number formats. Remember that East Africa is 8–11 hours ahead of North America, 3 hours ahead of Europe, 8 hours behind Australia, and as much as 6 hours behind East Asia.

Don't be surprised if some people don't return your calls from East Africa. The price of a single phone call can be a day's wages for the average person (though mobile phones are changing this), so many East Africans are reluctant to phone internationally unless it's absolutely necessary. Most climbing outfitters and hotels will fax you back a confirmation of a booking when you make one. A much better way to communicate with hoteliers, outfitters, and others in East Africa is via email, and most of those offering these services nowadays have websites from which you can get email addresses.

Mobile phones work all the way to the summit on Kili, so bring one (that is set for an East African connection) if you want to call home from the summit.[42]

Choos and *Pangas*

This might seem like a silly topic discuss, but a *choo* (Swahili for "toilet," pronounced "chaw") in Africa is different from anything most North Americans will experience at home. Generally, nice hotels and restaurants have flush toilets with seats. However, the less expensive the place, the more likely it won't have a seat, or a bowl at all. In many places, toilets are nothing more than a hole in the floor.

Likewise, the *panga* (Swahili for "machete") is another East African specialty. In Tanzania, Kenya, and Uganda many people carry *pangas*. Some are huge, reminiscent of pirate swords; others are small and hooked. Don't feel threatened by someone holding a *panga*. Get used to them. Like a cold Tusker or Safari beer, *pangas* will become a constant in your life.

Film and Photography

In general, pretty much all the latest types of films, batteries, and videotape are available in the modern camera shops in Nairobi, Dar, and Kampala—that is, if you subtract fifteen years from a Western camera shop experience. Once you get out in the country, however, finding a roll of anything but color print film is tricky. The best advice is bring everything—camera, memory cards, film, filters, whatever—you need from home.

Nairobi has only a few photography shops, namely Camera Works Services in Thande House (third floor) on Luthuli Avenue, and Luedecke & Co., Ltd., in Uganda House on Kenyatta Avenue.

Arusha's and Moshi's photography offerings are pretty limited. Burnham Photographic Services (on Kilima Street in Moshi, just uphill from the intersection with Mawenzi Street; and next to the Impala Hotel in Arusha) carries some slide film; as would be expected, prices are about double what you'd expect in North America and Europe.

Nanyuki, on the north side of Mount Kenya, has a couple of good photo shops, and most of the bigger towns around Mount Kenya (Chogoria, Meru, Embu) have photo shops, although slide film is almost impossible to get.

Despite being a big city, Kampala's photographic offerings are also pretty limited, and the shops seem to come and go (and move) regularly. Furys, Ltd., has a store at 56/60 Kampala Road; Techno Associates has a store at 29B Nassar Road; and Afro Studio, at 9/7 Bombo Road, stocks some film types.

When you're in East Africa, always ask your subject for permission before taking a photograph. You might have to pay a nominal fee, but it's considered the polite way to take a photograph. If you don't ask first, you might find yourself arguing with locals who want a modeling fee.

It's important in Tanzania that you don't photograph any buildings, people, or offices associated with the government. Because of its political history, the Tanzanian government is still fairly paranoid about its relationships with other countries, and taking photos of any government facility could land you in jail.[43]

Also, for photography in the Rwenzoris, come prepared with fast-speed film (if you're shooting film). Because of the extreme mistiness of these mountains, ASA 200 and 400 films are a must.[44]

AVOIDING RIP-OFFS

"Kenya is a nation of opportunists."

That is how a high-ranking Kenyan government official summed up the East African attitude toward business, tourism, and crime during an interview I conducted in 1997.

Although most Kenyans, Tanzanians, and Ugandans are honest, hard-working people, many are looking to make a buck by cutting corners in tourism, overcharging for products and services, and straightforward pilfering.

The rip-offs are simple and complex. Some are legal, some are not. The following are a few of the more prevalent ones to watch out for.

Pickpockets

Although taxis are relatively inexpensive in Nairobi, Kampala, and other towns, buses, *matatus* and *dalla-dallas* (a kind of minibus, in Kenya and Tanzania, respectively) are extremely cheap and an attractive alternative to those on a budget.

However, be aware that every bus and minivan in East Africa can harbor pickpockets who can perform their job easily because the vehicles are so wildly crowded that you're literally squeezed from every side. Make sure when you travel by bus or minivan that all your valuables are buried deep within tight-fitting clothing. Backpacks and hand luggage are especially risky propositions unless they are in your lap with your arms around them.[45] The bottom line? Take a taxi.

Bogus Currency

Obviously, exchanging U.S. or European currencies for shillings on the street in Tanzania, Kenya, or Uganda comes with the usual problem: bogus currency. Counterfeit bills are everywhere. You'll be especially hassled to exchange your money on the street in Nairobi, Namanga (a border town on the way to Moshi, between Nairobi and Arusha), Dar es Salaam, and Kampala.

It's recommended you exchange your cash at official Forex Bureaus or banks. Barclays, the huge English bank, has offices throughout the region.[46]

Sponsorship Requests

No matter where you go in East Africa, you'll be asked to sponsor something. Often, it's school children requesting sponsorship for school supplies. The child will usually have a school notebook with a list of sponsors scrawled on the first page. Sometimes, the list is bogus, and any money you might give the child goes into his pocket for everything but school supplies. Sometimes the request is genuine—too genuine. Beyond high school, education is anything but free in East Africa (like most places). You'll also be asked to sponsor immigrants to your home country, and just about anything else you can imagine. Choose your response wisely.[47]

Double-Standard Prices

Most of you who buy this guidebook are *mzungus* or *abbajungus* (Swahili and Bakonjo for "white person," respectively). To many East Africans, *mzungu* means money, so you'll often be charged more than the local people for products and services—sometimes triple. If you don't mind such overbilling, fine. Otherwise, try to get a guide or a porter to purchase goods and services for you (most are pleased to do it).

Likewise, some shops don't have prices on items. When you walk through the door, the prices can go up. Try to shop where the prices are marked.[48]

Illegitimate Tour Operators

Since a special license is required for guiding or portering on Mount Kenya (see Mount Kenya in Chapter 3), and by law there is only one outfitter in the Rwenzoris, the following rip-off applies primarily to Kilimanjaro and Mount Meru.

Tour operators—even tour operators running mountain trips—must have a government license to operate within Kilimanjaro and Arusha (Mount Meru) National Parks. However, there are many companies out there who don't have licenses and who will try to sell you a climb. Ask to see their license.

Many legitimate companies hang photocopies of their licenses on the office wall so the originals don't get too ratty. If you are concerned, ask to see the original document. Some unscrupulous firms will obtain a legitimate company's license, photocopy the document, white-out the other company's name, write in their own, then photocopy the document again so it looks the same as the legitimate firm's license hanging on the wall. Although climbing Kilimanjaro with an unlicensed firm will likely be no problem as far as park officials are concerned, some of these illegitimate companies are notorious for bad service.

On Mount Kenya, all guides and porters must have valid cards issued by Kenya Wildlife Service (KWS). Such cards mean an organization is licensed to offer guiding and portering services. With these, guides and porters are granted entry to the park at the guides/porters rate, and any problems with the guides/porters can be dealt with, as guides and porters on Mount Kenya are all known to the park service. Ask to see a guide or porter's card if you are unsure about hiring them.

Paying Park Fees

Because you are required to hire an outfitter to climb Kilimanjaro, Mount Meru, and peaks in the Rwenzoris, the national park fees will be handled for you by the outfitter as part of the overall price of the climb. Be leery, though, of the price you are quoted for an ascent of Kilimanjaro: a recent development is tour operators offering very low prices for an ascent of Kili that then turn out to not include park fees.[49]

On the other hand, Mount Kenya National Park rangers are extremely meticulous with the paperwork of trekkers and mountaineers. Don't entrust paying the park fees to your outfitter.[50]

Booking Your Own Climb

If, before you leave North America or Europe, you want to make a reservation for your climb on specific dates, shop around. You can pay anywhere from US$800 to several thousand dollars for an ascent of an East African peak or peaks, depending on how you go about it.

If you contact a travel agent in North America or Europe, for example, and ask to book a climb, you will likely be charged two to three times the amount you would pay if you booked your climb in Moshi or Arusha. This is because your local travel agent will need to call an adventure travel company that specializes in mountain climbing. Often the adventure travel company is also based in North America or Europe, so it will need to call another company in Nairobi or Dar to book your climb. That company, in turn, calls a tour operator in Moshi or Arusha and books your climb.

Although the local company that actually does all the work might only charge, say, the Nairobi company US$800 for your climb, the Nairobi company will turn around and charge the adventure travel company US$1,000. The adventure travel company will likewise turn around and charge your local travel agent US$1,300 for your climb. Your local travel agent might then turn around and charge you US$1,600.[51]

VISAS

A visa is nothing more than a stamp that representatives of a country place in your passport before you go to that country. Depending on where you get your visa, prices, requirements, and the time required to get the stamp can vary.

Probably the simplest way to get a visa is to log onto the website of the embassy of the particular country in which you plan to travel and download a tourist visa application (see Appendix A for embassy websites; always check them before undertaking any East Africa trip). Usually, you'll get a one- to several-page questionnaire that must be completed, then submitted to the embassy along with two photographs of yourself, the fee for the visa, and your passport. In the past, it was necessary to include a photocopy of your return tickets (although this requirement seems to be unnecessary nowadays). Also, note that most visa fees are generally payable only with cash or money orders, so check before you send in your payment.

I recommend submitting all this material to the Tanzanian, Kenyan, or Ugandan embassies via special courier. Make sure you include a prepaid return envelope.

You can request either single-entry or multiple-entry visas. A single-entry visa for Tanzania, Kenya, or Uganda costs (in late 2005) about US$50 if bought in the United States, the United Kingdom, Canada, Australia, and other Western countries and works fine if you're planning to go solely to Tanzania, Kenya, or Uganda. However, if you plan to go in and out of these countries (say, land in Nairobi, then travel by land to Kilimanjaro or Kasese, then return to Nairobi before flying home), you'll need the multiple-entry visa, which costs about US$90–100.[52]

You can also get your visa when you arrive in Tanzania, Kenya, or Uganda (which is no longer cheaper, by the way), but be prepared to wait, and have your photos, return ticket, and some cash for your visa fee ready. Some guidebooks have reported differences in prices depending on whether you get your visa at home or once you arrive.[53] This seems to change, so inquire with that East African nation's embassy before you choose one way or the other.[54]

Addresses for Tanzanian, Kenyan, and Ugandan embassies abroad are also listed in Appendix A.

HEALTH PRECAUTIONS

Fortunately, the ailments you're likely to encounter in East Africa are easily treated and rarely life-threatening. The most common ailment is simply an upset stomach, and most of the time this is the result of your body adapting to the bacteria of East African cuisine and water.

If you do feel ill, talk to your outfitter. Outfitters are used to dealing with all sorts of ailments and are familiar with problems that visiting Westerners are most likely to experience, and they know where the best and fastest medical help is. You don't have to cut your trip short if you get a bug—if you have it diagnosed early.

African medical facilities have a terrible reputation because of the prevalence of AIDS and other serious diseases. However, for the more common ailments you're likely to encounter, diagnosis and treatment can be accomplished without ever drawing blood or cutting into the body.

There are many great websites with info on high-altitude mountaineering that offer much more information than I can include here—including the High Altitude Medicine Guide (*www.high-altitude-medicine.com*), the British Mountaineering Council (*www.thebmc.co.uk*), and others—so make sure your trip is preceded by a dose of web reading. Also, check out the more mainstream health websites—like the World Health Organization (*www.who.int/en*) and the Centers for Disease Control and Prevention (*www.cdc.gov*)—for diseases not related to climbing / trekking.

Immunizations

There are several immunizations that you should get before leaving North America or Europe for East Africa. At the bare minimum, include vaccinations for yellow fever, cholera, hepatitis A, tetanus, polio, typhoid, and meningococcal meningitis. Although medical professionals the world over agree that cholera shots are generally unnecessary, many governments—including those of East Africa—require the cholera stamp on your health documents. (Health documents are simply records of the immunizations you have received. Every public or private medical facility that administers immunizations should provide you with these documents at no cost.)

Also, if you are planning to get the above-mentioned shots, plan early. Some of them require several courses spread over weeks, even months, and some can't be taken with other medicines.

Malaria

Many Westerners—acutely aware of the well-publicized effect of AIDS on Africans—seem to forget about malaria, but malaria is still one of the biggest killers in East Africa.[55] According to the World Health Organization (WHO), "there are at least 300 million acute cases of malaria each year globally, resulting in more than a million deaths. Around 90 percent of these deaths occur in Africa, mostly in young children."

Malaria tablets are easy to get both in East Africa and at home, before you leave (nearly all courses require starting several weeks before you travel). There are several brands available (you can buy them at chemists' shops and many hotels, restaurants, and bars in East Africa), and some even sell for pennies per tablet. However, according to some medical professionals, some brands of malaria medicine are not effective.

Larium is reportedly the best antimalarial; however, it is not readily available in East Africa. It is also remarkably expensive, costing around US$150–200 for the typical course ("generic" Larium is about half that). Ask your doctor before you go.

The best way to combat malaria, however, is to cover up and prevent mosquito bites in the first place.

Dengue Fever

Dengue fever (there are several forms of it) has become something of a world issue in recent years, and an estimated 2.5 billion people worldwide are at risk of contracting it, according to the WHO, which also estimates that "there may be 50 million cases of dengue infection worldwide every year." The fever manifests itself as a severe, flulike illness that affects people of all ages, but rarely causes death. There is no cure for dengue fever. Like malaria, it is transmitted by mosquitoes, so the best defense is to cover up against the insects and use repellent when covering up is not possible.

Trypanosomiasis (Sleeping Sickness)

Trypanosomiasis is spread by tsetse flies, and this disease has two distinct phases: early and neurological. The early phase includes fever, headache, itching, and pain in the joints. The neurological phase occurs when the parasite that causes trypanosomiasis leaves the blood and enters the central nervous system. When this happens, the victim can experience confusion, a lack of balance, and reduced sensory skills. This is also when the parasite wrecks the sleep cycle, hence the name.

If the disease is not treated, it is fatal. Worse, if treatment does not occur before the start of the neurological phase, neurological damage can be irreversible. Treated early on—the treatment consists of two sets of drugs, each combating the parasite in the two phases—the chance of recovery is high. If you think you have contracted trypanosomiasis, seek professional medical help immediately.

Dysentery

Perhaps the most common ailment besides diarrhea is dysentery (and, obviously, diarrhea occurs with dysentery). There are several kinds, but they all can be identified by severe stomach cramps and confirmed by a simple stool test, which can be done at any dispensary (pharmacy).[56]

Water

Tap water is generally regarded as questionable to drink in East Africa. If you ask whether the water has been chlorinated, as some guidebooks suggest, you will either get an emphatic yes, regardless of whether it has been chlorinated or not, or no answer at all, as many local people are not sure what chlorination is. These days, most travelers, including climbers, rely on bottled mineral water, which is readily available throughout the region.

High on Kilimanjaro, Mount Kenya, Mount Meru, and especially in the Rwenzoris, the water is extremely clean, except for those few places where it has been contaminated by human waste. The lower you are, elevation-wise, and the closer you are to campsites and popular trekking routes, the more likely it is not. Wherever you are, it's a good idea to boil or treat your water at all times.[57]

Water is readily available at most camps and huts. At worst, such as Barafu Huts on Kilimanjaro, it's a half hour's easy hiking away.

ACCIDENTS AND GETTING LOST

Kilimanjaro, Arusha (Mount Meru), Mount Kenya, and Rwenzori National Parks are set up to respond to emergencies. All have rescue teams, although their knowledge and experience is considerably less than one would expect of the European or North American equivalent.

If you are in an accident in which a member of your group is injured and can't be moved, you should contact park rescue personnel as quickly as possible.

On Kilimanjaro, rescue personnel are stationed at all the huts along the Marangu Route. You can also contact park personnel at any of the main gates: Marangu, Mweka, Umbwe, Machame, Shira, and Rongai.

On Mount Meru, rescue personnel are located at the huts up and down the mountain on the standard (Momella) route.

On Mount Kenya, rescue personnel are permanently stationed at the ranger station at the head of the Teleki Valley, on the Naro Moru Route, just up from Mackinder's Camp. You can also contact park personnel at any of the main gates: Chogoria, Sirimon, and Naro Moru.

In the Rwenzoris, rescue personnel are located at the park office in Nyaka-lengija. Also, despite being a vast wilderness, the porters in the Rwenzoris have an amazing ability to get to the park headquarters within a day, adding a level of comfort to any trip.

If there are more than two in your party, one member should stay with the injured person while the other goes for help. If there are only two of you, the uninjured member should provide the victim with easy access to food, water, and clothing before going for help. If you are leaving an injured climber on a technical mountaineering route, make sure the person is well anchored.

Before leaving an injured climber, write down all information on the victim's condition and location, and mark the location on a map.

Helicopter rescue at the Horombo Hut on Kilimanjaro. The helicopter flew from Nairobi for the rescue. (Photo © Filip Kovenhult)

If you can lend a hand in a rescue, by all means do so. It may be hours before official park personnel arrive on the scene, and by that time you and a few other volunteers could easily have carried a mountain sickness victim to a lower elevation and saved the person's life. Altitude sicknesses, which are by far the greatest threat to any Western climber on East African peaks, can kill someone in just a few hours.

If you get lost, stay where you are. Wandering around trying to regain a trail can get you more lost. Lay a brightly colored article of clothing near yourself so that searchers on the ground and in the air can see it. Try to find an open place, and do not wander into thick forest or jungle. It is typical that lost climbers will be out overnight.

In all cases, you will be expected to pay for your rescue. Fortunately, rescue costs in East Africa are much cheaper than in North America or Europe. (See Fees, under the Regulations and Fees sections of Chapter 3.)

WILDLIFE

During one of his attempts on Kibo from the northeast, first ascensionist Hans Meyer discovered the body of a small antelope near the summit. A leopard was also found near the summit in 1926 by Dr. Reusch. In the 1990s, a Kikuyu friend of mine saw a black serval near Austrian Hut on Mount Kenya. In 2005, I found hyena prints at roughly 3,354 meters while hiking up Mount Meru,[58] and later—with my trekking buddies—I dodged an elephant at about 3,048 meters. And, that same year, several friends and I discovered leopard prints at about 3,659 meters, after leaving Bigo Hut in the Rwenzoris, much to the surprise of our local hosts.

Despite these stories, big animals are rarely found very high on Kilimanjaro, Mount Meru, Mount Kenya, or in the Rwenzoris. It is in the forest and moorland areas that climbers need to be aware of East Africa's unpredictable wildlife.

On all these mountains—but especially on Mounts Meru and Kenya—the biggest danger is the Cape or African buffalo (*Syncerus caffer*). These creatures are monstrous, and can weigh up to 800 kilograms (1,764 pounds). They are herd animals that prefer open grassland areas and generally congregate around watering places. For the most part, buffalo are docile animals that will wander off when you approach. However, if they are surprised, or have young, they can charge. The best thing to do is make a lot of noise when wandering through forested areas and to keep your distance when you do see one.

As with buffalo, elephants (*Loxodonta africana*) are known to charge if surprised or with young. Again, make a lot of noise and keep your distance.

Baboons and monkeys can be found throughout the forests on East Africa's mountains. They pose little physical threat, but a few of the bolder ones might steal sunglasses, cameras, articles of clothing, and small backpacks.

Rock hyraxes (*Procavia capensis*) are strange little mammals, similar in size, shape, and color to American and European marmots. Oddly, they are the closest living relative to the elephant. They are extremely common on Mount Kenya, but rare on Kilimanjaro, where rumor has it that porters have eaten them all; they are also rare on Meru and in the Rwenzoris. Like marmots, hyraxes will rummage through campsites looking for things to eat. They have been known to chew into backpacks and bags left unattended. Stow your belongings carefully if you are planning to leave them for any length of time.

Big cats (lions, leopards, etc.) are rare on all East African mountains and should be of no concern, as they generally keep out of the way of humans and tend not to go very high on the mountains. Likewise, servals (*Felis serval*), long-legged wild cats about the size of a domestic cat, are common on East African mountains but are shy and retiring nocturnal creatures.[59]

Other animals you might see on Kilimanjaro include the dik-dik, bushbuck, duiker, warthog, chameleon, mongoose, and sunbird. Occasionally, a zebra or hyena will wander up onto the Shira Plateau.

On Mount Kenya, which has vastly more wildlife than Kilimanjaro, you might encounter all the creatures mentioned above, along with eland and waterbuck. Black rhinoceros (*Diceros bicornis*) have occasionally been reported on Mount Kenya; if you see one, you should consider yourself very lucky.

Chameleon on the Marangu Route, near the Mandara Hut, Kilimanjaro

In the Rwenzoris, animals are less used to human interaction than in any other mountain areas and you can expect to see virtually no animals.[60] The animals you might see on the lower slopes are similar to the animals one might find on other tall East African peaks and include various antelope species, buffalo, and elephant. In the southern part of the range, chimpanzees are common, although that's likely because few people travel through the places where they live. Among the birds you might see are the Rwenzori duck (dark-colored birds that travel almost exclusively in pairs), and the Rwenzori turaco.[61]

An ascent of Mount Meru, however, is a mountain climbing adventure crossed with a safari and is one of the finest experiences East Africa has to offer. Hiking up Meru you will wander past buffaloes, zebras, elephants, and a few other "mega" fauna species.

Bakonjo porters near Bigo Hut, Rwenzoris

Chapter 3

CLIMBING IN EAST AFRICA

PLANNING THE TRIP

The amount of time needed to climb an East African peak is much less than the amount of time needed to climb other high mountains of the world. I know of climbers who have done Mount Kenya's Chogoria–Naro Moru traverse with a quick run up to Point Lenana in 3 days in minimal hiking garb. On the other hand, trekkers have been known to leisurely stroll up Kilimanjaro so slowly that the ascent takes up to two weeks.

There are no absolutes, but most parties take 5 or 6 days to complete any of the standard trekking routes on either Kilimanjaro or Mount Kenya. If a technical mountaineering route is to be part of the ascent as well, add another 2–3 days. A standard ascent of Mount Meru takes about 4 days (3-day trips feel rushed on this beautiful peak). The standard trekking circuit in the Rwenzoris—which accesses the main peaks—is typically done in 6 or 7 days. If a mountaineering route is to be part of an ascent as well, add at least another day per peak climbed.

Besides the time needed on the mountain, it generally takes a day to reach East Africa from Europe (longer, obviously, from North America), then another day to get to Kilimanjaro, Mount Meru, Mount Kenya, or the Rwenzoris by road, plus another day to get back to your airport; a couple of days' rest here and there along the way is highly recommended.

Flying direct to Kilimanjaro International Airport (KIA) can greatly shorten Kilimanjaro and Mount Meru trips. From Europe, you can fly to KIA one day, be on either mountain the following day, and flying home after a little more than a week for Kili and under a week for Meru—if you're organized.

Most climbers going to Kili, Mount Meru, or Mount Kenya via Nairobi plan on spending a night in Nairobi, then travel to Moshi or Arusha the following morning. Climbers headed to the Rwenzoris have a longer approach and typically spend nights in both Kampala and Kasese before heading into the mountains. It's also beneficial to then spend at least one day in Moshi, Arusha, Marangu, or Kasese doing nothing but sleeping and resting before beginning a trek. The long flight from North America or Europe wears you down, but more importantly, your body needs at least a full day to adjust to the local food.

Because you're often traveling halfway around the globe, you may want to add an extra week onto your trip for a safari, the consummate East African experience.

Seasons and Weather

There are two climbing seasons in East Africa: mid-December through mid-March, and early June through mid-October (although these are not absolute). Both of these periods are considered "dry seasons" in East Africa. Mid-December through mid-March is dry and warm, whereas early June through mid-October is generally dry and cool. The highest tourist season on East African peaks is probably the warm dry season, especially around Christmas.

Despite these broad generalizations, there are always regional and local fluctuations in the weather. East African peaks are so tall and isolated from other ranges that they create their own weather. After a clear morning, at about 10:00 AM thick cloud cover often forms around their summits (4,000 meters and up), remaining until late in the day, when the summits clear for the night.

During the dry seasons, precipitation is infrequent, but not unheard of. Compared with mountains of a similar height in other parts of the world, East African peaks seem to have fewer windy periods. However, when wind does occasionally blow, it can be fierce.

The Rwenzoris are a bit different, weatherwise, from the other peaks described here. Sitting against the huge, lush Congo basin, they are forever shrouded in mist. A typical ascent might start out in the rain or snow flurries, be clear for a while, then disappear back into the mists for a day, a week, or a month.

Most routes on East African peaks can be climbed in either dry season—however, several locals have reported that with climate change the storms on East African peaks are becoming more violent than a decade ago (hence, the recommendation for a good outer shell). Technical routes, especially on Mount Kenya, are more weather-dependent. Rock routes that face south are best done in December, January, and February; routes that face north are best in July, August, and September. Ice climbs are just the opposite: south-facing routes are best done in July, August, and September; north-facing routes are best in December, January, and February.

Although all these East African peaks sit astride the equator, they can be extremely cold places, especially during the night. Generally, expect temperatures at night and in the early morning at the 4,600-meter level to be as low as minus 5 degrees Celsius (23 degrees Fahrenheit).

Daytime temperatures are much more reasonable. It's possible to wear shorts as far as the top huts (Kibo, Barafu, Austrian, John Matte, Saddle, and so forth) on East African mountains, where midday temperatures can reach 10 degrees Celsius (50 degrees Fahrenheit).

However, anyone climbing above the 4,600-meter level should have several thermal layers of clothing. Also, be prepared to feel cooler at noon than you do at, say, 9:00 AM or 4:00 PM. The moisture in the clouds that swirl around the summits during the day makes the air feel much colder than it really is.

Choosing a Climbing Partner

Visitors to Kilimanjaro National Park (commonly called KINAPA), Arusha National Park (Mount Meru), and Rwenzori National Park are required to travel with a registered guide anytime they go inside the park boundaries, even if it's for a short day hike, and even if there is more than one person in the group. Because of this requirement, a climbing partner is unnecessary on Kili, Mount Meru, and in the Rwenzoris, and many choose to climb these mountains with only their required guide. (For more on climbing regulations, see the Regulations and Fees sections later in this chapter.)

Because most of the guides and porters in East Africa have limited English, if you choose to climb the mountain without a partner, you'll spend a lot of time hanging out by yourself while the guide has a good time with his porter friends—it can be a lonely experience. I recommend going with at least one other person who can speak your language on any mountain route, even the trekking routes.

For the technical mountaineering routes on Kilimanjaro and in the Rwenzoris, knowledge of ice and alpine climbing techniques is essential. Unlike Mount Kenya, there are no technical routes on Kili that are purely rock climbs, and the Rwenzori routes described herein (except the standard route on Baker) require (very minimal) glacier travel knowledge and skills.

On Mount Kenya, park regulations don't require climbers to have guides or porters. You and your partner can go climb by yourselves, wherever you like. Some tour operators might try to convince you that you must have a guide or porters on Mount Kenya, which is untrue. However, because of safety concerns, park regulations prohibit anyone from entering the park alone. (For more on climbing regulations in Mount Kenya National Park, see Mount Kenya Regulations and Fees later this chapter.)

As with Kilimanjaro, for both trekking and technical mountaineering on Mount Meru, Mount Kenya, and in the Rwenzoris, I thoroughly recommend going with at least one partner, even if you just met the person locally.

For the trekking routes on all East African peaks in this book, experience with high altitude is not essential, but it can certainly help. Experience with long, hard day hikes, especially those that go above 3,000 meters, is extremely valuable.

For the technical mountaineering routes on East African peaks, basic rock and ice climbing skills are necessary, but high-altitude mountaineering experience is not a prerequisite. The one exception is the peaks in the Rwenzoris; the routes described in this guide are so straightforward that many first-timers can—after shown the proper use of crampon and ice ax—climb Mount Stanley and Mount Speke (Mount Baker is just a hike, albeit across very rough terrain).

In the previous edition of this book I left out mention of deaths on East African mountains, but there are some lessons to be learned from the few tidbits I gleaned during a recent trip. According to a knowledgeable friend and Moshi-based Kili guide, about three people per year die on Kili; in 2004, ten died.[62] The reasons for deaths are a combination of things,[63] but the two big killers are altitude (specifically, pulmonary edema) and hypothermia. Unbeknownst to most Westerners visiting East Africa, porters die regularly on Kili from these two problems (they often lack appropriate warm clothing and many have very limited knowledge and experience with altitude). KINAPA is addressing some of these issues (for example, porters aren't allowed to wear beach thongs any longer and those who do will, technically, be sent down).

OUTFITTERS

Nearly all outfitters in East Africa will include several basic items when you sign up for a mountain trek and / or climb. These include transportation to and from a trailhead (or trailheads, if you are doing a traverse of some kind), food for the entire journey, stoves and fuel, and hut accommodations (if you are staying in huts). The services that come with your trekking / climbing fee include guiding you up the mountain or mountains, carrying most of your gear, and all your cooking and dish-washing.[64] Of course, every trip is slightly different and every outfitter has a different way of operating, so it's important to discuss with your outfitter exactly what you're getting and anything that might be lacking.

Kilimanjaro and Mount Meru

One thing you'll notice when you arrive in Tanzania is that there are several hundred companies offering guided treks up Kilimanjaro and Mount Meru. Only Tanzanian-owned businesses are allowed to operate within Tanzanian national parks.

In the 1998 edition of this book, I asked Matthew Mombo, Kilimanjaro National Park warden, which tour operators working on Kilimanjaro were the best, and I made a list for the reader. In this edition, with so many more companies offering outfitter services, I have had to limit my list to a handful of firms that I have heard good reports about from other climbers / trekkers (see Appendix D) or have used myself.[65]

If you are interested in shopping around—which is highly recommended—I suggest you scour the web and get a few ideas about what you're looking for (prices, etc.). But I suggest *not* relying entirely on any website for a recommendation for an outfitter. Nearly every website providing information about climbing Kili lists outfitters as part of its editorial content. Obviously, most editorial content on the web is either directly or indirectly supported through paid advertising, and most Kili "info" sites make some kind of premium for promoting the agencies they list. The best method is to talk to other climbers who've done the mountain (and these days, they're everywhere) and ask them about their experiences and whether or not they'd recommend a firm (see also Appendix H). Remember too that the companies listed in most guidebooks constitute about one-twentieth of the companies that actually do the work (the bulk of the firms are simply booking agencies—and there are thousands of these—and they don't do any actual work).

Also, if you have any questions about tour operators, the park warden is available to discuss firms with you. You can write to him, but mail takes weeks, even months to get to Tanzania and back to North America or Europe.[66] The best thing to do is go to the park office at the Marangu Gate (on Kili) or the Momella Gate (on Meru) and try to catch the warden or one of his assistants there. Be prepared to wait around for a couple of hours.

The costs of climbing Kilimanjaro and Mount Meru with an outfitter vary wildly, depending on where and how you book your climb (see Avoiding Rip-offs in Chapter 2). Most outfitter-arranged climbs booked in Moshi, Arusha, or Marangu currently range between US$700 and US$1,000 per person. Although this may sound expensive, it's important to factor in how much of these costs are going to park fees (see the Regulations and Fees sections, below). Of, say, US$800 for a 5-day ascent of the Marangu Route, for example, you'll quickly see that about two-thirds of that is going into park fees. Since outfitters generally include the costs of trailhead transportation in the overall price of a climb and renting vehicles is phenomenally expensive, these prices should begin to seem like a bargain. Besides trailhead transportation and national park fees, the prices an outfitter quotes should include food, cooking equipment, and a tent, if one is needed.

There are also some differences in price between the Marangu Route and other routes, which are more difficult to access. Marangu is the cheapest, and likely always will be. The Machame–Mweka combination route is probably next cheapest (around US$1,000). The Shira Plateau and Rongai Routes are the most expensive (US$1,200 and up) because they require a half day's travel to reach the trailheads. Similarly, a typical ascent of Mount Meru's Momella Route will run anywhere from US$400 to US$600, but that includes everything. All prices are generally negotiable.

One of the most positive developments in recent years is the formation of the Mount Kilimanjaro Porters' Society (MKPS), a cooperative organization that benefits the porters by providing clothing, first-aid classes, conservation lessons, and even helps porters' families in the advent of a porter's death.

Another great development in recent years is the appearance of female porters—on all East African mountains. Some nonprofit organizations encourage Western visitors to specifically request female porters. Women typically take a subordinate role in East African societies, and the idea is to allow them to achieve some independence. Indeed, one nonprofit that has trained female porters (the San Francisco–based Climb High Foundation; *www.climbhighfoundation.org*) in the Rwenzoris reported that for many trainees it was their first time ever earning their own money.[67]

Mount Kenya

As noted earlier, all guides and porters in Mount Kenya National Park must have valid Kenya Wildlife Service–issued cards. There are many rogue porters and guides operating around the park, and many times these are urban youngsters who know little about the mountain or mountain travel issues; sometimes, they have a background that includes crime. A decade ago, dozens of tour operators, hoteliers, and porter/guide associations organized themselves into the Association of Mount Kenya Operators (AMKO) to promote tourism and improve the standards of tourist operators on and around Mount Kenya. Most of the outfitters listed in Appendix D are AMKO members.

You can also always get an outfitter recommendation from park officials. The park warden's office is located at the park gate on the Naro Moru Route.

There are some key differences between outfitters on Kili and Mount Meru and those on Mount Kenya. For one thing, most outfitters on Mount Kenya only take clients or groups up Point Lenana, the third-highest summit on the massif.

The standard 4-day trips up to Lenana run anywhere between US$400 and US$600, depending on the company (see Avoiding Rip-offs in Chapter 2).

In 1997, a British friend did a 4-day trip up Point Lenana for US$80. He saved money by taking *matatus* from Nairobi, then walked the entire 30 kilometers from Chogoria to the mountain; on his way out, he walked from the Sirimon Gate down to Nanyuki. His only expenses were park fees and the stingy US$5 per day he spent on a porter.

Ascents to the summits of Nelion and Batian are requested infrequently and are considered a specialty product. Guides will ask a wide variety of sums for the ascent (anywhere from US$100 to US$300 for the summit alone). The more expensive guides are white and/or Nairobi-based. Many locals living in the villages around Mount Kenya guide Nelion and Batian for very modest fees and make better company on the mountain than the Nairobi-based hotshots. However, they often lack basic gear.

Should you plan to put together your own trip up to Lenana or Batian/Nelion, which I recommend, you will likely pay US$8–9 per day for porters, and a few extra dollars per day for a seasoned guide (negotiable).

Outfitters who arrange porters and guides for you will add on a booking fee, as will most hotels that arrange porters and guides, which can double the daily cost of a porter or guide. The eastern side of the mountain is much less expensive for hiring porters and guides than the tourist-oriented western side with its expensive lodges and package tours.

Rwenzoris

The Rwenzoris are a heck of lot easier for the inexperienced East African mountaineer, simply because only one firm—a quasipublic entity called Rwenzori Mountaineering Services (RMS)—is allowed to operate as an outfitter in Rwenzori National Park. Better yet, they post their trekking/climbing rates on their website (see Appendix D).

The company employs many people in the town of Kasese (and has a big office there in Saad House), and it employs nearly all the residents in the small village of Nyakalengija, which lies at the start of the most popular trekking circuit in the mountains.[68]

EQUIPMENT

For both trekking and technical mountaineering on East African mountains, remarkably little gear is needed compared with climbing similar-sized mountains in other parts of the world.

However, Kilimanjaro is nearly 6,000 meters (19,680 feet) tall, and Mount Kenya and Mount Stanley are over 5,000 meters (16,400 feet), and all can be extremely cold at times.

The following suggestions are my recommendations of necessary equipment, divided into two sets: one for trekkers or nontechnical climbers and a second specifically for technical mountaineers. The latter will obviously want to bring most of the items listed in the trekkers' list.

On East African mountains, the three most important gear considerations are your shoes, your sleeping bag, and your clothing, as you'll spend two-thirds of the day in the first, one-third of the day in the second, and 24 hours a day in the third.

Footwear: Sturdy trekking shoes or boots are a must for both the approaches to East African mountains and the standard trekking routes themselves. Ankle-high boots are good for support, but also for keeping out gravel and mud (in the Rwenzoris), but are not entirely necessary (especially if you plan on bringing gaiters). A pair of lightweight footgear (such as the modern plastic sandals now made) are very useful for nighttime, in the huts or in camp, as long as you can fit socks inside.[69] I recommend against down and other types of thermal booties—they get dirty, wet, and useless too quickly, and they offer less functionality than a pair of utilitarian sandals (which can also be used on the journey to the mountains, and in the towns and on approaches to the peaks).

Also, make sure your footwear is well broken in before you travel to East Africa, and carry it in your hand luggage—losing it to flight delays or what have you can bring a halt to a trip up any mountain before you get started. Other gear is less critical than your footwear.[70]

Sleeping bags: How warm a bag do you need? Sadly, sleeping bag ratings are not a bombproof guideline for selecting a sleeping bag because the ratings themselves vary from shape to shape, fill to fill, regional conditions, body size, and how you use it.[71] More important still is how tired and how well nourished you are—tired trekkers and climbers who've hardly eaten all day are excellent candidates for the chills.

On Kilimanjaro, Mount Meru, and Mount Kenya, I recommend going with a bag rated to at least minus 23 degrees Celsius (minus 10 degrees Fahrenheit).[72] Down or artificial fiber seems not to matter, although I personally prefer artificial fiber simply because it's more useable when wet and can handle longer periods of stuffing without detriment to its thermal characteristics. In the Rwenzoris, you'll definitely want to bring an artificial fiber bag because of the incessant moisture. One rated to minus 12 degrees Celsius (10 degrees Fahrenheit) is adequate for the standard trekking circuit in the Rwenzoris. If you go up to Elena Hut or other high places, consider bringing one rated to minus 23 degrees Celsius (minus 10 degrees Fahrenheit). (Note: These days, most East African outfitters offer sleeping bags for rent.)

Clothes: On all East African mountains, the best clothing is a collection of items that can be layered one over the other as you ascend to colder areas. Fleece and polypropylene items work well, and you should plan on bringing at least three layers, not counting a shell system to go over the thermal layers. Cotton clothing is not a good idea at the higher and colder elevations. Although this warning will sound ridiculous to experienced mountaineers, I've seen dozens of climbers on all East Africa's mountains wearing cotton socks and cotton turtle-necked shirts.

In the Rwenzoris, be warned: you will get wet—or rather, wholly soaked—and the best strategy is to plan for it. That means bringing footwear that, when totally soaked, you know you won't mind sliding your cold feet into each morning. The best shoes to wear are gum boots (calf-high rubber boots, often called

Wellingtons after the Duke of Wellington, who had his bootmaker modify a Hession boot), bought at the local stores in Kasese—Rwenzori Mountaineering Services, the sole outfitter in Rwenzori National Park, can arrange to get you a pair; the cost is around Ush5,000 (US$3) to rent for a trek and about Ush12,000 (US$7) to purchase.[73] Likewise, bring *at least* two pairs of socks: one pair for daily soaking and another pair (at least) that will be kept dry, for camping (though this second pair will also get soaked). Third, bring a second pair of "walking" pants, whatever they are. Your first pair will be mud- and water-logged by the end of your first day, and it's nice to have a "non-bog" pair when the weather clears.

Also, for the Rwenzoris, bring a poncho! You will wear it almost the entire time you're walking. The best kinds are not the cheap, flimsy kind you get in outdoor shops; rather, look for military-model ponchos (with thick waterproof coatings), which are sturdier, usually camouflage-colored, and designed to cover small villages. Many websites sell them.

Tents: On Kili, for all routes other than the Marangu Route (whose huts must be booked in advance), it is advisable to bring a tent. There are huts on many of the routes other than Marangu, but these are in such a bad state of repair that few climbers use them. Porters and guides use the huts for cooking, so they have soot-coated walls and are pretty unappealing. However, most outfitters provide tents for Kili.

On Mount Kenya, I also recommend a tent, as you will be more assured of privacy and will avoid being hassled by local people illegally trying to extract hut fees from you (see Hut Reservations, below). Please note that if you are approaching the Mount Kenya massif via the Chogoria Route, this route is a tents-only route. Minto's Hut on the Chogoria Route is reserved for porters/guides. Also, since the last edition of this book, note that Two Tarn Hut and Kami Hut have been removed.

I recommend bringing a tent in the Rwenzoris too, because of the small size of the huts, and a tent is a must if you plan on doing some of the more adventurous routes. Don't bring a tent for Mount Meru; the huts are huge, clean, and comfortable, and you'll likely have them nearly to yourself.

Discuss with your outfitter other things you'll need to bring. Generally, you will not need to bring along your own cooking utensils or food, as they will be provided, unless you are doing something other than a standard trek or climb. However, you still might want to bring some of your own food in case the East African mountain food is not palatable.[74]

Backpacks: Because your porters will carry the bulk of your load (usually sleeping bags, tents, nighttime gear, etc.), you need to only bring a personal day pack for trekking on all East African mountains. You will have the carried bag delivered to you each night so you can use the gear. Please note, however, that the porters in the Rwenzoris will take whatever bag you give them and drop it into a burlap sack rigged with straps.[75] Thus, it's best not to keep your "to-be-portered-gear" in a standard large backpack in the Rwenzoris; rather, I recommend dry bags, designed for canoeing, kayaking, and whitewater rafting.

Stoves/Fuel: As a result of deforestation, stoves are now required on East

Porter weighing loads at the Marangu Gate, Kilimanjaro

African peaks (although in the Rwenzoris this rule has not yet become reality, and porters still cook meals over charcoal fires). But you need not bring either stove or fuel on any East African peak, unless you plan something quite out of the ordinary. In short, leave them at home.

Whereas ten years ago you needed to bring everything from home, as there were no climbing or outdoor equipment shops in East Africa, that has changed considerably, at least on Kili and Mount Meru. Most of the trekking/climbing outfitters have vast stores of clothing and equipment, all rentable, and at the Marangu Gate the Kilimanjaro Guides Cooperative Society (KGCS) runs a big booth in the parking lot with a huge selection of equipment and clothing. All the KGCS gear is for rent, and it includes headlamps, stoves, goggles, boots, gloves, sleeping bags, sleeping pads—just about anything you could ever need. Although it's not the absolute best gear around, it's all pretty sturdy stuff, so if your luggage gets lost, or you find yourself in northern Tanzania without mountain gear, the stuff at the KGCS store is wholly adequate.

The various porters and guide organizations around Mount Kenya have equipment that varies greatly in quality, age, and functionality, so ask when booking your trip what they have and what you'll need. Rwenzori Mountaineering Services has very limited gear.

TREKKERS / NONTECHNICAL CLIMBERS

Footwear
Sturdy trekking boots or walking shoes (plastic mountaineering boots are
   unnecessary; bring gum boots for the Rwenzoris)
Heavy-duty socks (3–4 pairs, wool or polypropylene)
Gaiters (to keep out gravel and snow and, in the Rwenzoris, mud)
Sturdy sandals (the kind you can walk / hike long distances in)

Clothing
Shell jacket (including a poncho for the Rwenzoris)
Shell pants
Long top and bottom underwear (expedition-weight
   polypropylene)
Two thermal layers (fleece shirt and pullover)
Long nylon or acrylic walking pants
T-shirt
Shorts
Warm hat
Gloves / mittens

Accessories
Sunglasses
Trekking poles (optional; in the Rwenzoris they are extremely helpful in
   the open bogs)
Headlamp or flashlight
Spare bulbs
Batteries

Camping / Sleeping Gear
Backpack
Tent
Sleeping bag
Sleeping pad
Matches / lighter in waterproof container
Water bottles
Water pump

Personal Hygiene
Toothbrush   Toilet paper
Toothpaste   Small backpacking towels
Dental floss   Sunblock (very important)
Shaving kit   Lip cream with sunblock
Soap

Miscellaneous
Map   Camera / film
Compass   Journals / pens
Whistle   Zippered plastic bags
Pocketknife   Sewing kit
First-aid kit   Extra food
Insect repellent   Extra clothing

TECHNICAL MOUNTAINEERS

Mountaineering boots (leather boots work fine)
Helmet
Harness
Crampons (flexible, twelve-point crampons work fine)
Ice tools / axes
Extra ice picks and accessories
Carabiners (20–30)
Slings or runners (6–10)
Ropes, 60 meters (200 feet) x 9 millimeters (2)
Set of wired stoppers (usually 8–10)
Ice screws (6–10)
Set of camming units (with half sizes for the more serious routes)
UV-blocking goggles or mountaineering glasses
Technical day pack
Bivy sack
Stove
Fuel containers / fuel
Cooking pots
Cooking kit

TREKKING VERSUS TECHNICAL MOUNTAINEERING

The biggest problem with putting together a book like this is differentiating between technical mountaineering (with ropes, hardware, and so forth) and trekking (without equipment), which is also called walking or hiking.

Also, there is scrambling, which is hiking on very steep ground, with use of the hands needed for balance and upward progress. Trekkers often consider scrambling at the upper end of their abilities; technical mountaineers consider it at the lower end.

Where I grew up, "climbers" were technical mountaineering types who used ropes, hardware, and special skills for an ascent. However, most people who reach the summit of Kilimanjaro consider themselves climbers. For this book, I have decided to lump everyone together as climbers, whether they are doing a walking route or a serious Grade VI technical climb. Thus, I've tried to make the extensive descriptions of trails and climbs extremely clear, so that the reader can tell what kind of ascent he's reading about.

In this guidebook, I have described six major forest and moorland trekking routes on Kilimanjaro (Marangu, Mweka, Umbwe, Machame, Shira Plateau, and Rongai), one trekking route on Mount Meru (Momella), five forest and moorland routes on Mount Kenya (Naro Moru, Sirimon, Burguret, Timau, and Chogoria), and a trekking circuit through the Rwenzoris that leads to the standard climbing routes on the three tallest peaks there. The peaks themselves are a different matter. On Kilimanjaro, there are two trekking routes to the summit of Kibo, Kili's highest peak: the Normal Route and the Barafu Route. A third route up Kibo, the Western Breach Route (aka the Great Western Arch), is often called a trekking route, but it involves scrambling and is therefore not pure trekking.

Land Rovers passing en route to the Rongai Route trailhead, Kilimanjaro

The Momella Route on Mount Meru (the standard route described in this guide) is a trekking route, and anyone who can walk at altitudes up to 4,573 meters (15,000 feet) can do it.[76]

There are no trekking routes to the two highest summits of Mount Kenya: Batian and Nelion. However, there are trekking routes on Mount Kenya's third-highest summit, Point Lenana.

Besides the standard Rwenzoris loop trail (the Bujuku–Mubuku Circuit), I have described climbs on Mounts Stanley, Speke, and Baker. The climbs on Stanley and Speke require glacier travel skills and scrambling experience; most fit adults will be able to handle these routes, and learning glacier travel skills can be accomplished on the ascent with a qualified guide. The standard route on Baker is a hike, albeit a rough, demanding one.

Distinctions as to whether a route requires technical mountaineering skills and equipment—or, conversely, can be done in just hiking boots—will become obvious in individual route descriptions.

CLIMBING GRADES

This guidebook uses the East African grading system for climbs. For technical mountaineering routes (hard climbs), the system uses numbers between Grade I and Grade VII. For routes that fall into the category of trekking (walks and hikes), the East African tradition is to use three simple descriptive phrases to grade climbs: "walk," "stiff walk," and "scramble."

Although American and European rock climbers might not appreciate the East African grading system at first, as it is vague in terms of individual moves, it actually makes a lot of sense in mountaineering situations. As any mountaineer knows, it's often possible to avoid one variation of a route and climb another, and conditions—and therefore grades—change. The East African system also takes into account objective dangers such as rockfall.

Perhaps the most unusual thing about East African grades is that both rock and ice routes are graded under the same system. In other parts of the world, rock ratings and ice ratings are separated. Although the East African system works well in a mountaineering sense, it is sometimes difficult to translate one mountaineer's understanding of a Grade III rock route into a Grade III ice climb. I have therefore added my own comparison of East African grades with American ice climbing grades, using the water ice (WI) prefix in the accompanying chart.

Aid ratings (A1 to A6) are based on American aid ratings, as these are now the most commonly used aid ratings in the world.

None of the routes on the mountains should be considered in terms of their grades alone. These are high mountains, and the weather, the season, your fitness, and your experience with climbing at altitude for extended periods all come into play.

EAST AFRICAN CLIMBING GRADES

East African	American	American Water Ice	English	French
Walk	Class 1		Walk	
Stiff walk	Class 2		Stiff walk	
Scramble	Class 3		Scramble	
Grade I	Class 4/5.1–5.2		Easy–moderate	F (facile)
Grade II	Class 5.3	WI 1	Moderate–difficult	PD (peu difficile)
Grade III	Class 5.3–5.4	WI 2	Difficult–very difficult	AD (assez difficile)
Grade IV	Class 5.5	WI 3	Very difficult–mild severe	D (difficile)
Grade V	Class 5.6–5.7	WI 4	Severe–very severe	TD (très difficile)
Grade VI	Class 5.8	WI 5	Very severe–hard very severe	ED (extrêmement difficile)
Grade VII	Class 5.9–5.11	WI 6	Extreme	ABO (abominable)

MAPS

Numerous maps of Kilimanjaro and Mount Kenya are available in East Africa, North America, and Europe. Many are poorly made and inaccurate—maps of the Rwenzoris and Mount Meru are a little tougher to come by. For Mount Kenya, Andrew Wielochowski and Mark Savage's *Mt. Kenya Map and Guide* is generally regarded as the best. This publication, which has been updated over the years, is actually three maps (one of which is a full-sized topographic map) and a condensed technical mountaineering guide all in one. Wielochowski has also created a similar product for Kilimanjaro, the *Kilimanjaro Map and Guide*, and one for the Rwenzoris (not surprisingly, the *Rwenzori Map and Guide*), which also include full-size topographic maps. These are usually rare in East African bookstores and are more easily acquired in Europe and North America via specialty shops that stock maps and climbing guides.

The best stand-alone Kilimanjaro map available is *The New Map of the Kilimanjaro National Park*, produced by Maco Editions, LLC, in conjunction with Nature Discovery. This excellent little map is about five guides in one and includes maps of the region, the park, and the summit routes on Kibo. It also has a chart matching altitudes with flora and fauna and elevation profiles of the different trekking routes up Kili. (For information on obtaining these and other related maps and guides in North America and the United Kingdom, see Appendix F.)

The maps included in this guidebook cover the major forest and moorland approach routes on Kilimanjaro, Mount Meru, Mount Kenya, and the Rwenzoris, as well as the locations of the various trekking routes on the peaks. Though a general road map can be helpful for travel in East Africa, it's not necessary to purchase one specifically for your trip to an East African mountain. Unfortunately, there are no road maps in existence that accurately and completely depict the intricate network of minor dirt roads that traverse the agricultural lower slopes of these mountains. In fact, most road maps available for East Africa depict only the major highways (usually the paved ones). In the case of all East African peaks, you are unlikely to be driving your own automobile to the trailheads anyway (see Getting to the Mountains, below). Although I have included directions for reaching the trailheads for all the major trails, you may need to stop and ask for directions from locals once you are on the mountains, as roads wash out, bridges collapse, and things, in general, change.

An excellent hand-drawn city map of Arusha has become available in recent years, produced by Hoopoe Safaris (see Appendix F). It's a map on one side and a whole lot of advertising on the reverse.

FOOD

Food prepared on the mountains of East Africa by the porters and guides is like the food in the cities, towns, and villages: good, but it takes some getting used to.

It's amazing to watch the local porters and guides lug pots, cans, and bottles up East African mountains, then prepare meals in the most basic way. Often, the food is set out on a picnic blanket, and it is always served with tea, a throwback to the colonial days.

Unless you specify otherwise, your guide and porters, who take on the role of cook at mealtime, will likely prepare breakfasts of eggs, sausages, toast, pancakes, and fruit. Lunches are pretty similar, with a chicken wing or lump of cheese thrown in for good measure, and a carrot replacing the fruit. Dinners are generally some kind of meat with rice, potatoes, *ugali* (a type of cornmeal common in East Africa), or *matoke* (a carbohydrate dish made from plantains and common in Uganda).

With most outfitters, you can request to bring your own food, or a special kind of diet. I can't vouch for how good the food will be if that's the case. I've always found it better and easier to eat what they give you. The servings are huge, and it's all cooked to death, so there is little threat of contamination.

If you do decide to bring your own special food on the mountain, bring it from home. There is no such thing as "backpacking" food or anything like it in East Africa.

PHYSICAL FITNESS

There are three factors you should consider when preparing to trek up or do a technical climb on any of East Africa's mountains: your fitness, the altitude, and how hard you push your body on the ascent. If you're a couch potato and live at sea level and want to run up Kili, clearly you're going to have a harder time than if you're a marathon runner living in Leadville, Colorado (elevation about 10,000 feet), who plans to slowly wander up the Marangu trail. Your success on East Africa's mountains lies at the intersection of fitness, altitude, and speed of ascent. Having said that, the other thing to remember about altitude is that it affects different people differently, and that it can affect you differently *on different occasions.*[77] In short, it's a very difficult challenge. Regardless of where you live, you should strive to be in as good a physical (aerobic) condition as you can be.

Additionally, it really helps to have *some* kind of experience with altitude. If you can, before your East Africa trip, try hiking a few peaks in your own area. In the western United States and Canada, Europe, and New Zealand, there are many high peaks that offer a chance to get some distance between yourself and the sea. Obviously, the United Kingdom, Australia, and South Africa lack the high places of North America and Europe, but a few Munros or a trek up Kosciosko (and some of its neighbors) or some sturdy hiking in the Drakensberg mountains can't hurt.

Finally, go slowly, and don't let anyone rush you. Climbing mountains is about experiencing them—being part of the natural world for awhile. Going slowly enhances (and lengthens) this remarkable experience, while at the same time increasing your likelihood of reaching a summit. *Pole-pole* (slowly, slowly) isn't just the mantra of the guides and porters; it's a way to ensure success. Traveling slowly doesn't just mean hiking at a relaxed pace; if you think you'll have difficulty with the altitude, consider staying extra nights at certain places—Kibo Hut on Kili, for example.

In the first edition of this book, written when I was thirty, I mentioned that I'd never trained for any climbing on any of these mountains. I'd found simply taking my time while walking through the forests en route to the mountains to be more helpful than any aerobic conditioning plan I might follow before leaving home.

Now, older, I do recommend aerobic training before visiting East Africa. I recommend running or walking 10–15 miles per week for 6–8 weeks before your departure—at least—if you are aerobically challenged.

HIGH-ALTITUDE PROBLEMS

The most frequent illnesses mountaineers going to East Africa's mountains will encounter are various altitude-related conditions. They are all a result of climbing too high, too fast. And the one common treatment that works best for all three of them is descent.

There are no hard and fast rules about who will be affected by these illnesses. Some Himalayan experts who have been climbing for years can experience altitude sickness; meanwhile, inexperienced climbers going high for the first time might feel fine all the way to the top of Kilimanjaro.

The major illnesses are outlined below, but these are such serious issues I recommend you research these ailments further. Some websites and references are listed in the appendixes.

Acute Mountain Sickness (AMS)

The most common altitude-related problem is acute mountain sickness (AMS). Like other altitude illnesses, AMS is caused by ascending to high elevations too quickly for the body to adjust. AMS can occur at any altitude but is most likely in the first 1,000 meters (3,280 feet) of elevation gain during a climb. Generally, its symptoms begin to occur at 2,500 meters (8,000 feet). Those who live at low elevations, fly to East Africa, and get straight on a mountain are especially vulnerable.

Symptoms of AMS include headache, breathlessness at rest, nausea, vomiting, dizziness, a rasping cough, insomnia, and a loss of appetite. To quote Dr. Charles Houston, a leading researcher on altitude-related sicknesses, "AMS is much like a bad hangover, and like a hangover usually subsides in a day or two."

A normal but unpleasant occurrence at altitude is Cheyne-Stokes breathing, also called periodic breathing, which causes a dozing-off climber to suddenly awake gasping for air. This occurs regularly above 2,700 meters (9,000 feet) and can be extremely frustrating but isn't dangerous (whereas such breathing is very abnormal if due to something other than being at altitude, such as a head injury).

AMS is easily cured by descending to a lower altitude and resting for a day or two. Generally, after this period of rest, a climb can be resumed.

It is also important to remember that not everything that feels like AMS is AMS. There are many bugs in East Africa, including a simple stomach bug, that can cause similar symptoms.

In recent years, some climbers and trekkers have begun using *Ginkgo biloba* leaf extract for the prevention of AMS. Some studies—formal and informal—have suggested it reduces incidents of AMS. Classified as a dietary supplement, and one of the most popular on earth, ginkgo is believed to function in several ways—notably as a bloodflow enhancer in microcapilleries—explaining how it might help against AMS. While formal testing in mountain settings might be limited, the fact that it's an innocuous herbal remedy means there is little argument against trying it, if you think it might help you. Remember, the evidence—informal or otherwise—that it can prevent or lessens the affects of HAPE or HACE is limited.[78]

High-Altitude Cerebral Edema (HACE)

High-altitude cerebral edema (HACE) is the most serious altitude-related illness and is caused by a lack of oxygen. The large and small arteries of the brain dilate so they can carry more blood and more oxygen, causing the brain to swell.[79]

One of the obvious results of this swelling, or cerebral edema, is a tremendous headache. Other symptoms are confusion, hallucination, an inability to control emotions, and a staggering walk. The staggering walk is often one of the most definitive ways of identifying a HACE victim. Ask the victim to walk heel to toe along a straight line; if the victim has a problem with that they are in trouble and need to descend.

As with HAPE, it is imperative to get the victim to a lower elevation as quickly as possible. Carry the person if you must! Don't wait for helicopters. The victim must descend until fully well and with absolutely no residual loss of coordination (ataxia).

High-Altitude Pulmonary Edema (HAPE)

High-altitude pulmonary edema (HAPE), an accumulation of fluid in the lungs, can come on quickly and kill a victim within a few hours. Symptoms include exhaustion, difficulty in breathing (at rest), chest pain, a gurgling noise in the chest, and a cough with bloody sputum (saliva mixed with mucus).

The best treatment (the only treatment) is to get the victim to a lower elevation as soon as possible, even if that means carrying the person. Oxygen is often used to treat HAPE on mountaineering expeditions (in conjunction with a hyperbaric bag if available), but the best treatment is a fast and immediate descent. The victim should be kept warm or the pressure in their pulmonary vessels may increase even further, and you don't want that. Adalat (nifedipine) is an important treatment and is used to decrease the pulmonary pressure by dilating the pulmonary blood vessels.

Acclimatization

There are a few simple rules that you should swear by if you plan to reach the summits of any peaks in East Africa.

First, climb slowly. The expression *pole-pole* ("slowly, slowly" in Swahili) is well known as a climber's mantra in East Africa. A slow ascent will always produce better results than a fast one.

Above 1,500 meters (5,000 feet), experts recommend taking a full day for every 300 meters (1,000 feet) of elevation increase. This is sometimes difficult because of time considerations. If time and budget allow, plan on spending one or two extra nights on the mountain. The extra time will help you acclimatize and increase your chances of reaching the summit.

"If one member of the party shows signs of HAPE or HACE, slow down, stop, or turn back before the problem escalates," Houston once wrote. "There will be other days, other mountains."

Also, don't let your guide rush you. Guides and porters are especially known for this on the descent, where it's only a problem in terms of fatigue. Certainly they're eager to get home, but occasionally they will set a pace on the ascent that is unreasonable. Set your own pace and don't be pressured into going at a speed you can't handle.

Second, drink a lot of water. Acclimatization is much easier for a well-hydrated body than a dehydrated body. Drink at least 4 liters per day—6 liters if you can. Avoid diuretics such as coffee and tea, as well as alcohol and recreational drugs.

Many climbers like to use drugs to help with acclimatization and to treat altitude-related problems when they occur. Such drugs include Diamox (acetazolamide), Decadron (dexamethasone), Adalat (nifedipine), and others. If you decide to use any of these drugs read as much as you can about them before you go (and before you use them), talk to your physician, and understand the side effects, good and bad. I still adhere to the get-in-shape regime.[80]

Hypothermia and Frostbite

East Africa's mountains lack the extremely cold temperatures found in many mountain ranges of the world, but hypothermia and frostbite can still occur.

Hypothermia is a condition in which the body's core temperature drops below normal. The victim becomes weak and often begins to shake. The obvious response is to warm the victim by providing warm liquids, high-energy foods, hot-water bottles, and even crawling into a sleeping bag with the person (both of you nude for better heat transfer).

In frostbite, soft tissue is destroyed as body fluids freeze into crystals around the cells of the tissue. In the initial stages, the skin is white and hard.

In mild frostbite, when the skin is still soft (sometimes called "frostnip"), the affected area can be rewarmed fairly easily by placing the part someplace warm—under an arm, in a sleeping bag, in the crotch, or against the bare skin of a companion (the chest is good). The rewarming process may be painful, but is usually without long-term problems.

When an appendage is seriously affected by frostbite, the best thing to do is to evacuate the victim without rewarming the frostbitten area. Rewarming a frostbitten area often causes more damage than the actual frostbite. Often, a victim can walk out on frostbitten feet but must be carried if the feet are rewarmed.

If your evacuation must include another night out, rewarming the frostbitten area is inevitable. Modern medical thinking now dictates that rewarming be done quickly. Use water between 38 and 41 degrees Celsius (100–105 degrees Fahrenheit) and soak the frostbitten part for 30 minutes. Do not massage the affected flesh in any way. Once the frostbitten area is warm, wrap it with a loose bandage and keep it warm until a full evacuation can be made. Refreezing of a frostbitten part will cause further damage.

The best prevention for both hypothermia and frostbite is to dress properly. Dress in wools and fleece fabrics; never wear cotton clothing! You should also keep yourself well hydrated and well fed.

Denial

Denial is a huge issue on big mountains, especially with people who are adamant about reaching the summit. You need to admit when there is a problem.

Don't succumb to denial just because you are weak or because you aren't leading the pack. Denial can lead to the very serious, life-threatening problems described above.

GETTING TO THE MOUNTAINS

Once you're in East Africa, getting to Kilimanjaro, Mount Meru, Mount Kenya, and the Rwenzoris is fairly easy, although the options are not limitless.

The Kilimanjaro/Mount Meru area is served by an international airport, Kilimanjaro International Airport (KIA), as well as by various buses and shuttles.

The Mount Kenya area is served by tiny airstrips, but many of these are private and arranging a flight to them is very difficult. Reaching the Rwenzoris requires traveling across the entire southwestern part of Uganda, which can take a full day (or longer) via regular local bus; the simplest way to reach them is via a private vehicle (e.g., taxi) rented in Kampala. Air access is very limited.

Only the most popular—and most cost-effective—ways of getting to the mountains are outlined here (see Appendix C for contact information).

To/From Kilimanjaro and Mount Meru

Flying: The single best way to get to and from Kilimanjaro and Mount Meru is via Kilimanjaro International Airport (KIA), 64 kilometers west of Moshi and about 40 kilometers from Arusha. Numerous airlines offer flights into KIA and the schedules for these flights change regularly.

From Europe, KLM offers daily service direct from Amsterdam to KIA and Dar es Salaam.

From various African cities (Nairobi, Dar, Zanzibar, Mombasa, Entebbe, Addis Ababa, etc.) there are many African airlines that offer service to KIA, including Air Tanzania, Kenya Airways, Ethiopian Airlines, South African Airlines, and Precision Air (to/from Nairobi). There is a bank (for exchanging money) as well as a post office in KIA, with strict post-office-like hours.[81]

Nairobi is another option to/from Kili. Jomo Kenyatta International Airport in Nairobi is served by dozens of airlines, including British Airways, which offers daily flights between London and Nairobi. Jomo Kenyatta International is pretty modern by East African standards (it even boasts an ATM and other services).

To reach the Rwenzoris, the best option is to fly to Entebbe, about an hour's drive from the capital, Kampala (which can be done direct from London on British Airways) and to travel by land to the mountains.

Airports in East Africa are fairly basic, although every year Jomo Kenyatta seems to get a new boutique or Western-style restaurant.[82] It's also possible to fly to Arusha, which has an airport serving domestic destinations by Precision Air. Precision Air, Air Tanzania, and Air Excel all fly from Dar to Arusha daily (prices are US$72–82, and schedules vary).

A much cheaper way to get to Arusha and Moshi from Nairobi, Dar, and other cities—and the only real option to flying—is one of the commercial shuttles or buses.

Buses from Dar es Salaam to Moshi and Arusha: There are several companies that offer Dar to Moshi/Arusha service. There are three bus stations in Dar; the Kisutu Terminal on the corner of Morogoro Road and Libya Street downtown is where you can catch buses to Kenya, Uganda, and northern and southern Tanzania, including Moshi and Arusha. There are both "express" and regular buses; however, both seem to take about the same amount of time and make the same number of stops. An express bus will cost you Tsh8,000–9,000 (about US$7–8). A regular bus will cost about half that. The ride to Moshi and Arusha on both express and nonexpress buses takes about 6–8 hours. Also, note that Scandinavia Express has its own terminal at the corner of Misimbazi Street and Nyerere Road. It offers extensive service throughout the region.

Buses from Nariobi to Moshi and Arusha: You can catch buses and *matatus* or *dalla-dallas* (*matautus* in Kenya, *dalla-dallas* in Tanzania) in the River Road/Accra Road area in Nairobi. Scandinavia Express and Riverside Shuttles offer daily services with rates ranging from Tsh8,000 to Tsh10,000 (about US$7–9).

The Davanu shuttle (US$35 one-way; 6-plus hours to Moshi; about 4 to Arusha) leaves from a depot near the Norfolk Hotel in Nairobi at 8:00 AM each morning, although pickup can be arranged at hotels in the city center, and is an excellent way to get to Tanzania. The return shuttle leaves Moshi at 11:00 AM and also picks up at hotels in Moshi. The shuttle runs every day, including holidays.

Riverside Shuttles offers decent service between Nairobi, Arusha, and Moshi. Nairobi to Arusha costs about US$25, and to KIA/Moshi US$35. Arusha to/from Moshi or Kilimanjaro is US$15 (these are one-way), and Nairobi to Kilimanjaro is US$35. The shuttles leave Nairobi at 8:00 AM from near the New Stanley Hotel, on Kenyatta Avenue downtown. Arrive 15 minutes before the departure time. In Arusha it stops at the Novotel, and in Moshi at the downtown clock tower. Hotel pickup is also available, if your hotel is nearby.

It's also possible to catch a *matatu* from Nairobi to Namanga, but getting one from Namanga south to Arusha is, apparently, somewhat difficult because you must walk across the border and take a Tanzanian *dalla-dalla* for the ride to Arusha. Few trekkers and climbers use *matatus* to get to Kilimanjaro, but they are popular for transportation to and from Mount Kenya. (For a greater explanation of *matatus*, see To/From Mount Kenya, later this chapter.)

It's also possible to take a bus from Mombasa direct to Moshi via Taveta, on the border, without going through Nairobi. This costs around Tsh2,000 (US$2). *Matatus* also travel the Mombasa–Moshi route, but it is often necessary to change *matatus* at Taveta or Voi, on the Nairobi–Mombasa Road.

Obviously, coming by road from Nairobi requires a border crossing, in this case at Namanga. If it's your first time in Africa, Namanga can be a bit unnerving. Imposing Masai men and women thrust beads, carvings, and trinkets of all manner in the shuttle windows at you with persistence. You will be required to get off the shuttle and go through both Kenyan and Tanzanian customs, but this process is fairly quick—as long as you can duck past the trinket sellers.

Buses to / from Moshi and Arusha: There are many bus options for the quick trip between Arusha and Moshi, most costing about Tsh1,000 (about US$1); all bus companies seem to converge in Arusha at the Novotel hotel, a skyscraper-type building where buses and shuttles stop for a break (lunch) and to pick up and drop off travelers going in either direction.

The bus station in Moshi—downtown, on Mawenzi Double Road near the mosque—is a bit more chaotic than the Novotel depot in Arusha, but it's easy enough to find the bus you need.

Private shuttles (Davanu, etc.) arrive and leave from their own offices. Davanu's offices (usually open 8:00 AM to 6:30 PM) are located in Kahawa House, which is on the main roundabout in downtown Moshi. Impala Shuttle's offices are in the Impala Hotel, which is on Sekou Toure Way, west of downtown. Riverside Shuttles has an office in the THB Building, on Boma Road, just west of the downtown clock tower. Scandinavia Express has a big station along JK Nyere Road, with service to and from Arusha, Dar, and Nairobi; though you can't catch buses here, it's a quiet place to read the schedules unmolested by trinket sellers.

You can reach the village of Marangu, at the start of Kili's Marangu Route, by bus from Moshi for Tsh1,178 (US$1). A taxi from Moshi to Marangu will cost you about Tsh15,000–20,000 (US$13–18). Taxis around Moshi and Arusha should run you about Tsh2,500–3,000 (US$3–4) for a 5- to 10-minute ride. Always ask the price before you get in. An excellent resource for planning travel in the region is East Africa Shuttles' website, and the Tanzania On-line Information Center has some useful information (see Appendix C).

To / From Mount Kenya

There are many options for getting to and from Mount Kenya from Nairobi. For one thing, a paved tarmac road leads north out of Nairobi to Sagana Junction, where it intersects with a paved tarmac ring road that circles Mount Kenya and connects all the towns (Naro Moru, Nanyuki, Timau, Meru, Chogoria, Chuka, Embu) scattered around the base of the mountain.

It's about 3.5–4 hours' drive from Nairobi to either Naro Moru or Chogoria, plus another 1–2 hours from Naro Moru to Nanyuki, on the northwest side of the mountain. (It's about a 3-hour drive from Chogoria to Nanyuki.)

By taxi: The easiest but most expensive option for getting to any town around the base of the mountain, even from Nairobi, is to hire a taxi. I've done this a couple of times. The first time I did, four German climbers told me not to pay more than Ksh9,585 (US$135) for the service. I actually ended up getting a cab for Ksh6,177 (US$87) from Nairobi to Chogoria. On the return trip, a friend was able to hire a taxi for Ksh3,834 (US$54).

By bus: A much cheaper, but more dangerous, way of getting to Mount Kenya is to go by *matatu*. *Matatus*—the equivalent of the Latin American collectivo taxi—are minibuses designed to carry about ten people, but generally they carry twenty-five or more.

Matatu drivers speed like demons, swerve around corners, force other drivers off the road, and generally wreak havoc. Half the time you're in one, someone is sitting on your lap because there's not enough room. *Matatus* have names like Rambo 2000, Excessive Force, and The Babe Coach. Every single day that you're in Kenya, you can pick up the newspaper and read about deaths from the previous day's *matatu* accidents. I remember one day in which the *matatu* death toll was eighteen!

Regardless, a *matatu* ride from Nairobi to Chogoria or Naro Moru will cost you between Ksh284 and 426 (US$4–6), but if you have a pack or two full of camping or climbing gear, you may be required to pay for the space taken up by your luggage. Once you're in Embu, Chuka, Chogoria, Meru, Nanyuki, Timau, Naro Moru, or any of the other small towns surrounding Mount Kenya, it's extremely easy to get a *matatu* to the next town, or back to Nairobi.

Most *matatus* heading out of Nairobi in any direction leave town from the River Road/Accra Road area, on the northeast side of town. Sometimes, catching one is a matter of walking around and finding one with a sign in the window indicating it's going to the town you're going to.

To/From the Rwenzoris

For the Rwenzoris, most trekkers/climbers will fly into Entebbe, about an hour's drive from the capital, Kampala. There are many transportation options between Entebbe and Kampala, including taxis (about US$25 one-way), buses, minibuses, and even flying. From Kampala (where most climbers will spend a night), you have to traverse the entire southwestern portion of Uganda to reach the Rwenzoris. Luckily, Uganda's a small country.

The best place to stage a trekking/climbing trip in the Rwenzoris is out of the small (and typically hot and dusty) town of Kasese, on the southeastern flank of the range and about 500 kilometers by road from Kampala (via Mbarara). It's also possible to organize your trek/climb out of one of the smaller towns in the area, including Nyakalengija.

From Kampala, the easiest way to Kasese is by road. There are many buses from Kampala to Kasese, but a better, safer way is to hire a taxi of some kind. Driving from Kampala to Kasese or one of the surrounding towns takes about 7 hours, depending on the weather, the state of your taxi, and the traffic in the Kampala suburbs. Buses and taxis for outlying destinations leave from one of three bus and taxi stations—all near each other—near the intersection of Naki-vubo and Namirembe Roads, just north of Nakivubo Stadium, on the western side of downtown. Buses and taxis headed west leave from the westernmost station of the three, Buganda Bus Park (near the "new" taxi stand). Buses from Kampala to Kasese typically cost Ush15,000–20,000 (US$8–11). You can expect to pay anywhere up to US$100 per person one way (US$200 round trip) to go by private taxi from Kampala to Kasese.[83]

It is also possible to charter a flight. Eagle Air and Mission Aviation Fellowship, Ugandan companies based in Kampala, fly to/from Kasese. Eagle used to offer regular once-a-week flights, but at present it seems chartering a plane is necessary. Expect to pay US$200 or more for the flight, depending on whether or not you have to charter your own flight or can buy a seat on someone else's charter.[84]

Renting a Car

I recommend against renting a car in East Africa.

On all East African mountains, outfitters provide transportation to and from the trailhead, so it's unnecessary to rent a car. Besides, if you rent one, you'll have to leave it at a trailhead, then make sure you come back out of the park via that trailhead. The best aspect of climbing these mountains is going up one route and down another so you get to see a completely different aspect of the mountain or range. Also, if you leave a rented vehicle in any of the small villages for any number of nights, it's likely you'll owe the rental agency a new car by the time you get off the mountain.[85]

Because Mount Kenya has a ring road encircling it, getting around Mount Kenya is very easy by *matatu* because the routes are more straightforward to use here than anywhere else in East Africa. Most *matatus* are either going clockwise or counterclockwise around the mountain.

Still, if you must rent a car, it's fairly easy. There are big rental agencies in Nairobi, Dar, Mombasa, Kampala, as well as all the smaller towns in the country. Even in the smallest village, it's usually easy to find someone who will rent you a vehicle, even though they might not be part of an official rental agency. Rates vary wildly, but plan on spending at the very least US$100 per day. The cheapest I've found was US$80 per day for an absolute junker, and most are more like US$200 per day.

KILIMANJARO REGULATIONS AND FEES

Kilimanjaro, Mount Meru, and the Rwenzoris are very much "package tour" mountains, and you're going to end up as part of a group, large or small, whether you like it or not.

The most immediate reason for the package tour status is that Kilimanjaro (KINAPA), Arusha (Mount Meru), and Rwenzori National Parks require you to climb with a local guide or outfitter. No independent climbing is allowed. Further, you must travel with a registered guide in the parks at all times, whether you're going 1 meter inside the park gate or doing a serious technical mountaineering route that will take days. Although this package tour mentality might sound restrictive, it has several benefits, the most important being that you'll save hundreds of dollars and dozens of hours of frustration that would be required to organize food, transportation, porters, and park permits if you did the mountain independently.

In addition, Kilimanjaro, Arusha, and Rwenzori National Parks require that you hire at least one porter to carry the guide's belongings. You are allowed to carry your own food and equipment, if you choose, but since porters are about the cheapest part of an ascent, you're better off hiring some for yourself as well. Two to three porters per climber is standard. The porters will take a load off your back and make your ascent extremely enjoyable.

Your outfitter will arrange a guide and porters for you. (See the list of outfitters in Appendix D.)

There is one other regulation you should be aware of: KINAPA does not allow children under age ten to go higher than 2,700 meters (9,000 feet) on the mountain. Right or wrong, park officials fear children this young might be severely affected by the altitude.

All the other regulations are similar to what you might expect in European and North American parks: carry your litter out, don't harass wildlife, don't start fires, use the latrines (not the woods), stay on trails, and so on.

Climbing Reservations

Besides guides and at least one porter, a reservation is required to climb any route on Kili. KINAPA limits the number of non-Tanzanian climbers to sixty on the Marangu Route, plus thirty-two more on the other routes combined. Your outfitter will arrange a reservation for you at park headquarters either the day you begin your ascent or, if it's in high season, possibly a day or two before.

These mountain reservations get filled up fairly quickly, so you should organize a climb with an outfitter as soon as you get to Arusha, Moshi, or Marangu. Reservations made through big tour operators in Europe and North America work fine, but you will pay a premium for booking from overseas. (See Avoiding Rip-offs in Chapter 2.)

Technical Mountaineering Reservations

Climbing any route on Kili besides the standard trekking routes requires an additional reservation at park headquarters in Marangu. Whereas literally anyone who has the money to pay for a trekking route on the mountain is allowed to go up, technical mountaineers must make a formal application with the park to do mountaineering routes. For obvious reasons, KINAPA officials don't like to let unqualified climbers try routes that are beyond their abilities.

To make the application, KINAPA recommends sending a letter describing your proposed climb, along with a resume of your climbing record, to the park warden (see Appendix B for contact information). Officials will then ascertain whether you are qualified for a technical mountaineering route. Few are ever turned down.

If you send a letter from home to Africa to let KINAPA know you're coming, more than likely you will not get a response. I've sent numerous letters over the years and have never received a reply. The best thing to do is to send a letter a few weeks before you leave for Africa so park officials know you're coming. Then arrange to meet with them once you are at park headquarters in Marangu.

Perhaps the strangest aspect of technical mountaineering on Kilimanjaro is that although you are required to hire a guide when you go inside the park—as you are on trekking routes—most local guides have no technical mountaineering experience. Therefore they will guide you to the base of your proposed route, leave you there, then walk around and meet you on the summit. The park does not require the guides to go with technical mountaineers on their proposed routes.

One other climbing regulation: electric power drills (for bolting) and leaving fixed ropes and other technical gear after an ascent are not allowed. Park philosophy is that fixed ropes—if left permanently—create visual impacts.

Hut Reservations

You will need hut reservations only for the huts on the Marangu Route. The huts on the other routes (Mweka, Umbwe, Machame, Shira Plateau—there are none on the Rongai Route) are merely burned-out metal shells often filled with trash. Most non-Tanzanians who use these other routes bring a tent, and the huts are used only by the guides and porters, who don't seem to mind their state of disrepair. If you do decide to use the huts on these other routes, it's a matter of first come, first served.

If you don't have a tent and really must stay in huts as you ascend the mountain, the ones on the Marangu Route are in good condition. There are three main huts (Mandara Hut, Horombo Hut, and Kibo Hut), spaced a day's walk apart. However, each of these huts is surrounded by a virtual village of buildings, and the names refer to the old huts that existed long before the other structures were built. Some of the additional buildings are for porters and guides to sleep in, others are for park officials, others for small shops. Tourists generally sleep in the original huts.

At the time of this writing, an overnight stay in one of the huts on the Marangu Route cost US$50 per person per night; reservations must be made at the park offices at the Marangu Gate. Your outfitter will arrange these reservations for you as part of your climb.

When you arrive at each hut complex on the Marangu Route, you or your guide must go straight to the caretaker's office and show your reservations to park officials, who will help you find your hut and sleeping quarters. As with most other things, your guide will take care of this for you.

There are no facilities in the huts except for bunks, so you will need to bring a sleeping bag and sleeping pad. Cooking must be done outside. At both Horombo and Mandara Huts, there are separate facilities for washing—small bathroom buildings, with cold showers and toilets. The toilets at Kibo Hut are like toilets on other routes on the mountain—big earthen pits. There is no natural water supply at Kibo Hut, so there are no showers.

Fees

The fees for just about anything on Kilimanjaro are steep, steeper than most of the routes in East Africa. In the mid-1990s, they were raised manyfold as East African governments became aware of the income national parks could generate.[86] The reliance on national parks for revenues means that fees will likely rise every other year or so, and the national parks administration did indeed boost prices again in January 2006. As of this edition, KINAPA fees were as follows:

- Entrance fee: US$60 per person (e.g., tourist) per day for ages sixteen and above; US$10 for visitors aged ten to fifteen
- "Crew" (guide/porter) entrance fee: US$1 per person per trip
- Camping fee: US$40 per person (e.g., tourist) per day (there is no camping fee now on the Marangu Route)
- Hut fee: US$50 per person (e.g., tourist) per day
- Rescue fee: US$20 per person (e.g., tourist) per trip
- Rescue fee deposit (for technical mountaineering only): US$250, US$200

of which will be returned to you after your climb if you have not used rescue services (the unreturned US$50 goes into rescue team supplies and training)
- Ranger fee (for Shira routes): US$20 per trip

Discuss with your outfitter at the time you make your reservation exactly how the park fees will be paid. Because many Tanzanian outfitters are strapped for cash, it's common for them to get you to pay park fees for the whole trip when you show up at the Marangu Gate. (If you are doing the paying, bring U.S. dollars or traveler's checks.)

If you are paying park fees yourself, they need to be deducted from the overall cost of your climb. If you are climbing a route other than the Marangu Route, your outfitter will usually add the park fees into the cost of a climb and send a runner to Marangu to pay them on your behalf.

ARUSHA NATIONAL PARK (MOUNT MERU) REGULATIONS AND FEES

Arusha National Park is very much like Kilimanjaro, and you can't go into the park unless accompanied by a local guide. Arusha National Park (like Rwenzori National Park) has an additional twist: you must travel with an armed ranger (in the case of Mount Meru, to protect you from the wildlife). The regulations for Arusha National Park are also similar to what you might expect in European and North American parks: carry your litter out, don't harass wildlife, don't start fires, use the latrines (not the woods), stay on trails, and so on.

Whereas Kili offers numerous routes, there is currently only one route on Meru open to tourists, the Momella Route. You are not allowed to stray from it (any great distance) and hiking into the crater floor is not allowed. Also, to avoid conflicts with wildlife, you're only allowed to start your hike during the midportion of the day, between 9:00 AM and 3:00 PM.

Hut Reservations

Because there are relatively few people going up Mount Meru, getting hut reservations isn't much of an issue—and the huts themselves have plenty of room. Your outfitter will arrange hut reservations for you.

Fees

The fees for Arusha National Park are very reasonable:
- Entrance fee: US$25 per person (e.g., tourist) per day
- Guide/porter park entrance fee: US$2 per person per day
- Hut fee: US$20 per day
- Rescue fee: US$20 per person (e.g., tourist) per trip

MOUNT KENYA NATIONAL PARK REGULATIONS AND FEES

Mount Kenya National Park is much more like national parks found in the United States and other Western countries and is well suited to "independent" or self-created climbing excursions.

Regulations

The regulations for Mount Kenya are pretty straightforward and are posted at every park gate:

- All visitors must sign in when they enter the park and sign out when they leave. All visitors must pay the park entrance fee. Do not attempt to enter the park via any other unofficial route without the authority of the senior warden.
- No harassing the wildlife.
- All litter must be carried out (you might be asked to show your litter at the gate when leaving the park).
- Driving within the park is prohibited after 6:00 PM (dark).
- No one is allowed to enter the park alone.
- No parasailing is allowed in the park.

No technical mountaineering or trekking permits are required. You must only pay the park entrance fee and the camping fees (see Fees, below). Unlike Kilimanjaro, guides and porters are not compulsory on Mount Kenya. About the only regulation of consequence for most visitors is that you are not allowed to enter or move within the park alone. Solo climbing is permitted but someone on the ground *must* know your intent and keep an eye out for you.

Mount Kenya National Park will not refund daily park entrance and camping fees if you leave the park earlier than you expect, and if you stay longer than expected within the park, you must pay for the additional days and nights on your way out. This is one of the great flexibilities of Mount Kenya National Park.

Hut Reservations

There are both large bunkhouses and smaller huts on Mount Kenya. All these buildings are owned by various groups.

On the Naro Moru Route, the bunkhouses at the Meteorological Station ("Met Station") and Mackinder's Camp are administered by the Naro Moru River Lodge; space can be reserved through the lodge (see Appendix D for contact information). The cost is around US$10–12 per night.

The Old Moses and Shipton's Camp bunkhouses on the Sirimon Route are administered by Mountain Rock Lodge; reservations can be made through the lodge (see Appendix D). The costs are US$10 and US$12, respectively, per night. If the bunkhouses are not full, it's possible to show up and simply arrange a sleeping space upon your arrival.

Recently, Austrian Hut was acquired by Kenya Wildlife Service (KWS), which has renovated it and furnished it with mattresses. There is a caretaker and a park ranger permanently based on-site with a radio for emergencies. Reservations for Austrian Hut are made at the park gates on entry and accommodation costs around US$12 per night. Impromptu overnight stops need to be paid for at the park gate on exit (the ranger radios this information down) and *not* directly to the people at the hut. Indeed, at all the bunkhouses and huts on Mount Kenya, you'll typically find local porters and guides who will offer to take your money so they can pay the organizations that own the huts. Don't pay them.

The only other huts on the mountain are Minto's Hut, which is for guide/porter accommodation only, and Liki North Hut, which is available on a first-come, first-served basis. Both these huts are decrepit.

Because of the hassle of dealing with huts, bookings, and fees, I thoroughly advocate bringing a tent and camping instead.

Fees
The fees for Mount Kenya aren't as steep as they are for Kilimanjaro, but they still hurt if you're on a budget. As of early 2006 they were as follows:
- Entrance fee: US$15 per person (e.g., tourist) per day
- Guide/porter park entrance fee: US$2 per person per day
- Camping fee: US$8 per person (e.g., tourist) per day
- Hut fee: US$8–12 per person (e.g., tourist) per day

For Kenyan citizens, the fees are Ksh100 (US$1.50) per day for adults; Ksh50 (US$0.70) for children and students. For Kenya residents, the fees are Ksh500 (US$7) per day for adults; Ksh200 (US$3) for children; and Ksh100 (US$1.50) for students. There is also a vehicle fee: Ksh200 (US$3) per day.

RWENZORI NATIONAL PARK REGULATIONS AND FEES
Rwenzori National Park is very much like Kilimanjaro and Arusha National Parks, and you can't go into the park unless accompanied by Rwenzori Mountaineering Service's (RMS) guides and porters. Like Arusha National Park, Rwenzori National Park requires you to travel with an armed ranger. In this case, not for wildlife protection reasons, but for protection from rebels who have historically used the park as a base for fighting the Ugandan government. The real surprise about the arms—usually Russian machine guns—though, is that the rangers carry them everywhere. Climbing snow-and-ice-clad Mount Stanley with a ranger dressed in mountaineering garb accentuated by a machine gun slung over his shoulder (held on by climbing webbing) is about the weirdest thing you'll see in these fabulous mountains.

Regulations
The most significant Rwenzori National Park regulation for climbers is that you can (as of early 2006) only enter the park on Mondays, Wednesdays, and Fridays. This is for two reasons: there aren't enough qualified rangers to accompany trekkers and the accommodations within the park are limited.

Hut Reservations
RMS will make all your arrangements in terms of huts and lodging. There are relatively few people trekking the Bujuku–Mubuku Circuit, so getting space is not generally a concern and RMS will know who's in what hut on any given night. Still, it's worth asking, because having to camp means being prepared in terms of good equipment (because the weather is so bad), and moving on to another hut (if one is full) is a hard notion after you've been slogging through mud all day.

Fees

The fees for Rwenzori National Park are commensurate with other East African peaks. One thing to note, though, is that porters and guides are paid in the number of "stages" they do. A stage is roughly the distance between any two huts—typically, one day's travel. It becomes noteworthy if you're planning something like a traverse of one of the main peaks or something out of the ordinary, because often that requires several extra stages, sometimes all in one day. Other fees are as follows (and the Uganda Wildlife Authority's website is a good reference for park tariffs, *www.uwa .or.ug/tariffs.htm*):

- Entrance fee: US$25 per day for foreign nonresidents (e.g., tourists); US$15 per day for East African residents; and Ush5,000 per day for Ugandan citizens
- Porter's fee: US$5 per stage
- Guide's fee: US$7 per stage
- Hut fee: US$15 per day

As with other East African peaks, the cost for the Bujuku–Mubuku Circuit isn't usually quoted on a piecemeal basis; rather, all costs are lumped together by RMS into one overall package price. Currently, the standard 6-day / 7-night circuit trek (without any climbing to summits) costs foreign nonresidents US$567, East African residents US$465, and Ugandans US$250. These prices cover guides' wages and food, two porters' wages and food, the national park entrance fee, accommodation on the mountain, and a "charcoal" fee (charcoal carried up from Nyakalengija is used for cooking).

For mountaineers, RMS offers a menu for ascents of various peaks, with the additional "mountaineering" expense tacked onto the trekking fees for the Bujuku–Mubuku Circuit. As of early 2006, the total per person (trekking plus peak fees) were as follows:

- Mount Gessi: US$699
- Margherita: US$692
- Albert: US$692
- Alexandra: US$692
- Mount Meobius: US$685
- Luigi di Savoia: US$685
- Mount Baker: US$656
- Mount Speke: US$656

Obviously, if you do more than one peak—say, Stanley and Speke, or Stanley, Speke, and Baker, or some other combination—the prices will be higher. They range from US$59 for Baker to US$117 for Gessi (about US$90 for Stanley's summits and Speke). These peak "premiums" don't seem exactly straightforward until you recognize that they're based on difficulty and the amount of effort that the guides will be putting into each ascent. Regardless, RMS can quickly and easily take your planned trip and give you a dollar figure for overall cost. To keep up to date on RMS's prices, visit their website (see Appendix D).

CONSERVATION

The old adage, "Pack it in, pack it out," applies as much on East Africa's mountains as any other place on earth. Perhaps especially here, because guides and porters—who have lately become aware of the trash issue—have made valiant efforts to clean up the mountains.

Make sure that after any meal or overnight camp that all your refuse is collected and carried along for the remainder of the trip.

Kilimanjaro, Arusha, Mount Kenya, and Rwenzori National Parks all require that trekkers and technical mountaineers show their trash on the way out of the park, although often the rule is not enforced. Kilimanjaro National Park does official cleanups on the mountain several times a year.

Evacuation and urination should be done in designated pit toilets, which are at all overnight camping areas on these mountains. If you are on the trail between overnight stops, make sure you eliminate at least 100 meters (328 feet) from any watercourse.

Chapter 4

KILIMANJARO

There, ahead, all he could see, as wide as all the world, great, high, and unbelievably white in the sun, was the square top of Kilimanjaro.
—Ernest Hemingway, *The Snows of Kilimanjaro*

Kilimanjaro. There are few mountains in the world whose name evokes as much passion, wonder, and awe. From Ernest Hemingway's famous short story to the classic John Wayne film *Hatari!*, Kilimanjaro has always held a unique place in both the Western and African psyche. When you get to Kili, you'll realize why.

It is often said that Kilimanjaro is the biggest freestanding mountain in the world, in that it is not connected to other peaks in a range. Rising dramatically more than 5,000 meters (16,400 feet) above the East African plain (itself about 800 meters/2,624 feet above sea level), the massif is 60 kilometers long and 40 kilometers wide. It lies about 330 kilometers south of the equator, wholly within the United Republic of Tanzania.

Kilimanjaro is a complex mountain. The name Kilimanjaro actually refers to an entire massif comprised of three separate extinct volcanoes: Kibo (5,895 meters/19,341 feet), Mawenzi (5,149 meters/16,893 feet), and Shira (3,962 meters/12,999 feet). To confuse matters, the summit of Kibo is often referred to as Uhuru Peak (5,895 meters/19,341 feet; formerly Kaiser Wilhelm Spitze), and the highest point on Mawenzi is called Hans Meyer Peak.

Because of the mountain's proximity to both the equator and the Indian Ocean and because of its tremendous height, Kilimanjaro boasts five major ecological zones, each of which occupies about 1,000 meters of altitude: the lower slopes (800–1,800 meters); the montane forest zone (1,800–2,700 meters); the heath and moorland zone (2,700–4,000 meters); the alpine desert zone (4,000–5,000 meters); and the summit zone (5,000–5,895 meters). Each is a world in itself, with unique flora and fauna found few other places in Africa.

In the early 1900s, the area around Kilimanjaro was established as a game preserve. In 1921, the Tanganyikan government changed that status to a forest and game preserve. In 1957, Tanganyika National Parks authorities, with support from many local and international conservation groups, formally proposed creating a national park that would include the mountain and the surrounding forest and game preserve.

It took until 1973 for the formal creation of Kilimanjaro National Park (KINAPA). Its boundaries were based on a fairly simple concept: any land above

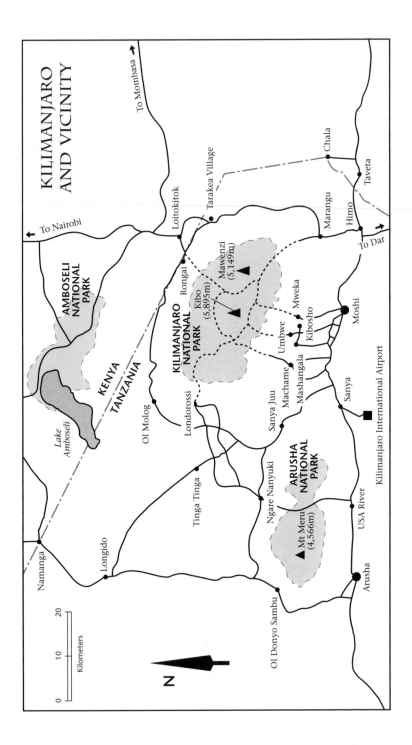

the 2,700-meter level is in the park. Altogether, the park comprises 756 square kilometers.

Kilimanjaro National Park was officially opened in 1977, and in 1989 it was declared a world heritage site by the World Heritage Convention.

THE NAME

Kilimanjaro's name has been a source of speculation for years. The Wachagga people of northern Tanzania—who emigrated to the Kilimanjaro area 250–300 years ago—claim to have no name for the entire mountain but are believed to be responsible for the individual names of Kipoo (Kibo) and Kimawenzi (Mawenzi).

Most historians and anthropologists believe the first part of the word Kilimanjaro—*kilima*—is a corruption of the Swahili word for "mountain"—*mlima*. However, the prefix *ki* is confusing because in Swahili, the addition of *ki* makes a noun diminutive, so *kilima* means "small mountain." Many believe the diminutive reference is one of affection for the mountain.

The second part of the word—*njaro*—is open to much greater speculation. Some believe *njaro* is derived from the Swahili word *ngara*, which means "to shine." Others believe it comes from the Wachagga word for caravan, since in the early days of East Africa exploration, caravans used the mountain as a landmark.

Some believe *njaro* refers to a demon who was thought by coastal residents to cause cold. Still others believe that *njaro* is a corruption of the Masai word for water, *ngare*, since Kilimanjaro is a water source for much of the Masai territory that lies north of it.

POPULARITY

Kilimanjaro is one of the most popular mountains in the world. In 1982, 4,600 nonresidents and 1,600 residents visited Kilimanjaro National Park. By 1991, the number of nonresident visitors had gone up to 10,800, while the number of resident visitors had decreased to 810.[87] Of the 10,800 nonresidents who visited KINAPA in 1991, 9,800 attempted to climb the Marangu/Normal Route to the summit, and about 1,000 took other routes. In 1994–1995, the park recorded a total of 14,578 visitors. In 2005, I was told by a reliable source that the number of people climbing Kili had jumped to somewhere between 25,000 and 27,000 people per year. Adding porters and guides, that likely means there are nearly 100,000 visitors to the park annually.

It is estimated that only 40–50 percent of all summit-bound climbers are successful in reaching Uhuru Peak.

In 1991, the park earned US$1.75 million from park fees. Reportedly the money goes into much more than maintaining the park, but to KINAPA's credit, it does cleanups on the Marangu Route twice a year.

In January 1997, park fees jumped by 50 percent (and were raised again in early 2006). Similarly large increases should be expected in the future as East African nations tap into the growing worldwide tourism boom.

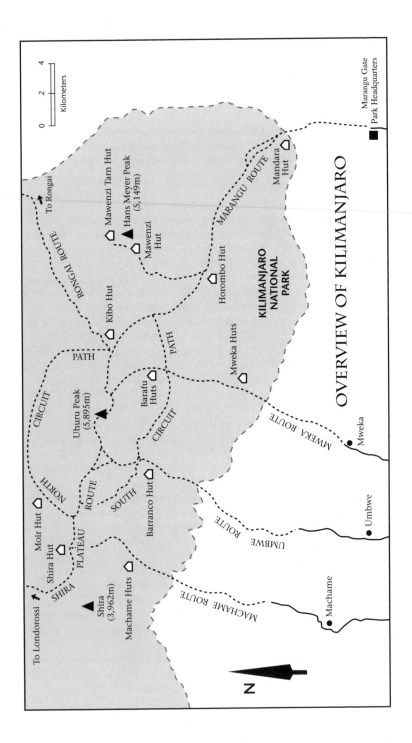

OVERVIEW OF KILIMANJARO

Marangu Gate
Park Headquarters

Kilometers
0   2   4

To Rongai

RONGAI ROUTE

Mawenzi Tarn Hut
Hans Meyer Peak
(5,149m)
Mawenzi Hut

MARANGU ROUTE

Mandara Hut

Kibo Hut

Horombo Hut

KILIMANJARO
NATIONAL
PARK

PATH

PATH

Mweka Huts

CIRCUIT

Uhuru Peak
(5,895m)

Barafu
Huts

CIRCUIT

MWEKA ROUTE

Mweka

NORTH

Moir Hut

ROUTE

Shira Hut

SOUTH

Barranco Hut

Umbwe

UMBWE ROUTE

PLATEAU

SHIRA

To Londorossi

Shira
(3,962m)

Machame Huts

MACHAME ROUTE

Machame

N

WILDLIFE SIGHTINGS

Although the wildlife you will see on Kilimanjaro won't compare to the wildlife you'll find on safari in East African game parks, the mountain is still home to many exotic creatures (see Wildlife, in Chapter 2). Dik-dik, duikers, bushbucks, blue monkeys, colobus monkeys, chameleons, mongeese, and sunbirds are all part of the average ascent.

The College of African Wildlife Management, located in Mweka Village, appreciates any reports of animal sightings you might experience on Kilimanjaro. To report sightings, write: College of African Wildlife Management, PO Box 3031, Moshi, Tanzania.

GEOGRAPHY

Although geographically, Kilimanjaro is very easy to understand, the way the routes are named is not. The half-dozen forest and moorland approach routes that penetrate the forest and moorland areas (Marangu, Mweka, Umbwe, Machame, Shira Plateau, and Rongai) and the way those routes connect to routes that climb the final 1,200 meters of the mountain can be extremely confusing for the first-time visitor.

All these forest and moorland routes get to about the 3,500–4,500-meter level, then join the South Circuit Path. They do not go to the summit. From the South Circuit Path, various walking, scrambling, and technical mountaineering routes then lead to the summit.

Trekkers usually climb the final 1,200 meters to the summit by one of the three easiest routes up Kibo: the Normal Route, the Barafu Route, or the Western Breach Route. Technical mountaineers can choose other routes. Discuss which summit route you want to take with your outfitter before you leave Moshi, since the company must make the appropriate arrangements with KINAPA.

The names of combination routes on Kilimanjaro are also extremely confusing because the names don't completely describe where the routes go. For instance, the popular Machame–Mweka Route isn't just a combination of the Machame and Mweka forest/moorland routes. The climb begins with the Machame Route, then takes in a part of the Shira Plateau Route, some of the South Circuit Path, then climbs the final section of Kibo via the Barafu Route. It then descends the Barafu Route to Barafu Huts before joining the Mweka Route to descend through the forest.

Likewise, the Rongai Route ascends through the forest, but at Kibo Hut, where the Rongai Route ends, climbers usually take the Normal Route to the summit. To confuse matters, the Normal Route is often referred to as the Marangu Route because it joins up neatly with the Marangu Route.

The best thing to do is study a map, which will sort out much of the confusion. Actually getting on the mountain will sort it out even more.

One reason these forest and moorland routes are arranged in combinations is because the Umbwe and Mweka Routes are so steep and rough that they are incredibly difficult to ascend. Most outfitters prefer to use them only for descents. If you're so inclined, you can easily arrange ascents of these two routes, but tip your guide and porters well!

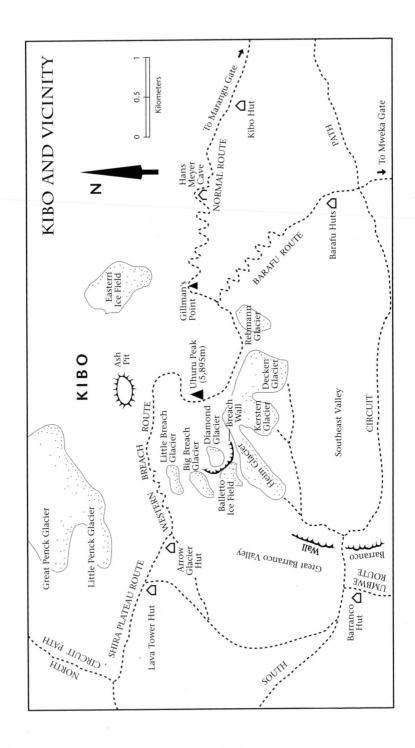

KIBO AND VICINITY

FOREST / MOORLAND ROUTES

The following route descriptions begin with the ever-popular Marangu Route, then move clockwise around the mountain through the southern glaciers to the Breach Wall and the northern glaciers, which lie on the western and northern side of Kibo.

A note about descents on the forest / moorland routes: The descriptions here—with details on elevation gain, time to travel between huts, and so forth—are for ascent only. On the descent, you will travel much more quickly and generally skip every other hut. For example, on the Marangu / Normal Route, after a night at Kibo Hut and a climb to Uhuru Peak in the morning, it is customary to descend to Horombo Hut that afternoon for one night, followed by a descent to the park gate the next day.

MARANGU ROUTE

Among the area's outfitters the Marangu Route is known as the Coca-Cola Route. Like the beverage, it's highly popular. Probably 90 percent of all Kili climbers follow it. It's also the cheapest product around.

Although the Marangu Route is often criticized as being crowded and sometimes as a bad experience, it's actually very beautiful and doesn't deserve its tourist-route reputation. One of the best things about the Marangu Route is that it's possible to stay in huts all the way up the mountain, and there are facilities for bathing (that is, cold water) at Mandara and Horombo Huts. The other benefit is that mineral water, beer, and carbonated soft drinks are available at all the main huts (Mandara, Horombo, Kibo), although you can expect to pay double what these products would cost down in Moshi.

The Marangu Route starts at the Marangu Gate, several kilometers above the village of the same name.

To reach Marangu, drive east from Moshi on the main Arusha–Taveta Road for 27 kilometers to the bustling roadside village of Himo. Between Moshi and Himo are some of Tanzania's biggest baobab trees. The logs hanging from various trees are locally constructed beehives.

The signed turnoff to Dar, on the right, is shortly before Himo. At Himo, turn left (north) and continue about 14 kilometers to the village of Marangu. This road is paved all the way, a reflection of the economic impact of the Marangu Route. The town of Marangu is spread out along the road. The Marangu Hotel—a popular place for climbers—is on the left. At the Y intersection in Marangu (the only intersection in town, near the post office), veer left, toward the Capricorn Hotel. Continue about 5 kilometers up the paved road to KINAPA's Marangu Gate, at about 1,900 meters elevation.

Here, either you or your guide will have to pay park fees and check in, which can take anywhere from 10 minutes to an hour.

Once the park formalities have been dealt with, the walking begins. In the following descriptions, the trails have been broken down into segments that most parties travel in a day.

MARANGU ROUTE: MARANGU GATE TO MANDARA HUT / DAY 1

Ascent: 1,900 meters to 2,700 meters
Distance: 8 kilometers
Time: 3 to 4 hours

From the park gate, the trail winds up through the forest on a paved road that quickly gives way to a wide dirt road. After 10 minutes of walking, a subsidiary trail branches off to the left. This trail joins the main trail higher up, and is much narrower, but many use it hoping to see more wildlife than on the main trail. You'll likely see just as much wildlife on the main path.

The main trail gradually narrows as it climbs through the forest toward Mandara Hut and is no more than a single-file track in some places. Mandara Hut is just one of many A-frame huts clustered together in the forest at 2,700 meters. This is the standard first-night stopping point on the Marangu Route, and the huts can accommodate dozens of people. There are many blue monkeys in the surrounding forest. If you get to camp early, wander up the trail toward Horombo Hut a hundred meters and you might see them in the lush vegetation.

MARANGU ROUTE: MANDARA HUT TO HOROMBO HUT / DAY 2

Ascent: 2,700 meters to 3,700 meters
Distance: 11 kilometers
Time: 5 to 7 hours

From Mandara Hut the trail continues northwest through the forest. A few minutes up the path, a trail going left leads to the Maundi Crater, a rounded knob rising above the forest that offers spectacular views. It is possible to take this trail, then rejoin the main trail higher up the mountain.

Just after the Maundi Crater, the trail enters a badly burned area that dates from a massive fire that burned about 200,000 acres of land on the southeast side of the mountain in January 1997.

The trail to Horombo Hut is well marked, and there are only short steep sections where the trail dips across creeks. The views of Kibo and Mawenzi are inspirational.

Like Mandara Hut, there is an entire village of huts around Horombo Hut (3,700 meters), with a camping area on the hillside above. A clear stream runs through the complex (but its water should be treated before use). Many parties spend only one night at Horombo, but if you think you might have trouble with altitude higher up the mountain, it's best to spend two nights. Arrange the extra night with your outfitter before you start up the mountain.

If you are headed to Mawenzi, the trail to Mawenzi Hut intersects the main Marangu Route trail just above the Horombo Hut camping area. From this point, it's about 2–3 hours to Mawenzi Hut.

MARANGU ROUTE: HOROMBO HUT TO KIBO HUT / DAY 3

Ascent: 3,700 meters to 4,700 meters
Distance: 11 kilometers
Time: 5 to 6 hours

The trail above Horombo Hut is well marked. After an hour's hike, at 4,000 meters the trail crosses the Maua River, a good place to get water. The official last water point on the Marangu Route lies a short walk farther up the trail and is well marked with two signs. However, it is a small, muddy creek with not much to recommend it.

About an hour beyond "last water," a sign indicates that the trail is entering the Saddle—the area between Mawenzi and Kibo. Near the Saddle sign, the South Circuit Path takes off to the left (southwest). The trail junction is not very prominent, and the Saddle sign is the best way to tell you've reached it. (From here, you can follow the South Circuit Path around the southern side of the mountain. This is a fairly straightforward way of accessing the southern glacier routes—the Rebmann, Decken, Kersten, and Heim Glaciers—on Kibo.)

Continuing straight, the Marangu Route crosses the Saddle and heads toward Kibo, reaching Kibo Hut at 4,700 meters. Like the other overnight stops on the Marangu Route, the Kibo Hut area is a collection of huts. Kibo Hut itself has about a half-dozen rooms, each with eight to fifteen bunks. From Kibo Hut, the Normal Route (also known as the Marangu Route) on Kibo leads to the crater rim at Gillman's Point and the summit. (See the Kibo section, later this chapter, for a description of the Normal Route from Kibo Hut to the summit.)

MWEKA ROUTE

The Mweka Route is steep and rough. Most outfitters and guides consider it a descent route only, although you can ascend it. It is the most direct way of getting to the Barafu Route and the Rebmann Glacier on Kibo.

The route starts at the Mweka Gate, on the Mweka Road in the village of the same name, located 13 kilometers north of Moshi.

In the forest on the Mweka Route, Kilimanjaro

MWEKA ROUTE: MWEKA GATE TO MWEKA HUTS / DAY 1

Ascent: 1,500 meters to 3,100 meters
Distance: 10 kilometers
Time: 4 to 5 hours

From the Mweka Gate, the route follows an old logging road for several kilometers, then goes for several kilometers on a narrow, often muddy track that is extremely uneven and slippery in places.

The trail continues along a ridge between two valleys before emerging at Mweka Huts (3,100 meters) after about 10 kilometers. The two huts are Uniports, like most huts on Kilimanjaro. There is water in a small valley 5 minutes to the southeast. This is the last water on the Mweka Route.

MWEKA ROUTE: MWEKA HUTS TO BARAFU HUTS / DAY 2

Ascent: 3,100 meters to 4,600 meters
Distance: 11 kilometers
Time: 6 to 8 hours

Above Mweka Huts, the trail winds its way up a rocky rib before emerging in the alpine desert on the eastern rib of the Southeast Valley.

After you cross the South Circuit Path, it is about 2 kilometers to Barafu Huts. (From Barafu Huts to the summit, see the description for Barafu Route in the Kibo section.)

The Barafu Huts with Kibo behind (Photo © Ann Burns)

UMBWE ROUTE

This route is easily one of the best experiences of a lifetime. It is breathtaking, wild, rough, and extremely steep. It displays Kilimanjaro's dramatic geological formations better than any other route on the mountain. And almost no one goes up this route.

Like the Mweka Route, the Umbwe Route is generally considered a descent route. Some tour operators might decline an ascent of this route, or charge you extra.

There are several roads from Moshi to Umbwe Village. The best way to get there is to drive west from Moshi on the Moshi–Arusha Road, and turn right on the Lyamungu Road. At the T intersection, turn right toward Mango, cross the Sere River, then turn left, past the Umbwe mission and school. A few kilometers farther up the road lies the park gate.

UMBWE ROUTE: UMBWE GATE TO CAMP I / DAY 1

Ascent: 1,400 meters to 3,000 meters
Distance: 11 kilometers
Time: 5 to 6 hours

From the gate at 1,400 meters, the trail winds up through the forest, following a ridge between two deep valleys. In many places it is necessary to pull yourself up on tree roots and branches. At around 3,000 meters, you will reach a small clearing and cave. This is generally the first night's camp, commonly called Camp I. There are campsites on the small hill above the cave, as well as right in front of it, and there are several obvious water sources around the cave.

UMBWE ROUTE: CAMP I TO BARRANCO HUT / DAY 2

Ascent: 3,000 meters to 3,900 meters
Distance: 7 kilometers
Time: 4 to 5 hours

The trail continues up the ridge, getting steeper and more interesting as it progresses up the mountain. In some places, the trail wanders along ledges with 600-meter drops on either side.

At about the 3,200-meter level, it is necessary to climb a short (10-meter) rock cliff. This cliff is only a scramble (American Class 3), and there is little exposure, but it requires climbing rock and pulling your way up a few branches and roots. Most visitors to Kilimanjaro who have never climbed rock have no problem with this section of the route.

The trail continues up the ridge, which gets increasingly easier and wider before arriving at Barranco Hut, where the trail joins the South Circuit Path.

Once at Barranco Hut, you can opt for either the Western Breach Route or the Barafu Route (if you're hiking) to the summit of Kibo, or you can do one of the southern glacier routes (technical mountaineering). (See the Kibo section.)

MACHAME ROUTE

While the Marangu Route is dubbed the Coca-Cola Route, the Machame Route is known as the Whiskey Route. It's more expensive to ascend, and its fantastic views are much more intoxicating.

Like other forest routes on this side of Kili, the Machame Route is generally considered an ascent route. When combined with the Barafu Route on Kibo to the summit and the Mweka Route as a descent through the forest (also known as the Machame–Mweka Route), it is easily the best forest/moorland route for acclimatization on Kilimanjaro, as well as one of the most scenic outings on the mountain.

It climbs slowly through the forest before emerging on the edge of the Shira Plateau and joining the Shira Plateau Route, then traverses the mountain, taking in the South Circuit Path, with overnight stops at Barranco Hut and Barafu Huts before a slow grind up Kibo to the summit. Because of the slow ascent, this combination route has the highest rate of success of any route on the mountain.

The Machame Route, by itself, is also the second most beautiful route on the mountain after the Umbwe Route. It starts above the village of Machame, on the southwestern slopes of Kilimanjaro. Like most villages in Africa, Machame has no real center but is strung along the road for several kilometers. To reach the village, drive west on the Arusha–Moshi Road from Moshi for 13 kilometers, then turn right onto the Machame Road (signed) and drive another about 7 kilometers. When you reach the village market, veer left between the buildings. Another few kilometers of steep dirt road will lead to the well-marked Machame Gate.

MACHAME ROUTE: MACHAME GATE TO MACHAME HUTS/DAY 1

Ascent: 1,800 meters to 3,000 meters
Distance: 10 kilometers
Time: 5 to 6 hours

The trail bypasses the park offices to the left (west), then follows a four-wheel-drive road for several kilometers before it begins thinning to a narrow jungle track that follows a ridge. The trail is well used, so losing it is not an issue. Five to 6 hours of hiking brings you to Machame Huts, at 3,000 meters. Like nearly all the huts on Kili—except those on the Marangu Route—they are Uniports in a state of disrepair. There are good camping sites on the hillside above the huts (to the east), and fresh water is available from the creek down the steep hill behind the huts to the northwest.

MACHAME ROUTE: MACHAME HUTS TO SHIRA HUT/DAY 2

Ascent: 3,000 meters to 3,800 meters
Distance: 7 kilometers
Time: 5 hours

From Machame Huts, the trail enters the moorlands and more or less follows a fin of volcanic rock protruding from the mountain. About 2 hours from Machame Huts, the trail reaches a semicircular rock wall that must be negotiated. The wall is a scramble (American Class 3), but it is short (8 meters), and exposure is not a problem. The average person—with no climbing experience whatsoever—can manage it. Above the wall is a scenic rest stop.

Next, the trail heads northwest, away from Kibo, and crosses two streams before emerging on the Shira Plateau, near Shira Cave. Shira Hut lies a few hundred meters to the northwest. Most parties camp near the cave, as Shira Hut is old and dirty.

At this point, the Machame Route has joined the Shira Plateau Route. (See Shira Plateau Route, below.)

SHIRA PLATEAU ROUTE

To reach the trailhead for the Shira Plateau Route, drive west from Moshi on the Arusha–Moshi Road for 26 kilometers, then turn right (north) for 22 kilometers to the town of Sanya Juu. Often your guide will stop in Sanya Juu for last-minute supplies or lunch. From Sanya Juu, it's another 40 kilometers or so to Londorossi, and the roads get progressively worse. To the first-time visitor, Londorossi looks like a town straight out of a Hollywood Western. It is constructed entirely of wood, and its dirt streets conjure up images of Tombstone. It's easy to go the wrong way in Londorossi, but watch for signs pointing to the Londorossi Gate.

It's possible to drive the 11 kilometers from the gate all the way to the trailhead at 3,500 meters; however, the road is extremely rough. (There are no facilities at the trailhead except an outhouse-style toilet.)

SHIRA PLATEAU ROUTE: TRAILHEAD TO SHIRA HUT/DAY 1
Ascent: 3,500 meters to 3,800 meters
Distance: 6 kilometers
Time: 4 hours

From the trailhead, the trail goes east, breaking out across the center of the Shira Plateau. About 3–4 hours' walk from the trailhead, you will reach Shira Hut. There are many campsites within the first few kilometers along the Shira Plateau Route, and a late start from Moshi often necessitates camping before reaching Shira Hut.

Shira Cave lies another 20 minutes' walk to the south-southeast of Shira Hut. Most parties camp here rather than at Shira Hut, which is old and dirty. There is camping near the cave (about 5 minutes' walk to the west-southwest of the cave), where a second large cave often serves as a kitchen/campsite for porters and guides. There is a tremendous pile of garbage at this camp, and at night, dozens of dik-dik roam about, picking at the mess. Camping in the Shira Cave is prohibited. There is a wooden toilet building next to it.

Water is available from several sources. If you've come up the Machame Route, there are two creeks back along the Machame Route, toward Machame Huts. The first stream is about a 10-minute walk from Shira Cave. A closer water source is a creek about 300 meters directly west of Shira Cave. Sometimes, however, this creek dries out.

From Shira Hut, it is possible to go in several different directions: to Lava Tower Hut, to Moir Hut, or to Barranco Hut. That's because just east of Shira Hut, the Shira Plateau trail meets the North Circuit Path, which gives numerous options.

Because most climbers who use the Shira Plateau trail (or portions of it) are either headed for the Western Breach Route on Kibo or are doing the Machame–Mweka combination route, those two sections of trail are covered below.

SHIRA PLATEAU ROUTE: SHIRA HUT TO ARROW GLACIER HUT / DAY 2, OPTION 1

Ascent: 3,800 meters to 4,800 meters
Distance: 6 kilometers
Time: 3 to 4 hours

Closure note: *Because of rockfall on the Arrow Glacier that caused several fatalities in early 2006, KINAPA closed the Western Breach Route (aka the Great Western Arch Route) on January 5, 2006. It was scheduled to reopen in spring 2006. Check with the park before attempting the Western Breach Route.*

From the Shira Cave area, the Shira Plateau trail skirts right (south) of the cave and then follows a long, low, thin fin of rock for several kilometers before it slowly trends southeast, aiming for a striking tower of rock, Lava Tower. About halfway between Shira Cave and Lava Tower, the North and South Circuit Paths join the Shira Plateau trail. The junction is not well marked. In fact, the only indication that you have intersected the North and South Circuit Paths is some red spray paint on a rock stating "Moya Hut" (Moir Hut).

At this point, you can follow the North Circuit Path left (north) to Moir Hut or the South Circuit Path right (south) to Barranco Hut, or you can go straight, which takes you toward Lava Tower Hut and the trail up to Arrow Glacier Hut and the Western Breach Route.

After intersecting with the North and South Circuit Paths, the Shira Plateau trail flattens out a little bit and continues east-southeast to Lava Tower.

Just after the intersection, the trail crosses a fairly deep valley, and climbing out of it is a grind. Above this hill, the path crosses two broad, flat valleys before reaching Lava Tower Hut (4,500 meters). The hut is a ruin, and the area is rarely used for camping.

Lava Tower Hut is the access point for the Western Breach area (also known as the Arrow Glacier area) and the Western Breach Route. Just east of Lava Tower, the small trail to Arrow Glacier Hut angles off up the hill to the northeast. It's a couple of hours' walk to Arrow Glacier Hut (4,800 meters), which is nothing more than a ruin.

SHIRA PLATEAU ROUTE: SHIRA HUT TO BARRANCO HUT / DAY 2, OPTION 2

Ascent: 3,800 meters to 3,900 meters
Distance: 10 kilometers
Time: 5 to 6 hours

There are two ways of getting to Barranco Hut from Shira Hut. Each offers a different way to go around Lava Tower.

The first way is to follow the trail described above, which leads to Lava Tower Hut. From Lava Tower Hut, stay on the main trail as it descends east and south around Lava Tower. The trail to Arrow Glacier Hut will go up the steep hill to the left. This route around Lava Tower is highly recommended as it aids in acclimatization and is very scenic.

The other way is to follow the Shira Plateau trail east, toward the intersection with the North and South Circuit Paths (see Day 2, Option 1, above), then go south and east on the South Circuit Path, around the south side of Lava Tower.

Both routes around Lava Tower join up east of Lava Tower and continue down a beautiful valley to the Barranco Wall area and Barranco Hut, another dirty metal shell.

RONGAI ROUTE

The Rongai Route is a very different experience from the routes on the southwest side of the mountain. It's drier, it's covered with tall grass and elephant scat (and the elephants that produced the scat), and there are no huts. The best thing about the Rongai Route is that it offers spectacular views out over the broad, flat Masai lands north of the Tanzania-Kenya border.

Ann Burns climbing the Barranco Wall, Kilimanjaro

The Rongai Route is one of several standard routes on the north side of Kilimanjaro. Getting to the trailhead requires driving along the Tanzania-Kenya border.

To reach the trailhead, drive through the village of Marangu, veer right at the Marangu Post Office, then traverse around the entire eastern side of the mountain by way of several small, but interesting villages. The road is wildly rough.

The Tanzania-Kenya border is on the north side of Tarakea Village, which lies on the northeastern side of the Kilimanjaro massif. Instead of driving through the border gate into Kenya, take the road to Rongai, which leads off to the left just before the gate. After many kilometers, the wooden town of Rongai is reached. A stop at the park gate (up the road to the left a short distance from Rongai) is required before you can begin hiking. Then it's necessary to drive back down to Rongai and continue left around the mountain for several more kilometers, to a turnout area on the left, where a big white metal sign proclaims the virtues of the "Snow-Cap Mountain Climbing Camp—Rongai."

RONGAI ROUTE: TRAILHEAD TO FIRST CAVE / DAY 1
Ascent: 2,000 meters to 2,880 meters
Distance: 8 kilometers
Time: 4 to 5 hours

From the trailhead, the route follows an old four-wheel-drive road as it winds through the forest for about 1.5 kilometers of jungle before emerging in the heather at about 2,500 meters. The trail is not at all steep, but is rather a gentle hike through beautiful country. There can be tons (literally) of elephant manure on this section of the trail. The first night's camp is at First Cave, at about 2,880 meters. You'll find some excellent campsites just above First Cave with breathtaking views over the plains to the north. There are a toilet structure and a wooden table with benches, but no hut. Water is just down the trail below First Cave.

RONGAI ROUTE: FIRST CAVE TO THIRD CAVE / DAY 2
Ascent: 2,880 meters to 3,875 meters
Distance: 8 kilometers
Time: 4 to 5 hours

The trail continues up toward Kibo, passing Second Cave en route, and reaching Third Cave at about 3,875 meters. Most parties spend their second night on the Rongai Route here. Facilities are minimum (toilets only). Water is in the obvious stream below the cave, although you might have to wander downhill to find some.

About 20 minutes' walk above (west of) Third Cave, the North Circuit Path leads off to the right (north). There is also a difficult-to-locate trail that leads from Third Cave to Mawenzi Tarn Hut.

From Third Cave, the trail to Kibo Hut is fairly straightforward and traverses up the far northwestern portion of the Saddle between Mawenzi and Kibo. (From Kibo Hut to the summit, see the Kibo section.)

SOUTH CIRCUIT PATH

If you climb any route other than the Marangu Route, you will likely take in some portion of the South Circuit Path. As the name implies, the trail circumnavigates the southern side of Kibo and connects the Shira, Lava Tower, and Barranco Huts, as well as the Barafu and Marangu Routes. The South Circuit Path is extremely well marked and easy to follow.

On its eastern end, the path starts at its intersection with the Marangu Route, near the Saddle. On its western end, the path connects with the Shira Plateau trail as the latter reaches the eastern end of the Shira Plateau, below the Western Breach area.

Because most parties that use the South Circuit Path will travel it from west to east, I have described the trail in this direction.

The South Circuit Path begins on the Shira Plateau, just east of the North Circuit Path–Shira Plateau trail intersection, east of the red spray paint stating "Moya Hut." The start of the trail is not well marked, and many parties miss it.

From the above intersection, the trail winds down a rocky hill and goes south around Lava Tower, connecting to a junction with the Barranco Hut–Lava Tower Hut trail on a ridge. From this junction, which has several signs and is well marked, it is 2 hours or so of easy hiking down the valley to the east to reach the Barranco Hut area.

The Barranco Hut area is fairly spread out. A camping area lies close to the South Circuit Path; however, the hut itself is located about 10 minutes' walk down the Great Barranco Valley, on the west side of the valley. Two small valleys are crossed to reach the hut from the South Circuit Path.

On the eastern side of the Great Barranco Valley is the Barranco Wall, a 300-meter barrier of volcanic rock that must be negotiated to continue east on the South Circuit Path. From the Barranco Hut area, the path heads north for a few hundred meters, then crosses a river before switchbacking up the wall. Although it's tall and looks incredibly steep, this wall is very easy to climb up or down. It's similar to climbing a set of stairs with the occasional short section of ladder thrown in for good measure. There is very little exposure.

The South Circuit Path then crests the Barranco Wall and arrives at a high alpine desert area, best described as a plateau, although it has several small valleys cutting across it from north to south.

The top of the Barranco Wall is the best place to access the southern glacier routes (Rebmann, Decken, Kersten, and Heim Glaciers) on Kibo, and a trail leading north toward the glaciers is cairned.

The South Circuit Path then descends and winds its way through the many small valleys crisscrossing the high alpine desert. The last valley on the plateau is the deepest and has a stream running through it, which is the last water for many kilometers. After another few kilometers, the trail meets the Mweka trail on a ridge. This is the way to access Barafu Huts and the Barafu Route. If you are doing the Machame–Mweka combination, turn left (north) and follow this trail.

If you are headed for the Marangu Route, continue east until the Marangu Route is intersected in the Saddle.

If you are going west on the South Circuit Path from the Marangu Route, you may have a hard time finding the start of the trail. It starts in the area of the Saddle, where it is best identified by a small wooden sign saying "Saddle." The South Circuit Path heads east behind this sign.

NORTH CIRCUIT PATH

The North Circuit Path links Third Cave on the Rongai Route to the Shira Plateau trail, between Lava Tower and Shira Hut via the north side of Kibo.

The trail is straightforward to follow, but it takes either a full, hard day of walking, or 2 fairly easy days to make the circuit from Third Cave to the intersection with the South Circuit Path.

The North Circuit Path crosses numerous rock ribs and gullies on the north side of Kibo but maintains an elevation of around 4,300 meters for most of the circuit. Moir Hut is the only hut on the North Circuit Path, and it is located on the extreme western end of the circuit, near the junction with the Shira Plateau trail. Like most other huts on Kili, it is a metal shell.

On the east end, the trail can easily be accessed from Kibo Hut, Outward Bound Hut (which lies a few hundred meters north of Kibo Hut), or Third Cave. Small trails that contour around Kibo lead from each of these three places to the North Circuit Path. To access the North Circuit Path from the west (Shira Plateau), see the description for the Shira Plateau Route.

Joined to the South Circuit Path, the North Circuit Path makes an interesting circumnavigation of Kibo. Most parties take 3 days to do the entire circumnavigation, with stops at Kibo, Moir, and Barranco Huts.

KIBO

There are numerous options to reach the summit of Kibo (5,895 meters / 19,341 feet), and thus Kilimanjaro's highest point, from the high huts on the forest and moorland routes.

Ninety percent of those trying the mountain will opt for the Normal Route, the continuation of the Marangu Route. Probably another 9 percent will opt for either the Barafu Route (from the Barafu Huts to the summit) or the Western Breach Route, a slightly more difficult route that ascends the western side of the mountain, but which has an unwarranted reputation among nontechnical climbers as being very difficult. All three routes require nothing more than lots of warm clothing and a good pair of trekking shoes or boots. ***Closure note: KINAPA closed the Western Breach Route as of January 5, 2006. Check with the park before attempting this route.***

Other major, but rarely climbed, routes on Kibo include the southern glacier routes (Rebmann, Decken, Kersten, and Heim Glaciers) and the Breach Wall area routes.

All the southern glacier and Breach Wall routes have elevation gains of about 1,300 to 1,400 meters, require 5 to 7 kilometers of travel, and take, for the most part, 2 days. The other routes on Kibo (including hiking routes) have elevation gains of about 550 to 1,000 meters, require about 5 kilometers of travel, and take 1 day.

The following route descriptions begin with the Normal Route (also known as the Marangu Route) and move clockwise around the mountain.

The standard descent for all the technical mountaineering routes on Kibo is to follow one of the walking or scrambling routes (Normal, Barafu, or Western Breach) down.

1. NORMAL ROUTE (WALK)

Although this route has traditionally been called the Normal Route, many people simply call it the Marangu Route, as it's something of an extension of the Marangu forest/moorland route to the summit of Kibo. It was first climbed by M. Lange and Weigele on July 6, 1909.

The trail leaves the Kibo Hut area at 4,700 meters and heads north between the porter/guides buildings, then turns left (west) toward Kibo. Most parties will want to leave the Kibo Hut area at around midnight or 1:00 AM to catch sunrise over the summit of Mawenzi, and also because they'll likely be going much more slowly than expected. Also, in the wee hours of the morning, the trail is frozen, so hiking it is not as strenuous as later in the day.

After leaving the buildings, the trail follows fairly gentle terrain up to the Hans Meyer Cave, at about 5,150 meters. Above the cave, the trail steepens considerably as it switchbacks up to Gillman's Point (5,680 meters), on the crater rim.

Hikers on the crater rim between Gillman's Point and Uhuru Peak, Kilimanjaro

The attrition rate on the last section of the route to Gillman's Point is tremendous, and it's not uncommon to see dozens of climbers turn back. At Gillman's Point, the summit will come into view across the crater. The trail drops down a few meters into the crater and then follows along the crater rim, passing Stella Point, where the Barafu Route reaches the crater rim and the minor knobs of Hans Meyer Point and Elveda Point.

Although the walk around the crater rim to the summit is not particularly steep anywhere, it is extremely tiring, and it's necessary to rest frequently. It takes about 2 hours for the average person to get from Gillman's Point to Uhuru Peak (5,895 meters / 19,341 feet), the highest point on Kilimanjaro.

2. BARAFU ROUTE (WALK)

Like the Marangu Route, the Barafu Route up to the summit is essentially a continuation of a lower route—the Mweka Route—through the forest, and thus it is often referred to as the Mweka Route.

The Barafu Route starts at Barafu Huts (4,600 meters), which sit atop a prominent ridge on the eastern side of the Southeast Valley. The Southeast Valley lies off to the left as you look at the summit from Barafu Huts. The Barafu Route is steep but does not entail anything harder than hiking.

The route climbs the rocky prow of the rib above the hut before winding its way up a very steep gravel trail to the rim. The trail follows the far right side of the Rebmann Glacier; off to the far right is the Ratzel Glacier, which has melted away so considerably in the last ten years that it's hard to tell it's a glacier.

The Barafu Route (Route 2) above the Barafu Huts, Kilimanjaro

It takes about 5–6 hours to get to Stella Point (5,795 meters), on the rim of the crater, then another hour or so to reach Uhuru Peak (5,895 meters/ 19,341 feet).

KIBO / SOUTHERN GLACIERS

The southern glaciers lie on the southern side of Kibo and are visible from many places around the mountain. There are three major glaciers (from west to east: the Heim, Kersten, and Decken Glaciers) and one smaller, minor glacier, the Rebmann Glacier, which lies east of the Decken Glacier.

The southern glaciers sit above a large, wide, relatively flat, rocky depression called the Southeast Valley. The Southeast Valley is bounded on the west by the Barranco Wall, and on the east by a rib that runs up Kibo next to the Barafu Route.

The three big glaciers (Heim, Kersten, and Decken) are best approached from the Barranco Hut area (3,900 meters). From the Barranco Hut area, follow the South Circuit Path up the Barranco Wall to the point where the trail crests the Barranco Wall. The Southeast Valley will lie before you to the east.

From the crest, follow a rocky ridge that leads off to the left (north) directly toward the Heim Glacier. There is a line of rock cairns marking the way. The Heim Glacier will be directly ahead; the Kersten and Decken Glaciers will be off to the right (northeast). After 1 kilometer or so, the ridge gives way to the broad gravelly slopes that lie below the glaciers. From this point, the approach to all three glaciers involves hiking across these slopes to the base of each glacier.

The Decken and Kersten Glaciers can also be accessed from the east. From the junction of the Marangu or Mweka Routes, follow the South Circuit Path west until you are in the Southeast Valley and the glaciers are visible to the north, then hike straight toward the glacier you intend to climb.

In the eastern side of the Southeast Valley (the Barafu Huts side), there are several areas of low volcanic canyons, just north of the South Circuit Path. These canyons must be negotiated to reach the glaciers. However, they can be crossed in numerous places along the trail and should not create a difficult obstacle.

The Rebmann Glacier is best accessed from the Barafu Huts area (see route description, below).

One important word of caution regarding the southern glacier routes: the glaciers are retreating rapidly, and climbing conditions are changing considerably. In general, this means that where icy ramps existed just ten years ago, steep icefalls and blank rock walls might exist now. The general consensus among climbers worldwide has been that such melting is making climbs harder and more dangerous, as rocks and ice become detached from the mountains. Also, conditions vary from year to year, and from season to season.

Most of the southern glaciers drop off sharply around the rim of Kibo's crater, forming massive seracs. Climbing below these seracs in the late morning and afternoon should be avoided for obvious reasons (they may calve off and crush you).

Most parties hike up to the base of the glaciers and bivouac for the night before starting an ascent.

3. REBMANN GLACIER (GRADE II)

The two-pronged Rebmann Glacier is the easternmost of the southern glacier routes on Kibo and is the easiest of the southern glaciers to climb. Indeed, the crux of the climb is reaching the glacier.

Unlike the other southern glacier routes, the Rebmann Glacier is best accessed from Barafu Huts (4,600 meters); however, getting to the glacier requires dropping down off the rock spur on which the huts sit and into the Southeast Valley. This can be done near Barafu Huts or partway up the Barafu Route where the rock rib drops down enough to allow you to climb down to the Rebmann Glacier. Care should be taken picking a route off the rock spur. The glacier starts at around 5,200 meters and peters out near the crater rim (5,700 meters), where the Normal Route is joined and followed to Uhuru Peak (5,895 meters / 19,341 feet). The hardest climbing (Grade II) is at the start of the glacier. The angle lessens as height is gained.

This route takes a half day from Barafu Huts. The first-ascent party is unknown.

4. DECKEN GLACIER, RIGHT SIDE (GRADE III–IV)

The right side of the Decken Glacier was first climbed by M. Tudo, J. Montford, F. Shock, and J. Kuhn in August 1974.

The route skirts the difficult rock and ice walls found halfway up the Decken Glacier by traversing right onto an easy ice field that leads to several pitches of steep ice climbing, then tops out at 5,650 meters near the Wedge, a prominent rock fin that separates the Decken and Kersten Glaciers. From the glacier, the Normal Route is followed around the crater rim to Uhuru Peak (5,895 meters / 19,341 feet).

5. DECKEN GLACIER, ORIGINAL ROUTE (GRADE III–IV)

The Decken Glacier was first climbed by E. Eisenmann and T. Schnackig on January 12, 1938. The first solo ascent was by Ante Mahote in 1964.

This route starts directly below the lower left-hand side of the Decken Glacier, at about 4,650 meters, and follows the line of least resistance up the left-hand side of the glacier. The first half of the route consists of snow climbing up to 65 degrees. Cruxes (Grade III–IV) are encountered where the glacier has melted out to form icefalls. There are several moderate rock pitches, and rock gear should be carried. About halfway up, at about the 5,200-meter level, the angle of the glacier kicks back dramatically, and the route becomes nothing more than a snow hike, though care should be taken in case of crevasses. Continue north toward Kibo's crater, then join the Normal Route to Uhuru Peak (5,895 meters / 19,341 feet).

Allow 2 days for an ascent of this route from one of the high huts. There are several rock bivouac sites on the right side of the glacier, about midway up the route.

The southern glaciers of Kibo, Kilimanjaro, with Routes 4–10 marked

6. KERSTEN GLACIER, RIGHT SIDE (GRADE V)

First climbed by Mark Savage and Iain Allan in 2 days, July 28–29, 1976, this ascent requires excellent routefinding skills. It starts at about 4,650 meters, below the large rock buttress separating the Kersten and Decken Glaciers, then follows a jumble of seracs and ice steps up and left for many pitches until it gains the prominent ice field below the crest of the glacier. This ice field is very dangerous because of the serac above and afternoon melting.

At the top of the ice field, a gully leads up and left past a series of seracs. Near the top of the gully, move up and right, through a break in the seracs, which leads to easier ground. Above this, the angle lessens, and a steep hike leads to Uhuru Peak (5,895 meters/19,341 feet).

7. KERSTEN GLACIER, DIRECT ROUTE (GRADE VI)

This route was first climbed by Ian Howell, Bill O'Connor, and John Cleare on December 20–21, 1975.

Start below the middle of the Kersten Glacier, at about 4,700 meters, and climb straight up a couloir that angles right. At the head of the couloir, climb a steep ice pitch on the left, then the rock wall above to a snow ledge. Move right into a gully and climb steep ice, then traverse farther right, back into the main gully. Climb up the gully to a rock overhang, then skirt it by going left and around it, on snow. Climb straight up for four pitches to a large ice cave at about 5,100 meters, which can be used as a bivouac spot. Move right and climb snow slopes to the crater rim (5,700 meters). The Normal Route is then followed to Uhuru Peak (5,895 meters/19,341 feet).

8. KERSTEN GLACIER, ORIGINAL ROUTE (GRADE VI)

This route ascends easy ground on the left side of the glacier, skirting two steep icefalls and avoiding any serious difficulties. It was first climbed by Walter Welsch and Leo Herncarek on September 20–22, 1962.

Start below the left-hand edge of the glacier (4,700 meters) and climb up to the first icefall. Traverse left up a steep ice slope, then back across right to surmount the icefall. At the second icefall, traverse right, then back left.

Continue through the serac falls at the top of the glacier and cross the summit ice field to the crater rim (5,700 meters). Continue via the Normal Route to Uhuru Peak (5,895 meters/19,341 feet).

9. HEIM GLACIER, DIRECT ROUTE (GRADE VI)

This route has one of the hardest ice leads of any of the southern glacier routes up a vertical icicle at 5,200 meters. It was first climbed by Robert Barton and David Morris on December 29–30, 1977.

Separating the Kersten and Heim Glaciers is a huge rock buttress. The toe of the Heim Glacier lies several hundred meters left of the left edge of this buttress, at about 4,650 meters. Climb the snow and ice fields right of the glacier's toe, until below the tall, broad rock wall that houses the seracs of the upper portion of the Heim Glacier. Climb up and right, to an obvious gully with a vertical icicle hanging down it. Climb the 30-meter icicle (Grade VI).

Above the icicle, it is necessary to work around several seracs that bar access to the upper portion of the Heim Glacier. The upper snowfield leads to Uhuru Peak (5,895 meters / 19,341 feet).

10. HEIM GLACIER (GRADE III)

This is the classic glacier climb on Kilimanjaro, the equivalent of the Polish Glacier on Aconcagua. It was first climbed on September 20–25, 1957, by A. Nelson, H. J. Cooke, and D. N. Goodall over a period of 6 days. The route can be climbed in 1 day, but generally 2 are taken. It is often soloed.

The best place to spend a night before attempting this route is Barranco Hut (3,900 meters) or in a bivouac directly below the glacier itself. From a point at the top of the Barranco Wall on the South Circuit Path at about 4,200 meters, a line of cairns (some missing) marks an indistinct trail that follows a rock rib toward the foot of the glacier. The rock rib peters out, so the last part of the approach lies on gravel and scree.

From the toe of the glacier, climb up and left in a long gully that follows the right side of the Window Buttress, which separates the Heim Glacier from the Breach Wall area. There are occasional ice steps up the gully, which can be avoided in places by traversing out left on rock, especially in dry years. At the head of the gully is the steepest section of the glacier, which can be traversed around by going either right or left, following the line of least resistance.

Once atop the steepest section of the route, you will find several bivouac sites to the left, on top of the Window Buttress, at about 5,150 meters. From this point, the route ascends the low-angled upper section of the Heim Glacier, staying between the east end of the Breach Wall and ice cliffs on the right side of the upper part of the glacier. There are several bivouac opportunities on this section of the route.

The top of the glacier has retreated from the rim, so the final section of the route is a walk across rubble to the edge of the crater, then on to Uhuru Peak (5,895 meters / 19,341 feet) via the Normal Route.

KIBO / BREACH WALL

Although the difficult Messner / Renzler Route is often referred to as "the Breach Wall," there are, in fact, several routes up the Breach Wall, the Messner / Renzler Route being the most notorious and direct.

The Breach Wall is a massive block of stone that protrudes from the south-western edge of Kibo. It contains two glaciers on its slopes—the Balletto Ice Field, which is halfway up the wall, and the Diamond Glacier, which sits atop the Breach Wall and provides moisture for the famous Breach Wall Icicle. Ironically, the three routes that climb portions of the wall are, for the most part, snow-and-ice routes.

The Breach Wall is best accessed from the Barranco Hut area (3,900 meters), which lies just down the Great Barranco Valley from the wall. To reach the Breach Wall, hike up the South Circuit Path, as if you are heading for Lava Tower, for about 1 kilometer. When the Breach Wall is visible off to the right, hike toward it. There are several small drainages that must be crossed before

the base of the wall is reached, but which pose little problem. Crampons can be helpful for this approach.

11. BREACH WALL, EAST END (GRADE V+)

The first ascent of this route was made by John Temple and Anthony Charlton on December 22–23, 1974.

At the base of the Breach Wall (4,600 meters), is a huge, cascading icefall that leads from the talus slopes at the foot of the wall to the Balletto Ice Field. Climb the icefall to the ice field, then climb up and right to the foot of the upper wall (5,450 meters), where it is possible to bivouac.

Move right along the foot of the upper wall to the left-hand edge of the Heim Glacier. Follow the Heim Glacier, or the scree slopes to its left, to Uhuru Peak (5,895 meters / 19,341 feet).

12. BREACH WALL, DIRECT ROUTE (GRADE VI)

The first ascent of this difficult climb was made by Reinhold Messner and Konrad Renzler on January 31, 1978.

At the base of the Breach Wall (4,600 meters) is a huge, cascading icefall that leads from the talus slopes at the foot of the wall to the Balletto Ice Field. Climb the icefall to the ice field, then carefully climb the ice field up and left to the Breach Wall Icicle (5,450 meters). Climb the 90-meter icicle to the Diamond Glacier and continue north to Uhuru Peak (5,895 meters / 19,341 feet).

It is reportedly possible to bivouac behind the Icicle itself, or down to the right of the Balletto Ice Field (5,400 meters), near the Window Buttress.

There is much rockfall on this route, especially on the lower half. Anyone contemplating an ascent would do well to spend a couple of nights at Barranco Hut, studying the route. On the trail between Barranco Hut and Lava Tower, you can hear rocks and ice crashing down the wall throughout the day.

13. BREACH WALL, BALLETTO ICE FIELD (GRADE VI)

First ascent by John Temple and Dave Cheesmond on April 1–4, 1975.

This route climbs the rock wall to the left of the icefall that constitutes the start of the Breach Wall Direct Route. From 4,700 meters, six pitches up the rock wall (using aid in places) lead to a notch looking down over the icefall. From here, work up onto the ice field itself and climb to the base of the upper wall that houses the Direct Route's Icicle. Traverse right along the base of the wall to a gully. Climb the gully on a mixture of rock and ice pitches to easier ground near Uhuru Peak (5,895 meters / 19,341 feet). There are several bivouac sites on this route, at the base of the upper wall and near the base of the gully.

14. LORTSCHER ROUTE (GRADE V)

This route was first ascended by Fritz Lortscher, solo, on January 11–12, 1972. Beginning at 4,700 meters, skirt the lower left-hand edge of the Breach Wall, following broken ledges and easy ground to the western edge of the Diamond Glacier. Then continue north to Uhuru Peak (5,895 meters / 19,341 feet).

The Breach Wall area, Kilimanjaro, with Routes 10, 12, and 14–16 marked

15. BREACH GLACIERS ROUTE (GRADE III)

The route was first climbed by Fritz Lortscher and J. Mayer on January 10, 1972.

A straightforward and direct route, the Breach Glaciers Route climbs the huge gully left (west) of the Breach Wall, beginning at about 4,700 meters and following the gully all the way to its top, near Uhuru Peak. It may be necessary to exit the top of the gully to the right, which puts one on the Diamond Glacier, depending on conditions. From the top of the gully (and the Diamond Glacier), Uhuru Peak (5,895 meters / 19,341 feet) will be a short hike to the east.

16. WESTERN BREACH ROUTE (SCRAMBLE)

Closure note: *Because of rockfall on the Arrow Glacier that caused several fatalities in early 2006, KINAPA closed the Western Breach Route (aka the Great Western Arch Route) on January 5, 2006. It was scheduled to reopen in spring 2006. Check with the park before attempting the Western Breach Route.*

Also known as the Arrow Glacier Route and the Great Western Arch, this excellent route is a classic scramble. It does not actually climb the Arrow Glacier, but scree and easy rock up and left of the glacier.

The final hill leading to the summit, Western Breach Route (Route 16), Kilimanjaro

Opposite: *Western Breach Route (Route 16), Kilimanjaro*

The route is exposed, but the climbing is no harder than a scramble (American Class 3). Trekkers will likely feel a little bit out of place on this route; technical mountaineers will run right up it. Crampons are not necessary; however, they can make the descent easier.

The route starts at the ruinous Arrow Glacier Hut (which is the best place to camp the night before an ascent), at 4,900 meters. At the Arrow Glacier, examine the huge amphitheater above. It runs from the western end of the massive Breach Wall around to a major, but broken rock buttress on the left end (which might not be visible from the hut itself). Halfway across this huge amphitheater, and almost directly above Arrow Glacier Hut, is a low-angled minor rock rib that runs vertically up into the amphitheater wall.

Climb the small talus and scree hill above Arrow Glacier Hut, then follow the left-hand edge of the rock rib for about 600 meters until the foot of the amphitheater wall is reached and the rib steepens. At this point, it is necessary to move right, onto the rib itself, and to follow the well-worn trail as it negotiates the steepest section of the route. The climbing is only scrambling, but it is somewhat exposed in places. The rib ends at the crater rim, at 5,700 meters, where the trail flattens out and skirts right of a summit ice field along the edge of the Western Breach. After 20 minutes of walking, the final hill leading to Uhuru Peak (5,895 meters / 19,341 feet) will be obvious off to the left. The trail ascends the easy ground left of the prominent buttress via a series of strenuous switchbacks. At the top of the switchbacks, the summit is an easy half hour's walk away, to the northeast. Be sure to keep an eye on landmarks as you approach the summit, as getting back to the top of the switchbacks can be confusing.

KIBO / NORTHWESTERN GLACIERS

The northwestern glaciers on Kibo are rarely visited, simply because they lie so far from any trailheads and most trails on the mountain.

Perhaps the most significant thing about the northwestern glaciers is that they have retreated so much since they were originally named and mapped that they bear very little resemblance to their original selves. Indeed, maps of these glaciers from the 1960s show them all connected, far from the situation today.

The northwestern glaciers are best accessed from the North Circuit Path, which can be reached from most of the other trails on Kilimanjaro.

17. LITTLE PENCK GLACIER (GRADE III)

This two-pronged glacier lying immediately west of the massive Western Breach area was first climbed on June 20, 1969, by D. Payne and D. King. The route taken by the first ascent party started at the foot of the Great Penck Glacier (4,900 meters) and traversed rock and ice cliffs up and right to reach the snout of the left prong of the Little Penck Glacier. The remainder of the glacier offers a steep (50–60 degrees) hike up to the crater rim at about 5,700 meters. Once on the rim, walk southeast, along the top of the Western Breach area, to Uhuru Peak (5,895 meters / 19,341 feet).

The right-hand side of the glacier (Grade III) has also been climbed.

Kibo from the Shira Plateau, Kilimanjaro, with Routes 12 and 16–19 marked

18. GREAT PENCK GLACIER (GRADE II)

This glacier has retreated considerably in recent times. It is the obvious tongue of ice left of the Little Penck Glacier and offers a steep hike from about 4,900 meters. It was first climbed by J. Pike and P. A. Campbell on September 14, 1960. The upper part of the glacier has melted away, so it requires scrambling on scree up to the crater rim, which is reached at about 5,700 meters. Once on the crater rim, hike southeast, passing along the top of the Western Breach area, to Uhuru Peak (5,895 meters/19,341 feet).

19. CREDNER GLACIER (GRADE II)

Along the North Circuit Path about 1 kilometer past the Great Penck Glacier is the Credner Glacier. This long glacier offers an easy hike from 4,900 meters to the crater rim (5,700 meters) on Kibo. Once on the rim, walk southeast, along the top of the Western Breach area, to Uhuru Peak (5,895 meters/19,341 feet).

The first-ascent party is unknown.

MAWENZI

Mawenzi is rarely climbed: because there are no trekking routes up the mountain, it probably receives only one or two ascents a year. All the routes on Mawenzi require technical rock climbing (ropes, hardware, and so forth), which is usually mixed in with a little ice climbing, depending on the conditions.

The other feature that distinguishes Mawenzi from its big sister Kibo is that Mawenzi is a complex mass of summits, most of which are difficult to reach from one another. It is basically a north-south rock ridge, with spurs of rock rising from the main ridge. The highest summit is Hans Meyer Peak (5,149 meters/16,893 feet), named after the geographer who made the first ascent of Kibo.

Although it is overlooked by most climbers, Mawenzi is the fourth-highest summit on the African continent after Kibo and Mount Kenya's two summits, Batian and Nelion.

Only the two most frequently climbed routes on Hans Meyer Peak—Oehler Gully and the Northwest Ridge—are described here.

There are two bases from which an ascent of Mawenzi can be easily made: Mawenzi Hut (4,600 meters), on the western side of the peak, and Mawenzi Tarn Hut (4,300 meters), on the north side of the peak. Both huts are small and primitive. Both are reached by hiking north on the obvious marked trail from Horombo Hut on the Marangu Route. From Horombo Hut (3,700 meters) to Mawenzi Hut, it is a 2- to 3-hour hike. To reach Mawenzi Tarn Hut, continue north on the trail from Mawenzi Hut, passing several buttresses and crossing Mawenzi's northwest ridge to reach Mawenzi Tarn, and the hut. Water is available at both huts.

Mawenzi Tarn Hut can also be reached from the area of Third Cave on the Rongai Route; however, this trail is rarely used and not well marked.

Descents on Mawenzi are via the route of ascent.

Mawenzi from the Saddle, Kilimanjaro, with Routes 20 and 21 marked

20. HANS MEYER PEAK / NORDECKE PEAK,
OEHLER GULLY ROUTE (GRADE IV)

The standard route on Hans Meyer Peak, the tallest point on Mawenzi, is the Oehler Gully. This prominent gully leads to a notch in the ridge between Nordecke Peak (to the north) and the summit of Hans Meyer Peak (to the south). It was first climbed by Edward Oehler and Fritz Klute on July 29, 1912.

From Mawenzi Hut (4,600 meters), traverse north (left) along the scree field below the west face to the massive west buttress. Climb up and right, into the col above the west buttress, then traverse along the top of the ridge to a rock wall called the Big Step. Skirt the Big Step to the right and enter the Oehler Gully. Climb the gully for several pitches to the notch between Nordecke (to the left, or north) and Hans Meyer Peak (to the right, or south). Scramble up to the summit (5,149 meters / 16,893 feet). The difficulty of the gully depends on conditions. Generally, with more ice and snow, it is easier.

Descent is made via the gully, although it is common to climb out of the gully onto the walls to each side if rockfall is hazardous.

21. HANS MEYER PEAK / NORDECKE PEAK,
NORTHWEST RIDGE ROUTE (GRADE II)

The first ascent of this route was by R. F. Davies, solo, in January 1953.

From Mawenzi Hut (4,600 meters), climb the Oehler Gully Route past the Big Step to a point 25 meters left of the Oehler Gully, then climb up a gully following a dike that leads to the northwest ridge proper. Follow the ridge all the way to the summit of Nordecke (5,140 meters / 16,863 feet), then traverse across the notch at the top of the Oehler Gully to Hans Meyer Peak (5,149 meters / 16,893 feet).

Chapter 5

MOUNT MERU

We found the climb up the steep southern face hard going, with the first part through cedar and loliondo forest. We reached the bamboo belt at about 8,000 feet and it was so thick that the only way to walk through it was to follow the winding game tracks, which were difficult to negotiate and required constant attention to avoid meeting the rhino, elephant and buffalo that also used them.

—David Read, describing a 1938 ascent of
Mount Meru, *Beating About the Bush*, 2000

Climbing Mount Meru (4,566 meters / 14,976 feet) is one of the most rewarding activities for hikers in northern Tanzania, and yet, the peak is hardly known by tourists. There are few things as wondrous as being atop Little Meru watching the sun rise over Meru's big sister to the east, Kilimanjaro, and few summits as rewarding to reach as Socialism Peak (as the highest Meru summit is called). The climb to Meru's summit is, arguably, more grueling than the climb to Kili's Uhuru Peak, even though Meru sits at a lower elevation.

Geographically, Mount Meru has an almost classic volcano cone shape, except that in Meru's case the eastern side has blown out, so the mountain takes more the form of a horseshoe or a big bowl that's had one half of it lopped off at an angle. This horseshoe shape makes it, in many ways, much more interesting to climb than Kili because the standard climbing / trekking route follows one edge of the massive bowl. It's possible to peer far into the 2,500-meter-deep crater from many points along the "ridge" as you ascend.

Also, unlike other East African volcanoes, Mount Meru is not extinct. Eruptions, rumbling, and gaseous releases have all been reported ever since the time of the first European exploration. Of course, whether or not it will erupt—and to what extent—is about as easy as predicting the weather a year from now.

Most parties take 4 days for the sole route—the Momella Route—that is open to tourists.

THE NAME

The name Meru reportedly translates as "that which does not make a noise," an ironic title considering that Meru is volcanically active and that rumblings have been reported throughout history. According to Henry Fosbrooke in his 1972 *Ngorongoro: The Eighth Wonder*, the Masai call Meru Oldoiny'orok, "the black mountain."

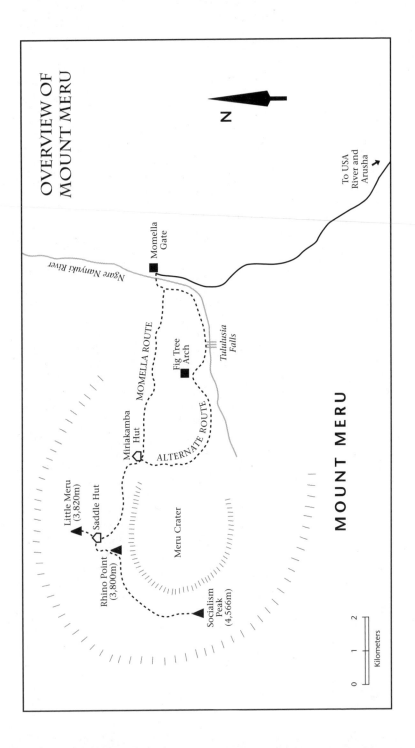

OVERVIEW OF MOUNT MERU

N

To USA River and Arusha

Ngare Nanyuki River

Momella Gate

MOMELLA ROUTE

Fig Tree Arch

Tululusia Falls

ALTERNATE ROUTE

Miriakamba Hut

Little Meru (3,820m)

Saddle Hut

Meru Crater

Rhino Point (3,800m)

Socialism Peak (4,566m)

MOUNT MERU

0   1   2
Kilometers

Porter hiking low on the Momella Route, Mount Meru

WILDLIFE SIGHTINGS

If you have to decide between a post-Kilimanjaro safari and doing something else, climbing Mount Meru is a fair compromise. On this mountain, more than most others in East Africa, you're likely to see a decent selection of East African wildlife. Low on Meru, buffalo, giraffe, zebras, warthogs, bushbucks, gazelles, and baboons are common. Higher on the mountain—depending on grazing conditions in the region—you might see a variety of small mammals, from hyraxes to galagos (a small, possumlike mammal) not to mention larger mammals, like elephants and hyenas.

Even up near Rhino Point, it's not uncommon to run into various antelope species, like klipspringers and duikers—and other large mammals, for that matter. You will likely see colobus monkeys on your drive into the park head-quarters, at Momella.

The College of African Wildlife Management, located in Mweka Village, appreciates any reports of animal sightings you might experience on Mount Meru. To report sightings, write: College of African Wildlife Management, PO Box 3031, Moshi, Tanzania.

MOMELLA ROUTE

The Momella Route is the standard route on Mount Meru. It's a fairly challeng-ing trek that leads from the (main) gate in Arusha National Park to the summit of Mount Meru, a distance of about 31 kilometers round trip with an altitude gain of nearly 3,000 meters (9,900 feet). It is a trekkers' route—with no technical

Starting the Momella Route, Mount Meru

climbing whatsoever—but it is steep, long, and exhausting and will challenge any trekker who thought Kilimanjaro was easy.

The route boasts two alternative starts: one travels up the eastern ridge of the old volcano; and a second, which I've called the Alternate Route below, heads toward the crater itself, then skirts north and climbs the wall of the crater. Both alternatives meet at Miriakamba Hut, then the trek follows a single route the rest of the way up.

To reach the Momella Route, head east from Arusha or west from Moshi (toward each other, respectively). Just east of Arusha, turn north onto the well-marked Arusha National Park access road (near a town called USA River). It takes about 45 minutes of driving through dry, dusty bush to reach the Momella Gate, where you'll meet your porters and your ranger, and his weapon.

MOMELLA ROUTE: MOMELLA GATE TO MIRIAKAMBA HUT/DAY 1
Ascent: 1,550 meters to 2,500 meters
Distance: 5 kilometers
Time: 4 to 5 hours

From Momella Gate (the main gate), the trail crosses the Ngare Nanyuki River (usually a small stream) north of the ranger station (via a bridge), then wanders across a broad field with considerable game. You're likely to see buffalo, giraffe, warthogs, bushbucks, and baboons—at the very least.

On the other side of the 500-meter-wide field, the trail begins a pretty steady and somewhat steep climb for about 5–6 kilometers up an open ridge. After about 2.5 hours of this grunt, the trail enters a forested area, through which it winds for a short distance before emerging at the Miriakamba Hut.

There are actually about six huts here, with much accommodation and good cooking facilities—and a very clean bathroom (toilets, washbasins, etc.—no showers). Buffalo are everywhere around Miriakamba Hut during the night, so be careful when going out after dark.

The Alternate Route to Miriakamba also crosses the Ngare Nanyuki River and wanders through the open field of animals, but then turns left, passes some campsites, and then begins climbing into the forest. There is a short side trail (off to the left, after crossing the 500-meter-wide field) that leads to the beautiful Tululusia Falls along this route. However, it is very difficult to find, so ask your guide.

After about an hour you reach Fig Tree Arch, a giant fig tree that strangled several other trees, which subsequently died, and now stands alone in the forest in this strange configuration. About 20 minutes on through the woods, you reach Itikoni Clearing, which can also boast impressive numbers of wild animals.

Another half hour on, you reach Maio Falls, then Kitoto Camp, which has a now-defunct hut. Continue wandering north, uphill, until you come to a split in the trail. The left track goes to Meru's crater's floor, the right track wanders up the north ridge of the crater and, about an hour from Kitoto Camp, joins the main branch of the trail at Miriakamba Hut.

Tululusia Falls, Mount Meru

MOMELLA ROUTE: MIRIAKAMBA HUT TO SADDLE HUT / DAY 2
Ascent: 2,500 meters to 3,500 meters
Distance: 5 kilometers
Time: 3 to 4 hours

From Miriakamba Hut, the trail heads northwest, along a grassy road and downhill for several hundred meters. Then begins the "5,000 Steps" (my term), a series of stairs built into the east ridge of the mountain. This is pretty steep hiking—well, stair climbing—for about 600 meters of elevation gain.

Roughly halfway to the next hut, Saddle Hut, there is a wonderful overlook at the appropriately titled Mgongo wa Tembo (Elephant Ridge) viewpoint (and commemorative bench), where, according to local lore, an elephant fell into the crater.[88]

Just after Mgongo wa Tembo, the trail breaks through forest, then crosses a small stream, then steepens again and begins to go through an area of deep trail ruts (the trail, a series of trenches, really, sinks as much as 1 meter into the ground).[89] The hiking is arduous and requires good balance.

The ruts lead, eventually, to Saddle Hut (3,500 meters), another collection of clean, spacious huts. The main hut for *mzungus* is compartmentalized, so you and three other friends can actually have your own room, with four bunk beds for a night. Because the huts come with lockable doors and keys, you can even lock your sleeping gear here while you head to the summit the next day, which is very useful.

MOMELLA ROUTE: SADDLE HUT TO SUMMIT TO SADDLE HUT / DAY 3
Ascent / descent: 3,500 meters to 4,566 meters and back to Saddle Hut
Distance: 11 kilometers round trip
Time: 6 to 7 hours

This is a pretty long and grueling hike, even if you're acclimatized.[90] From Saddle Hut, go north, between the huts, and join a gently angled track heading for the col between Meru and (off to the right) Little Meru (3,820 meters / 12,530 feet), a subsidiary summit of Mount Meru. The trail winds around a bit in the col, but after a few hundred meters it heads west and begins to climb in earnest, up the same kind of rutted trail that you experienced just before Saddle Hut.

After winding and grinding up these rutted trails, the track emerges at Rhino Point (3,800 meters) on the rim of the crater—a magnificent viewpoint from which it's possible to see down into the crater.

The trail then drops down 100 meters or so and crosses several rocky slopes, then starts climbing steeply again. The climbing on Meru is of the big-step-small-slide-backward variety and can be frustrating. Continue up and west along the ridge, across scree slopes, then rock ribs, then more scree slopes—the trail is very well marked with spray paint—until, after nearly 6 kilometers, you reach the summit.

This summit of Mount Meru—like all East African summits—has a name separate from the mountain massif itself: in this case, Socialism Peak (4,566 meters / 14,976 feet).

The descent follows the same route.

Hiking from Saddle Hut (visible at far right), at the base of Little Meru, to Rhino Point

MOMELLA ROUTE: SADDLE HUT TO LITTLE MERU TO
MOMELLA GATE / DAY 4

Ascent / descent: 3,500 meters to 3,820 meters to 1,550 meters
Distance: 12 kilometers
Time: 4 hours

Depending on how you feel after hiking to Meru's summit the previous day, you might consider a side trip, early on your last day, up Little Meru. This is an excellent place to watch the sun rise over Kilimanjaro, to the east.

The hike is fairly easy (after the summit day on Meru). It follows an easily found trail, northwest of the Saddle Hut area, up the closest side of Little Meru. The hike up to Little Meru is about 1 kilometer and takes about 40 minutes. After sunrise on Little Meru, you'll likely have breakfast at Saddle Hut before heading down the mountain.

From Saddle Hut, the descent to Momella Gate is the same as the ascent, and much more grueling if you have knee issues. Still, from Saddle Hut to Momella Gate can be done remarkably quickly.[91]

Chapter 6

MOUNT KENYA

*We passed the night without disturbance, and rose with the sun. Kenya peak
glittered superbly in the sky....*
—Halford John Mackinder in his diary, August 26, 1899

Mount Kenya is a mountaineers' mountain.

Steep, craggy, and with twin summit spires, it's the kind of peak mountaineers might conjure up when they dream of serious climbing adventures. It resembles some of the legendary peaks of Patagonia, the Matterhorn, and certain mountains in the Canadian Rockies.

At 5,199 meters (17,058 feet), Mount Kenya is also the second-highest mountain in Africa after Kilimanjaro.

Mount Kenya is much more intriguing to mountaineers than Kilimanjaro. For one thing, it took until nearly the end of the nineteenth century for explorers to even confirm the existence of the peak. Felice Benuzzi's famed 1953 story of three Italian war prisoners escaping from a British prison camp near Nanyuki so they could climb the mountain, then their "escape" back into prison after bagging Point Lenana—having been beaten back by bad weather on the west face of Batian—adds to the allure (see Appendix H).

Besides an interesting history, Mount Kenya has interesting geographic characteristics. Mount Kenya's peaks lie just 17 kilometers south of the equator. The high point is 600 meters (1,968 feet) lower than Kili, and yet Mount Kenya boasts the best ice climbs in Africa, and some of the finest in the world.

Like many other mountains in East Africa, Mount Kenya is an extinct volcano which was active 2.6 to 3.1 million years ago. The volcanic uplift created an island ecosystem, known today as the Central Highlands. Mount Kenya forms the eastern part of these highlands.

The Mount Kenya massif is circular in shape, about 70 kilometers in diameter, and rises about 5,000 meters from the 800-meter surrounding plains.

Like Kilimanjaro, Mount Kenya boasts several distinct zones of flora and fauna: the cultivated slopes around the national park boundaries, the bamboo forests, the high moorlands around the main peaks, and finally the alpine desert zone, which is mostly rock and ice.

Mount Kenya National Park was created in 1949 and in 1997 was designated a World Heritage Site by UNESCO for being "one of the most impressive landscapes of Eastern Africa with its rugged glacier-clad summits, Afro-alpine moorlands and diverse forests which illustrate outstanding ecological processes." In 1978 it was also declared an international biosphere reserve by UNESCO.

The park covers 715 square kilometers and takes in most of the land area above 3,200 meters. In July 2000, all the surrounding natural forests were added to the conservation area, which is now known as Mount Kenya National Reserve. Thus the area of the national park and the national reserve combined is 2,800 square kilometers.

Mount Kenya encompasses more than just one peak. It contains multiple rock spires and summits, ten glaciers, and numerous pristine valleys. The three highest peaks are Batian (5,199 meters/17,058 feet), Nelion (5,188 meters/17,022 feet), and Point Lenana (4,985 meters/16,355 feet).

The big difference between Mount Kenya and Kilimanjaro is that the summits of Batian and Nelion can't be reached by trekkers; they require technical mountaineering skills and equipment.

Point Lenana can be climbed by trekkers without any special mountaineering skills or equipment. Often when trekkers say they have "climbed Mount Kenya," they are really referring to an ascent of Lenana. The Mountain Club of Kenya has a regularly updated website (*www.mck.or.ke*).

THE NAME

To the indigenous people who lived in central Kenya for thousands of years, Mount Kenya had various names.

The Kikuyu, who make up the bulk of Kenya's modern-day population, called the mountain Kirinyaga, which, roughly translated, means "white or bright mountain." They believed the mountain to be the home of their god Ngai, and out of respect, some still build their houses so that the doors face Mount Kenya.

The Embu called the mountain Kirenia (mountain of whiteness), and the Masai called it Oldonyo Eibor (white mountain) and Oldonyo Egere (speckled mountain).

Anthropologists and linguists believe the modern name Kenya comes from the Kamba or Wakamba tribe, who called the mountain Kiinyaa (mountain of the ostrich) because the dark rock and speckled ice fields closely resemble the tail feathers of the male ostrich.

The three highest points on Mount Kenya—Batian, Nelion, and Point Lenana—were all named by Halford Mackinder after legendary Masai *laibons*, or medicine men, following the first ascent of the mountain. The Masai who lived around Mount Kenya believed that their divine ancestors dwelt on Mount Kenya and that their people came down from the mountain at the beginning of time.[92]

Most of the other subsidiary summits around Mount Kenya are named for more contemporary European explorers and climbers.

POPULARITY

According to Mount Kenya National Park estimates, about 25,000 people visit the park annually—15,000 of those ascend to the upper mountain. Most climb Point Lenana, and probably 60 percent make its summit. About 500 each year attempt to climb the Normal Route on Nelion, and about 200 of these reach

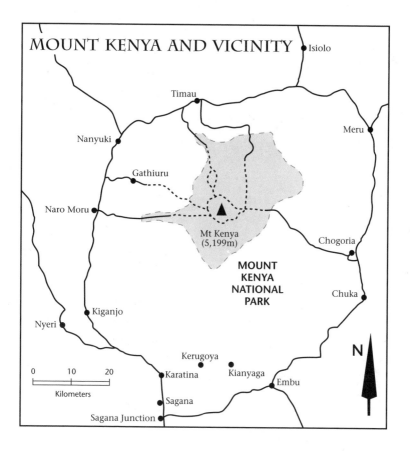

its summit. Surprisingly to most serious mountaineers, only an estimated fifty climbers reach the summit of Batian each year, most by following the North Face Standard Route or the Normal Route to Nelion, then traversing across the Gate of the Mists.

One of the best things about climbing Batian or Nelion is that if you have a few days to wait, you can usually find a day when you will have the mountain all to yourself!

GEOGRAPHY

There are five major approach routes (Naro Moru, Chogoria, Sirimon, Burguret, and Timau) that penetrate the forest and moorland areas on Mount Kenya. These routes, which can all be done by trekkers, do not go to the summit of any peak, not even Point Lenana. They all end at the Summit Circuit Path, which circumnavigates the main peaks of Mount Kenya.

From the Summit Circuit Path there are dozens of options, from hiking up to Point Lenana from Austrian Hut or Shipton's Camp, to climbing Batian and

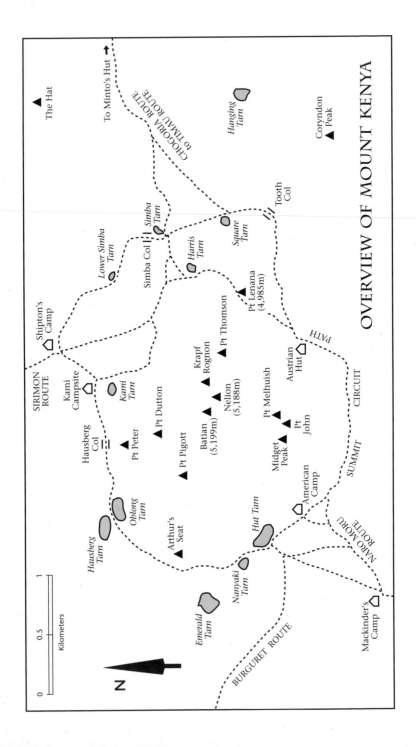

OVERVIEW OF MOUNT KENYA

Left: *Mount Kenya and the Gorges Valley*

Overleaf: *Day 1 of the Bujuku–Mubuku Circuit, Rwenzoris*

Below: *Benny Bach starting the South Face Route, Mount Kenya*

Above: *Climbing toward
Shipton's Notch, West Ridge
Route, Mount Kenya*
(Photo © Bart O'Brien)

Right: *Waterfall near the
Chogoria Route roadhead,
Mount Kenya*

Above: *Second cave,*
Rongai Route, Kilimanjaro

Left: *Mount Kenya*
(Photo © Doug Scott)

Right: *William Sandy descending the Arrow Glacier Route, Kilimanjaro*

Below: *Mobuku Valley, Rwenzoris*

Left: *Benny Bach on the Southeast Gully Route, Point John*

Below: *P. Cummings approaching Firman's Tower, Mount Kenya* (Photo © Bart O'Brien)

Mount Stanley summit, Rwenzoris

Kitandara Hut on the Bujuku–Mubuku Circuit, Rwenzoris

Next page: *Normal Route on Mount Stanley, Rwenzoris*

Nelion. If you are doing a trek or climb with an outfitter or guide, you must decide which route or routes you want to take to any of Mount Kenya's various summits (if any) with your outfitter before you leave Naro Moru, Chogoria, Nanyuki, Nairobi, or wherever.

FOREST/MOORLAND ROUTES

The three main forest and moorland routes leading to the main peaks of Mount Kenya are the Naro Moru, Chogoria, and Sirimon Routes. These routes are well established and well marked, and offer easy-to-follow trails into the high country. The other two approach routes, the Burguret and Timau Routes, are not well established, and even getting to their trailheads is an experiment in exploration. Regardless of how good your map-reading and navigational skills are, you will invariably get lost at some point on either of the two routes.

Perhaps the most important thing to remember about the Naro Moru, Chogoria, and Sirimon Routes is that they have national park gates, where you can pay your park fees upon entrance to the park. If you use the Burguret or Timau Routes, however, you must make sure that either you, or a hired outfitter, pays the fees at the Naro Moru Gate. Under no circumstances should you attempt any "unofficial" routes without the authority of the Kenya Wildlife Service senior warden in charge of the park. You must confirm assurances by local outfitters that this has been done. Don't rely on their word alone.

Many climbers will want to combine two of the forest and moorland routes to make a complete traverse of the massif. There are numerous options, obviously, but probably the prettiest traverse is the Chogoria–Sirimon traverse.

All of the trailheads are accessed from the tarmac ring road that circles Mount Kenya. From the south (Nairobi), this ring road starts at Sagana Junction, a small village north of Nairobi. The main Nairobi–Nanyuki Road becomes the western half of the ring road at Sagana Junction; the eastern half of the ring road is a subsidiary road at this point.

To quickly reach Chogoria, Meru, and other points around the eastern half of the mountain, turn right at Sagana Junction. To reach Naro Moru, Nanyuki, Timau, and other villages on the northern and western side of the mountain, go straight at Sagana Junction.

The following routes are described in order of popularity. Each route description is broken down into days, the way a typical party would ascend the mountain to the Summit Circuit Path.

NARO MORU ROUTE

The Naro Moru Route is the most popular way to the higher elevations on Mount Kenya. It ascends through the mountain's forest and moorland areas from the west. The route is not the most scenic but is generally the one chosen by most tour and outfitting companies because of its ease of access and fancy tourist accommodations at the base of the mountain.

Naro Moru itself is little more than a collection of shacks and shops strung out along the road. It lies about 200 kilometers north of Nairobi, and about 60 kilometers north of Sagana Junction.

The road to the park gate is well marked. Officially, it is Route D448, and a big sign announces that it is 12 kilometers to Munyu (a tiny village en route to the Naro Moru Gate).

Just west of the main Naro Moru intersection, where the ring road meets Route D448, is the popular but expensive Naro Moru River Lodge. Porters and guides can be arranged here, along with transport to and from trailheads. Also, just 7.2 kilometers north of the Naro Moru intersection is the Mountain Rock Lodge. It is similar to the Naro Moru River Lodge, and guides and porters can be arranged here as well.

To reach Mount Kenya National Park headquarters and the Naro Moru Gate from the Naro Moru intersection, drive east on the dirt road for 7 kilometers to a split in the road. Take the right road and drive another 3 kilometers to another split. Take the left branch and 2.5 kilometers after this is the Youth Hostel Camp. About 5 kilometers beyond the Youth Hostel Camp, the road leads to the park headquarters (2,500 meters) and the park gate.

For acclimatization purposes, most climbers begin hiking at the park gate, although it is possible to drive a vehicle 9 kilometers farther, as far as the Met Station (3,050 meters).

NARO MORU ROUTE: NARO MORU GATE TO MET STATION / DAY 1
Ascent: 2,500 meters to 3,050 meters
Distance: 10 kilometers
Time: 3 to 4 hours

From the Naro Moru Gate, the trail leads through the forest along a ridge between the two branches of the Naro Moru River. About 6–7 kilometers from the park gate, the trail crosses Percival's Bridge, then continues north, then east again, as it gains the lower Teleki Valley. The trail soon reaches the Meteorological Station ("Met Station") at 3,050 meters. The Met Station has a large lodge, managed by the Naro Moru River Lodge, and it accommodates about thirty people. There are also several latrines. Water is readily available from taps near each *banda* (cabin). Most parties are encouraged to spend their first night on the Naro Moru Route here.

NARO MORU ROUTE: MET STATION TO MACKINDER'S CAMP / DAY 2
Ascent: 3,050 meters to 4,200 meters
Distance: 10 kilometers
Time: 5 hours

The normal second day's hiking continues east, up the trail, passing a radio tower and emerging from the forest at about 3,200 meters. It's best to start this hike by 7:00 AM at the latest, as this will spare you the worst of the weather. The steepest, wettest portion of the moorland is called the Vertical Bog, for obvious reasons. Just picture yourself here in the rainy season! Continuing east, the trail splits at an obvious rest-point overlooking the Teleki Valley: the left branch descends to the Naro Moru River losing a lot of your hard-earned elevation; the more popular right branch goes into the valley to the south side and joins the river higher up. After a full 5 or 6 hours, Mackinder's Camp (4,200 meters) is reached.

Mackinder's Camp has a large stone bunkhouse, as well as many possible campsites. Most parties spend their second night on the mountain here.

From Mackinder's Camp, the trail continues up the Teleki Valley, moving along the left side of the valley toward the base of the peaks, where it joins the Summit Circuit Path. At the Summit Circuit Path, you have the option of going north around the west side of the mountain, past American Camp and Hut Tarn, or continuing east around the south side of the mountain to Austrian Hut and the Lewis Glacier area.

If you are trekking, your third day will most likely be the hike up to Point Lenana, commencing at 3:00 AM, then an afternoon return to the Met Station for one night before hiking out to Naro Moru the next day (unless you have arranged for collection by vehicle and a night of luxury in a good hotel). Most climbers at Mackinder's Camp who are headed to Point Lenana get up extremely early so they can catch the sunrise over the mountain. It takes about 4–5 hours to reach Point Lenana from Mackinder's Camp, and the elevation gain is about 800 meters. The trail to Lenana—which goes east, around the south side of the main peaks—is extremely steep and on loose gravel, so it is important to go slowly.

If you are doing technical mountaineering, your third day will most likely be a matter of getting to one of the huts below your proposed route and setting up camp for the night.

SIRIMON ROUTE

After the Chogoria Route, the Sirimon Route is probably the second most scenic route accessing the upper portions of Mount Kenya.

To reach the Sirimon Route, drive 15.8 kilometers northeast from Nanyuki on the Mount Kenya ring road to a sign-posted dirt road leading to the Sirimon Gate, 9 kilometers farther on. The road to the Sirimon Gate is well marked with a huge wooden sign.

SIRIMON ROUTE: SIRIMON GATE TO JUDMAIER CAMP / OLD MOSES / DAY 1

Ascent: 2,700 meters to 3,300 meters
Distance: 9 kilometers
Time: 3 to 4 hours

It is 9 kilometers from the Sirimon Gate through the forest to the Judmaier Camp/Old Moses area (3,300 meters). Many people choose to drive this section of the road, but some walk it to aid acclimatization (which is recommended). The road is obvious and well maintained.

Most parties spend their first night on the Sirimon Route at Judmaier Camp, a cleared camping area on the left side of the road, or at the Old Moses bunk-house, another few hundred meters farther up the road.

SIRIMON ROUTE: JUDMAIER CAMP / OLD MOSES TO SHIPTON'S CAMP / DAY 2

Ascent: 3,300 meters to 4,200 meters
Distance: 12 kilometers
Time: 5 to 6 hours

From Old Moses, the main summits of Batian, Nelion, and Point Lenana are visible, as are the subsidiary peaks of Terere and Sendeyo, to the left of the main peaks.

From the Judmaier Camp / Old Moses area, there are two alternative trails to Shipton's Camp: the first via the Mackinder Valley turns right from the Global Atmosphere Watch (GAW) station; the second via Liki North Hut leads straight on up the ridge before turning right higher up. Most parties follow the Mackinder Valley Route, as the trail is much easier to follow. Some porters will not follow the Liki North Hut alternative and must be met at Shipton's Camp if you use this route. A map and compass are helpful.

The main trail, via the Mackinder Valley, follows a rough four-wheel-drive road and continues south (keep right, as other roads lead off left) before petering out as it circles around a creekbed, the Ontulili River. A hundred meters beyond the creek, the trail leaves the old roadbed, going left. It is not well marked but should be obvious. The trail contours along the northern slopes of the massif for about 4 kilometers, gradually turning south and cresting an insignificant ridge. Descend the next valley, cross the Liki North River, then climb out of the valley to the south. The trail crests another ridge, this one above the spectacular Mackinder Valley.

The trail contours into the Mackinder Valley and follows the eastern side of the valley for about 7 kilometers to Shipton's Camp (4,200 meters).

The Liki North Hut variation starts up the same rough four-wheel-drive road and continues from the GAW station heading toward the Barrow, a rounded hill above you. It skirts right of the Barrow, along the southwest side of the hill, then crosses the heads of the Ontulili and Liki North Valleys before reaching Liki North Hut (4,000 meters). The small hut doesn't offer much shelter, but there are plenty of campsites around it. From Liki North Hut, the trail climbs out of the Liki North Valley, crests a ridge, then descends into the Mackinder Valley, where it joins the Mackinder Valley Route.

It's a straightforward walk up the valley to Shipton's Camp, where there are a bunkhouse and several camping areas. Most parties spend their second night on the Sirimon Route here.

From Shipton's Camp, you have several options. You can continue up the main trail southeast, which climbs to Simba Col, then joins the Chogoria Route near Square Tarn. Or you can hike up the hill to the right, which leads to a campsite where the Kami Hut used to be below the north face of Batian. In between these two options is a trail that climbs Point Lenana. It leads up (south-southeast) through a narrow gully, then switchbacks up a steep gravel hill before reaching Harris Tarn. The trail goes around the north side of Harris Tarn, then scrambles up the northeast side of Point Lenana.

Shipton's Camp, Mount Kenya, with Terere and Sendeyo behind

CHOGORIA ROUTE

The Chogoria Route is by far the most scenic and interesting route through the forests and moorland areas of Mount Kenya National Park, although it has limited views of the main peaks. It is reached from the Chogoria Village area, on the east side of the mountain.

Note: The Chogoria Route's huts are no longer available for visitors; they are for porters and guides only. You must bring camping equipment (i.e., a tent) to do this route.

To reach Chogoria, drive north from Nairobi and turn right at Sagana Junction. Follow this road for many kilometers, through the towns of Embu and Chuka. About 16 kilometers past Chuka is a turnoff on the left. Look for signs pointing to the Transit Motel. The Transit Motel, located about 2 kilometers up this road, is an excellent place to stay, with very reasonable rates and a friendly staff. Chogoria Village is about 2 kilometers north of the Transit Motel turnoff on the Mount Kenya ring road, then up a dirt road to the east.

Guides, porters, and lifts to the park gate can be arranged at the Marimebu Lodge, which is up the Chogoria road, past the Transit Motel, about 1 kilometer before the park gate. The entire village of Chogoria is in the Mount Kenya guiding/portering business, and everyone here is related. Apparently a couple of generations ago, Chogoria chief Mbogori Mwenda had thirty-seven wives and greatly contributed to the town's population.

From the Transit Motel, the road continues west. After about 2 kilometers, turn left, and drive past Mutindwa Market and Village. The road will circle around to the south, then reaches a turnoff to the right leading to the Mount Kenya National Park gate. Recently, Mount Kenya National Park was extended down to this gate, and KWS was (at the time of this writing) in the process of constructing a new park entrance.

You will need to sign in at the park gate.

CHOGORIA ROUTE: PARK GATE TO MERU MOUNT KENYA LODGE/DAY 1
  Ascent: 1,700 meters to 3,000 meters
  Distance: 23 kilometers
  Time: 10 to 11 hours

Although many groups walk from Chogoria Village to the park gate on their first day, and from the park gate to Meru Mount Kenya Lodge on the second day, most parties get a lift at least to the park gate. (In mid-2005, the park boundaries were extended from the Meru Mount Kenya Lodge area all the way down to the former forest gate and a new park gate was constructed.)

From the park gate, it's about 20 kilometers up the dirt road to the Meru Mount Kenya Lodge area. This section of dirt road passes through some wild forests, and it is not uncommon to encounter elephant and buffalo here.

After 20 kilometers you'll enter a wide, open area and, off to the right, is the Meru Mount Kenya Lodge—actually a collection of cabins (more commonly known as the *bandas*) built around a grassy common. They offer showers, kitchens, bedrooms, and small lounges and cost about US$15 per night per person (plus another US$3 if you use gas for cooking). Most parties climbing the

Chogoria Route stay here their first night, and if you are slow at acclimatizing, it is wise to spend 2 nights here. The open area in which the *bandas* are located attracts many buffalo and other animals (so wandering outside, especially at night, has certain risks). Behind the *bandas* (to the north, down a big hill) is a dried-out lake, where many animals gather. This is a good place to watch wildlife in the early morning and evening hours.

CHOGORIA ROUTE: MERU MOUNT KENYA LODGE TO MINTO'S HUT / DAY 2

Ascent: 3,000 meters to 4,300 meters
Distance: 15 kilometers
Time: 6 to 7 hours

From the *bandas*, it's an easy 7-kilometer stroll up the four-wheel-drive road to the end of the road. You can also drive as far as the roadhead, which is the only one on Mount Kenya where tourists regularly leave vehicles (ensure that no valuables are left in the vehicle and any good gear should be stored out of sight).

Near the roadhead is an interesting side trip that many climbers may want to take. Just downhill from the roadhead is a beautiful waterfall. A trail on the south side of the stream follows it for about 0.5 kilometer to the top of the falls. A small, very steep trail goes down the west (right) side of the falls to the bottom. Also, just west of the falls is an amphitheater containing a cave used by the Mau Mau rebels in the early 1950s. The cave—filled with goat dung—was bombed by the British; some guides might not want to take you here for fear of there still being live shells in the area.

From the roadhead, the Chogoria trail crosses the creek to the south, then climbs a long east-west ridge for several kilometers. The trail eventually crests a ridge that overlooks the spectacular Gorges Valley. The trail then follows the north (right) side of the gorge for several more kilometers to Hall Tarn and Minto's Hut, the normal second night's stay on the Chogoria Route. Minto's Hut is small, basic, and pretty filthy and is a guides and porters shelter only. Visitors need tents. There are many campsites around the hut.

CHOGORIA ROUTE: MINTO'S HUT TO AUSTRIAN HUT / DAY 3

Ascent: 4,300 meters to 4,800 meters
Distance: 3 kilometers
Time: 2 to 3 hours

From Minto's Hut, most parties continue on to Austrian Hut, although there are other options.

From Minto's, the trail continues west to a large flat area known as Temple Fields, where it meets the Summit Circuit Path. At this point, there are two options. In the first, you can hike southwest (following the left branch of the trail) to reach Tooth Col and Austrian Hut. This route climbs a steep scree field before crossing Tooth Col between several rock towers. In the second option, the right branch of the trail (which heads north) goes to Simba Col and then drops down a long hill to Shipton's Camp.

Tooth Col from Temple Fields, Chogoria Route, Mount Kenya

Most trekking groups take the first option to Austrian Hut, where they spend a third night before climbing Point Lenana the next morning. Technical mountaineers headed for the Normal Route on Batian / Nelion also usually go to Austrian Hut.

BURGURET ROUTE

The Burguret Route should not be considered a trail, track, or path like the other routes on the mountain. It is a "route" only in the sense that it is one way you can go. Put another way, the Burguret Route is little more than a route through the woods on its most pronounced sections. On its least pronounced sections, the trail is nonexistent. You will need special authority from the senior warden to use this or any other "unofficial" route.

The route begins near the little settlement of Gathiuru (1,500 meters), southeast of Nanyuki. There is no official trailhead for this route, and getting on the route is a matter of trial and error.

To reach Gathiuru from Nanyuki, drive southwest on the Mount Kenya ring road for 8.5 kilometers. To reach Gathiuru from Naro Moru, drive northeast on the Mount Kenya ring road for 7.2 kilometers. The road to Gathiuru is well signed. Officially, it is called Route E642. There is also a green-and-white sign pointing to "Ministry of Environment and Natural Resources, Forest Department's Gathiuru Forest Station."

Follow this dirt road southeast for 11.1 kilometers to the forest gate. Immediately after the forest gate, turn sharp right. The road immediately splits; take the left branch. The road will pass a small village on the left that looks like an early American pilgrim settlement. Then, 0.4 kilometer past the gate, the main road veers right while a small, very rough road continues straight toward the mountain. Take the rough road straight for 2.3 kilometers, then turn right into a forest.

The forest is only about half a kilometer wide, and the road soon reemerges into cultivated fields. However, about halfway through the forest, an old, impassable road leads off right. This is the start of the Burguret Route. There are no signs, no facilities. Nothing. (To get an idea of where the Burguret Route goes, continue driving through the forest to the fields on the east side. From this cleared agricultural area, you can look up at the lower slopes of the mountain. A small, rounded hill is where the route goes.)

The Burguret Route is close to the route taken by Felice Benuzzi and his compatriots when they escaped from a POW camp in 1943 (see Appendix H). Most guides' and porters' organizations around Mount Kenya have guides / porters who will know this route.

Hiking the Burguret Route with Highland Castle behind, Mount Kenya

BURGURET ROUTE: ROAD END TO KAMPI YA MACHENGENI / DAY 1

Ascent: 2,000 meters to 3,000 meters
Distance: 9 kilometers
Time: 7 to 8 hours

Although extremely difficult to follow at times, the route ascends an indistinct ridge between the Burguret and Nanyuki Rivers. Much of the walking requires bushwhacking through bamboo forests, and inevitably everyone gets lost. The "trail" emerges at a sloping clearing between the bamboo forests and the heather forests above, called Kampi Ya Machengeni.

BURGURET ROUTE: KAMPI YA MACHENGENI TO HIGHLAND CASTLE / DAY 2

Ascent: 3,000 meters to 3,700 meters
Distance: 7 kilometers
Time: 7 hours

As the bamboo forest gives way to heather, the "trail" does not become any more pronounced, except that much of the route is marked with ancient wooden elevation signs. Some of these signs are so old and worn they are easily missed.

The route emerges from the heather (3,500 meters) and continues up the upper Burguret River drainage. Eventually, Highland Castle (3,700 meters)—a long, low rock wall on the left side of the valley—is reached. Most parties spend their second night at Highland Castle.

BURGURET ROUTE: HIGHLAND CASTLE TO HUT TARN / DAY 3

Ascent: 3,700 meters to 4,500 meters
Distance: 9 kilometers
Time: 7 hours

From Highland Castle, the route follows the ridge above Highland Castle and aims straight for the main peaks. After a half day's walk, you reach Hut Tarn (where the Two Tarn Hut used to be), on the west side of the mountain. The Summit Circuit Path is joined, and any portion of the mountain can be reached from this.

TIMAU ROUTE

This route is rarely used, and is not recommended because of the horrendously long, rough, dirt road approach, which takes you all over the northern side of the mountain, through endless farm country and numerous villages. Also, the trail is not well established, and in some places, is nonexistent. A map and compass are required for this route.

Like the Burguret Route, the Timau Route is a wilderness experience. There is also a new park gate at the base of this route known as Marania Gate.

To get to the trailhead, drive west on the Mount Kenya ring road from the town of Meru for about 35 kilometers, or east from Nanyuki for about 30 kilometers, to a dirt road. This road leads south just 100 meters from a quaint little petrol station with a shop that stands in a grove of trees in the middle of wheat fields.

Continue along this road toward three rounded hills, past wheat fields, and then into residential farmland country. After about 15 kilometers, you will see tall radio masts on your left. Take the turn to the right, which leads to the forest barrier after a few hundred meters. One kilometer farther, turn right again and continue for about 7 kilometers until you reach the national park gate. Leave your vehicle here if you are going up the Timau Route.

Near the gate, a left turn then leads you up a track through the last of the forest until you emerge into the zone of giant heather. This road continues in an easterly direction and you need to turn off it after about 3 kilometers and follow an old track to the right of a small hill for another kilometer, then left onto yet another old track. This leads onward generally toward the main peaks. (The road you leave earlier eventually ends up 15 kilometers away at the Rutundu Fishing Bandas, which are booked only on an exclusive basis. This is way off the Timau Route and so would not necessarily be part of an ascent/descent of this route.)

TIMAU ROUTE: ROAD END TO MINTO'S HUT / DAY 1
Ascent: 3,300 meters to 4,300 meters
Distance: 16 kilometers
Time: 10 hours

The trail, where it exists, heads south, and slightly southeast, as it traverses around the tops of the Kazita East and Kazita West Valleys. The route follows the Kazita East Valley, the more southerly and larger of the two, in a southwesterly direction for about 3 kilometers, until it crests a high col and drops down into the Hinde Valley, where it crosses the north branch of the Nithi River, then continues south over relatively level country before joining the Chogoria Route at Minto's Hut. From this point, follow descriptions for the Chogoria Route.

SUMMIT CIRCUIT PATH

Although circumnavigations of Kibo on Kilimanjaro are not common, circumnavigations of the main peaks of Mount Kenya are somewhat popular. This is mostly because Mount Kenya is much smaller than Kibo, and also because the forest and moorland routes to Mount Kenya's main peaks converge from all directions, so the Summit Circuit Path must be used to link together trails, huts, and routes. On Kili, most of the forest and moorland routes all come in from the south, so only the South Circuit Path is regularly used. On Mount Kenya, the Summit Circuit Path is regularly used, and the entire cluster of main peaks on Mount Kenya can be easily circumnavigated in one day.

The following description of the Summit Circuit Path begins at the 4,300-meter intersection of the Naro Moru Route, near American Camp, since most people will first encounter the circuit path at this point, and will go around the mountain counterclockwise. This circumnavigation includes about 2,132 meters of elevation gain and loss and about 10 kilometers of travel.

From the end of the Naro Moru Route in the upper Teleki Valley, the Summit Circuit Path is more like a continuation of the Naro Moru Route than its own separate trail. From the unmarked junction of the two routes, the circuit path

Terere

Sendeyo

Hausberg Col

heads off up a major scree slope to the right of the main peaks, switchbacking and scrambling for a vertical gain of about 600 meters. This incline is easily the worst hiking experience you will have on Mount Kenya.

After cresting a ridge, the trail wanders through stacks of jumbled blocks and emerges at Austrian Hut (4,800 meters).

From Austrian Hut, the path drops down to the south, into the very top portion of the wide, beautiful Hobley Valley. The route contours across the head of the valley on a rocky, but fairly level trail that leads to Tooth Col. From Tooth Col, the trail drops down the hill and soon reaches Square Tarn. The Chogoria Route joins the Summit Circuit Path here. From Square Tarn, the Summit Circuit Path heads north, crosses another (minor) junction with the Chogoria Route at Simba Tarn, then climbs up steeply over Simba Col (4,650 meters). The views of Batian and Nelion from Simba Col are terrific. The trail then drops down a steep scree slope to Shipton's Camp.

From Shipton's Camp, a faint trail leads up the scree slope to the southwest, heading straight toward the main peaks. After an hour, it reaches the Kami campsite, where an old tin shack (the late Kami Hut) used to stand. Past the Kami campsite, the trail heads west-southwest and climbs up switchbacks in fine scree before topping out on Hausberg Col (4,590 meters). Point Peter (4,757 meters) will be the obvious triangular peak just to the south. From Hausberg Col, it's a very steep descent into the upper Hausberg Valley, where the aptly named Oblong and Hausberg Tarns are located. The trail then climbs out of the valley, passing the north side of Point Pigott on the way, to crest a ridge at Arthur's Seat. After topping the ridge, the trail winds along a beautiful series of rock ledges before passing Emerald Tarn (off to the right down the valley), Nanyuki Tarn, and Hut Tarn. Two Tarn Hut used to be located at Hut Tarn; today the site is a scenic campsite with spectacular views of the southeast face of Batian.

The Summit Circuit Path skirts the west side of Hut Tarn, then drops off into the Teleki Valley, down a steep hill to the south. At the bottom of this long hill is American Camp (4,350 meters). There are no facilities at American Camp, just a flat spot in the valley. Some parties bivouac here before attempting south-face routes on Nelion and Batian, like the Diamond Couloir (although it's better to hike up into the massive south-face amphitheater and bivouac closer to the routes).

From American Camp, the Summit Circuit Path continues south, where it meets the Naro Moru Route. There are about ten different variations of the trail between Hut Tarn, American Camp, and the upper part of the Naro Moru Route. A map and compass can be helpful in this area; however, just using the major landmarks is probably the easiest way to tell where you are, provided that the clouds have not rolled in.

As mentioned, the Summit Circuit Path can be done in 1 long day, or it can be broken up with overnight stops at any of the huts along the way. Some parties spend 3 days circumnavigating the mountain. There is no technical climbing on any portion of the Summit Circuit Path, and it can be done in walking shoes.

Looking toward Hausberg Col from Arthur's Seat on the Summit Circuit Path, Mount Kenya

Mackinder's Valley, Sirimon Route, Mount Kenya

MOUNT KENYA PEAKS

Contrary to the understanding most safari-going tourists visiting Kenya have of the mountain, Mount Kenya is not just one single peak. It is, in fact, a dizzying cluster of peaks, towers, and summits, each of which has its own unique character.

Although most climbers visiting the Mount Kenya area head for Point Lenana (4,985 meters/16,355 feet)—the third-highest summit, which can be scrambled up—or Batian (5,199 meters/17,058 feet) and Nelion (5,188 meters/17,022 feet)—the twin highest points of Mount Kenya, which require technical climbing equipment and skills—there are many other interesting peaks and towers with exceptional routes on them.

The hiking, scrambling, rock climbing, and ice climbing routes are all generally excellent on Mount Kenya. However, that doesn't necessarily mean the rock is always solid. In many places it's rotten and loose, and rockfall on climbing routes is very common.

Routes on Mount Kenya's various summits are described in the following sections according to the various summits. Point Lenana, the trekkers' peak, is described first. Next, Nelion and Batian are described together because many of the routes on these peaks (for example, the South Face or the Ice Window) can be climbed to either summit. Indeed, the Normal Route on Mount Kenya takes in both summits.

Following the descriptions of these three major summits, the most popular climbs on Mount Kenya's subsidiary summits are described in a clockwise direction around the massif.

POINT LENANA

Point Lenana (4,985 meters/16,355 feet), as the third-highest peak of the massif, is the standard trekkers' objective and provides spectacular views of Batian and Nelion from its summit. It is most commonly climbed from Austrian Hut (4,800 meters), from which the summit is just a 45-minute walk to the northeast. However, there are dozens of different possibilities for an ascent of Lenana.

Many parties start very early from Mackinder's Camp (4,200 meters) and climb the hill (via the Summit Circuit Path) to Austrian Hut before sunrise, continue on up to the top of Point Lenana to watch the sun rise, then return to Mackinder's Camp before descending back down the Naro Moru Route.

1. POINT LENANA, SOUTHWEST RIDGE (SCRAMBLE)

From Austrian Hut (4,800 meters), the route to the summit follows the ridge to the right of the Lewis Glacier. There are many variations. It's important to stay as close to the ridge as possible. If you stray too close to the edge of the Lewis Glacier, you'll soon find that the gravelly slopes between the ridge and the glacier lie on top of ice. Go too close to the glacier and you'll be slipping and sliding. Point Lenana has a summit block, and 2-meter walls bar easy access to the very top (4,985 meters/16,355 feet). The easiest way up this block is on the northwestern corner (on the left side, at the far end if you're coming from Austrian Hut), where the block is stepped and can be negotiated easily.

Hausberg Col

Point Peter

Batian

Nelion

Krapf Rognon

Krapf Glacier

Thomson's Flake

Point Thomson

2. POINT LENANA, NORTH RIDGE (SCRAMBLE)

Compared with the southwest ridge, this route is rarely used except in the summer months when it's free of snow. It can be climbed from Shipton's Camp or can be combined with the southwest ridge in either direction for a traverse of the peak.

From Shipton's Camp (4,200 meters), the trail to Point Lenana climbs up a narrow gorge with a small stream running through it, just southeast of the camp. After breaking through this gorge, the route climbs a very steep hill via many switchbacks, and eventually reaches Harris Tarn. From Harris Tarn, the trail continues up the slope behind (west of) Harris Tarn, and moves left (south) before scrambling up a gully to the right and then a rising ramp to the top of a ridge, the north ridge of Lenana. Turn left and scramble up the summit block (4,985 meters / 16,355 feet). This route receives a lot of sunshine in the morning and is a much warmer experience than the southeast ridge.

NELION / BATIAN

Batian (5,199 meters / 17,058 feet) is the true summit, the highest point on Mount Kenya. It is separated from Nelion (5,188 meters / 17,022 feet—the second-highest summit) by a gap of only 140 meters, the famed and beautiful Gate of the Mists.

A note on Batian / Nelion descents: The best descent from Batian and Nelion for all routes has traditionally been via the Normal Route of ascent on Nelion (see below). That means, if you are on Batian, you must traverse back to Nelion to make the descent.

In the mid-1990s, a team of Austrian climbers created a standardized rappel route from the summit of Nelion, which diverges slightly from the Normal Route. This rappel route, comprised of stainless steel rappel rings, is almost free of rockfall. From the summit of Nelion, follow the green paint markers to the first rappel. The other rappels should be obvious. One word of caution, however: on the second rappel (easily identified because it's the steepest), make sure your ropes are well placed over the edge of the ledge. They easily get caught!

3. NORMAL ROUTE (GRADE IV)

The Normal Route is standard for ascents of Nelion and Batian. It was first climbed by Eric Shipton and Percy Wyn Harris on January 6, 1929, before they continued across the Gate of the Mists to achieve the second ascent of Batian. Today, the route is generally climbed in twenty roped pitches and gains some 400 meters of elevation. Most parties climb Batian in 2 days and Nelion in 1 day. It should be noted that when Halford Mackinder made the first ascent of Mount Kenya in 1899, he climbed portions of this route before traversing over the long south ridge of Nelion and crossing the upper Darwin Glacier on the south side of Nelion, then angling up to the Diamond Glacier, the Gate of the Mists, and the summit of Batian.

Main features of Mount Kenya from the east

Normal Route (Route 3), southeast face of Nelion, Mount Kenya

The route begins in a small amphitheater (4,800 meters) above the Lewis Glacier, between the Brocherel Couloir and Point Melhuish. The amphitheater is more or less straight across the Lewis Glacier from Austrian Hut.

The first pitch (often climbed unroped) ascends a low-angled, well-worn wall (Grade I) in the back (north side) of the amphitheater to a huge ledge covered with broken boulders. The second pitch (also very easy) follows a left-angling gully that leads up from the left (west) end of the ledge. This gully is often filled with snow or ice, but it is easy to negotiate these sections in rock shoes. At the top of this short pitch, an unlevel ledge is reached, the normal roping-up point. Pitch 3 traverses blocks—climbing up, down, and sideways—to the right, then steps across an airy drop to reach the base of Mackinder's Chimney. Mackinder's Chimney is very steep, and is often ice filled. It is rarely climbed and is not recommended.

From the base of the chimney, pitch 4 climbs down 3 meters and right about 10 meters, passing old pitons on the way, then straight up a low-angled crack that bypasses the right side of a triangular roof. Atop pitch 4 is a huge ledge and the One O'Clock Gully, which leads up and right for two pitches. After climbing two rope lengths up the gully (100 meters), move right onto a prominent flat block, which has many slings attached to it. Pitch 7 leads up and right onto easy (Grade I) ground. Climb two more very easy pitches up and right to Baillie's Bivy, the ruinous metal hut sitting on the crest of Nelion's south ridge. Sleeping in a hut is not advised.

From Baillie's Bivy, pitch 10 crosses the crest of the south ridge and descends about 25 meters onto rock ledges above the Upper Darwin Glacier. From this point, your goal is the notch between Mackinder's Gendarme and the upper south ridge.

You can either climb rock straight up for two pitches, following the left side of the gendarme (there are several fixed pitons) at Grade IV, or skirt the rock by descending down to the steep, obvious snow gully to the left (Grade III), then scrambling up to the notch. Pitch 13 is a perfect crack in a shallow dihedral, directly above the notch. Climb loose blocks and ledges up the ridge above for two pitches (100 meters), until the wall above steepens. Down and to the right is an unobvious traverse (pitch 16) that is the key to routefinding. Climb down 20 meters, then traverse right to gain easy ground and several big ledges.

Follow one pitch up and left, in the obvious gully, to a broad, flat, white-colored ledge. The short Grade IV chimney to the left (north) is the last crux on the route and can't be climbed with a pack on.

Above the chimney, scramble up and left on easy ground until you are overlooking the Diamond Glacier. A short, easy pitch up and right takes you to the summit of Nelion (5,188 meters / 17,022 feet).

If you are planning to cross the Gate of the Mists and ascend Batian, a night in Howell Hut on Nelion's summit is highly recommended. The hut is very low, but well built, and offers foam padding (albeit dirty) on the floor. It can comfortably hold four people.

From Nelion's summit, scramble down the ridge 18 meters, then move to the right (east) side of the ridge (belaying is advisable). The descent quickly

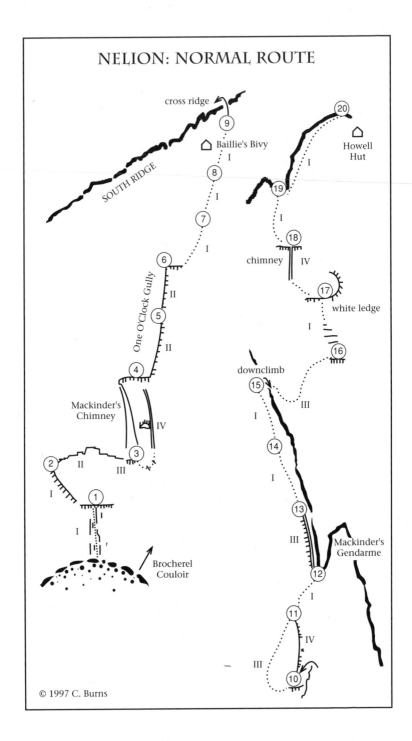

NELION: NORMAL ROUTE

cross ridge

SOUTH RIDGE

(9)

□ Baillie's Bivy

I

(8)

I

(7)

I

(6)

One O'Clock Gully

II

(5)

II

(4)

Mackinder's
Chimney

IV

(2) II

III

(3)

I

(1)

I

Brocherel
Couloir

(20)

□ Howell
Hut

I

(19)

I

(18)

chimney IV

(17)

white ledge

I

(16)

downclimb

(15)

I

(14)

I

(13)

III

Mackinder's
Gendarme

(12)

I

(11)

IV

III

(10)

© 1997 C. Burns

turns from rock to ice, and crampons are highly recommended. Continue down into the Gate of the Mists by rappeling. If you have not brought crampons, you'll want to leave a rope fixed down the last section of ice leading to the col, as it is fairly steep (about 70 degrees). Cross the Gate of the Mists, then skirt the huge gendarme that sits on the Batian side of the Gate of the Mists to its right (northeast). Climb back up to the south ridge. Generally, crampons and ice gear can be left here for the return trip to Nelion. Several easy short pitches climb the left side of Batian's south ridge and lead to the summit (5,199 meters / 17,058 feet).

The following climbs on Batian / Nelion's south face (Routes 4 through 8) start at about 4,600 meters in the huge, 600-meter-tall south-face amphitheater that contains the Diamond Couloir and Ice Window Routes.

It is best to bivouac at American Camp (4,350 meters) or higher, or to spend the night at Hut Tarn (4,500 meters) before starting these ascents. Most parties can do these routes in 1 day, but many people bivouac in the ice cave that is the Ice Window's namesake or on the summit of Batian or Nelion, to make the descent more leisurely.

4. SOUTH FACE ROUTE (GRADE IV)

The first ascent of the South Face Route was made by Arthur Firmin and John W. Howard in 1946. Originally Firmin and Howard climbed a line right of the lower section of the Ice Window Route, up the rock buttress between the Allan / Howell Variation (4A) and the Ice Window Route. Most modern parties climb the lower section of the Ice Window, then traverse right.

Like most other routes in this area, this route can be used to reach either Batian or Nelion, or both. It is usually climbed in about ten roped pitches, with much scrambling.

Start on the right side of the Lower Darwin Glacier, at about 4,600 meters, and climb it into a steep amphitheater that sits below the icefall joining the Upper and Lower Darwin Glaciers. Climb into the amphitheater's upper left-hand corner, where an obvious ramp leads up and left. Old slings and pieces of rope will make the route obvious. Turn the corner to join the lower section of the Ice Window icefall. A rocky gully just to the icefall's right can also be climbed. After several pitches, easy ground allows you to move right, to the bottom of the Upper Darwin Glacier. At the top of the Upper Darwin Glacier, move left, to the top of a rocky buttress overlooking the Diamond Glacier. This is where Mackinder's Original Route joins the South Face Route. The Diamond Glacier can be crossed diagonally, or it is possible to climb up to the Gate of the Mists, then continue on to Batian (5,199 meters / 17,058 feet) from there.

5. THE ICE WINDOW (GRADE V)

One of the true classics on the mountain, the Ice Window Route was first climbed by Phil Snyder, B. LeDain, and Y. Laulan on August 20, 1973.

Follow the description for the South Face Route until the lower part of the Ice Window icefall (4,800 meters) is gained. Follow the icefall for a half-dozen

South face of Mount Kenya with Routes 4–6 marked

pitches to a large, icy stance. This used to be an ice cave, in which climbers regularly bivouacked. It is now nearly gone, so bivouacking here is less an exotic thrill than a reality nowadays. Anyway, exit the stance—whatever's left of it—at its left end by chopping a hole in the icicles and turn the lip of the cave to gain the lower end of the Diamond Glacier. Four to five pitches lead to the Gate of the Mists. Altogether, most parties climb fifteen to eighteen pitches roped.

6. DIAMOND COULOIR (GRADE VI)

Easily the most beautiful ice climb in Africa, the Diamond Couloir was first climbed by Phil Snyder and P. Thumbi on October 4–5, 1973. The first woman to climb the route was Hillary Collins, in 1976. The route has also been so-loed several times. Yvon Chouinard and Michael Covington climbed the ice headwall directly below the Diamond Glacier, which creates a direct route, in January 1975.

The route—a striking ribbon of steep ice—starts above the left (northwest) side of the Lower Darwin Glacier, at the 4,750-meter level. The first section of the route is steep and can be almost entirely rock during dry years. Atop the first pitch is a piton belay on the left side of the couloir. At the top of the second pitch is a cave that can be used for a bivouac. Four to five leads above the first cave, the route splits, with the original route leading out left on a ramp and the headwall (6A) directly above. Both routes meet again on the Diamond Couloir. There is a second cave on the original route on the lower left side of the Diamond Glacier, which can be used as a bivouac.

Most parties climb fifteen to eighteen roped pitches.

7. SOUTHERN SLABS (GRADE VI-)

First climbed by Robert "Rusty" Baillie and R. M. Kamke on January 4, 1961, this route ascends the low-angled slabs left of the Diamond Couloir.

Starting from the 4,700-meter level in the huge south-face amphitheater, climb the Darwin Glacier's left (west) side, then the easy, right-trending ramp left of the bottom of the Diamond Couloir. When the ramp gets to within 12 meters of the Diamond Couloir, climb up a steep dihedral (Grade V) to the left for one pitch. Continue up a slab to a short wall, which is climbed on its left. Traverse right around a rib to another slab, and climb the slab to another short wall. Traverse left into a corner and up to a bulging face which is climbed by cracks (Grade VI-) to a stance.

Traverse 30 meters right into a gully and climb the gully for 30 meters to a prominent ledge. Continue up and right following a gully and slabs for 60 meters. Climb the overhang above via the obvious chockstone on the left. Above is a yellow face. About 100 meters from the left-hand edge of this face is a hidden chimney, which is climbed to a traverse to the right, then an obvious crack. Climb down and right to a ledge, then traverse right to a slab. Climb the slab, then the 5-meter wall above to gain another ledge. Traverse down and right into a steep gully. Climb the gully to a sloping ledge, then traverse left onto a block, and climb the face above the block.

Above are two steep gullies leading to the southwest ridge. Climb the right-hand gully to join the ridge and follow it to the summit of Batian (5,199 meters / 17,058 feet).

Portions of this route can be ice covered, and crampons are recommended. Most parties take 1–2 days for this ascent.

Climbing the Diamond Buttress, Mount Kenya (Photo © James Garrett)

8. DIAMOND BUTTRESS
(GRADE VI, A1 OR GRADE VII)

This is the classic outing on the Diamond Buttress, the large wall left of the Diamond Couloir. The first ascent was by John Temple and Ian Howell on March 13–14, 1976.

Diamond Buttress (Route 8), and Routes 5, 6, and 6A, Mount Kenya
(Photo © James Garrett)

From Hut Tarn (4,500 meters), climb up the left-hand edge of the Darwin Glacier. On the right side of the Diamond Buttress is a prominent V-slot/right-facing corner. Climb it for five pitches to a wall. Traverse left (poorly protected) and up into a chimney. Follow the left branch of the chimney to its top, then move right and climb a short wall to a ledge. Move right to a crack and climb it (Grade VI) until a pendulum allows you to traverse right across a blank wall and into a chimney. Done free, this traverse is Grade VII.

At the top of the chimney are several bivouac sites on ledges. Above the ledges, move left up slabs to an obvious corner. Climb the corner, then traverse left about 30 meters to the base of another crack. Climb the crack and continue up and left for several pitches to a short chimney that gains a leftward-leaning ramp. Climb the ramp to a blank slab. Traverse right across a steep wall and around a corner into a crack system, then climb up to a ledge. Traverse right to a thin crack and climb it to a ledge. Climb the wall above the ledge, passing the overhang by going left (Grade VI). Several pitches of scrambling lead up and left to gain the southwest ridge, which is followed to the summit of Batian (5,199 meters/17,058 feet).

Most parties take 1 long day or 2 short days to complete this route. Note: There are few fixed anchors on this route.

9. SOUTHWEST RIDGE (GRADE IV)

This route was first climbed by Arthur Firmin and John W. Howard, on January 8, 1946. It was probably first soloed by Dave Cheesmond in the mid-1970s.

From Hut Tarn (4,500 meters), climb up into the huge amphitheater below the Diamond Couloir and other south-face routes. Climb up the left (west) side of the Darwin Glacier until easy slabs allow one to scramble up to the notch between Point Slade (a subsidiary summit) and Batian. Climb the ridge above until it is possible to traverse left across an amphitheater to a minor ridge separating the amphitheater from the west face. Climb a steep buttress at the head of the amphitheater and follow the crest of the ridge to the summit of Batian (5,199 meters/17,058 feet).

This route can easily be climbed in a day.

10. WEST FACE (GRADE V)

This classic route was first climbed by R. A. Caukwell and G. W. Rose on January 7, 1955. It was probably first soloed by Dave Cheesmond in the mid-1970s.

From Hut Tarn (4,500 meters), climb the Tyndall Glacier to an obvious snow slope that leads up and right between the Forel and Heim Glaciers. Climb the slope to a rib on the upper portion of the face, then climb past the rib to the right and continue up to the summit of Batian (5,199 meters/17,058 feet). There are many options.

This route requires 1 full day to ascend.

West face of Mount Kenya with Routes 5, 6, 9–12, and 21 marked

11. THE UNTRAVELLED WORLD (GRADE VI)

This difficult and serious route was first climbed by Robert Barton and David Morris on January 10–11, 1978.

From Hut Tarn (4,500 meters), climb to the top of the Tyndall Glacier. From the top of the glacier, a thin gully leads to the lower left-hand edge of the hanging seracs of the Forel Glacier, above.

Climb the thin gully for four pitches, then make an exposed traverse right to gain a right-trending ramp that leads up and through the serac barrier to the Forel Glacier proper. Climb the Forel Glacier to its top, then climb several difficult mixed pitches up and right (west) to gain the southwest ridge. A scramble leads to the summit of Batian (5,199 meters/17,058 feet).

Allow 2 days for the ascent.

12. WEST RIDGE (GRADE V)

The first ascent of the west ridge, one of the most classic climbs on Mount Kenya, was made on August 1, 1930, by Eric Shipton and Bill Tilman.

The easiest and most straightforward approach is from the Kami campsite (4,400 meters). Hike up to the base of the Northey Glacier and traverse up and right (west) along the west side of the glacier to the col between the Petit Gendarme and Point Dutton. From the col, climb up and left, on easy slabs, toward the summit of the Petit Gendarme. Follow moderate rock on the south side of the crest until just below the summit of the Petit Gendarme, where an easy route leads around to the north and down into a spectacular exposed notch. A short wall leads up and left to an obvious bivy ledge. From the ledge, traverse up and along the base of the Grand Gendarme for several exposed but easy pitches. When the wall steepens, look for a ledge that leads right to a corner system that rises for 60 meters to the top of the Grand Gendarme.

Two difficult pitches (Grade V) end at a comfortable but exposed ledge atop the gendarme. From here, follow the ridge crest for about 40 meters to the base of the "12 Meter Pinnacle." A few strenuous moves (Grade V) on the left side of the pinnacle lead to easier rock and the arête. Follow this until it is possible to rappel into Shipton's Notch. A short, steep wall (with the only poor-quality rock on the entire route) leads out of the notch and back onto the ridge crest. Follow the right (south) side of the ridge for about four pitches to the summit of Batian (5,199 meters/17,058 feet). Descend by the Normal Route on Nelion.

This route requires 1–2 days.

13. NORTH FACE STANDARD ROUTE (GRADE IV+)

This is the standard route used by climbers during the Northern Hemisphere's summer. The first ascent was made by Arthur Firmin and P. H. Hicks on July 31, 1944.

From the Kami campsite (4,400 meters), traverse south along the east side of the mountain, and up into the wide gully between the Krapf Rognon and the main peak. A circle with a cross in it is chipped into the rock at the start of the route.

Climb up 10 meters, then move right (don't go left!) into a couloir. Follow the couloir for about 60 meters, and continue up to a right-facing corner that is climbed for 30 meters to easy slabs. On the slabs, move right about 5 meters to gain a series of easy grassy ledges below a wall. Continue up and left, then traverse right to a steep chimney that leads to a large hanging amphitheater that looks down on both the east and north sides of the mountain. This is where many parties bivouac on the route.

Traverse left across the amphitheater and climb an easy slabby gully that leads up and left. Near the top of the gully, traverse back right and up to the base of Firmin's Tower. Climb the left of two cracks on Firmin's Tower for 20 meters, then move to the right crack, a chimney, for 15 meters, then move left again into the first crack for 10 meters. Easy scrambling leads to the top of Firmin's Tower.

From the top of the tower, follow the ridge to a steep wall and climb up this to the right, where another, smaller, amphitheater is gained. Continue up the ridge above the amphitheater to reach the west ridge proper, where there is an excellent bivouac site. Traverse left on easy ground to Shipton's Notch. From Shipton's Notch, traverse left on ledges to reach the summit of Batian (5,199 meters / 17,058 feet).

Allow 1 full day for the ascent. This route can also be used as a descent route.

14. FRENCH ROUTE (GRADE V, A1)

This route was first climbed by Maurice Martin and Roger Rangaux on August 28, 1952.

From the Kami campsite (4,400 meters), traverse up and left below the start of the North Face Standard Route, to the next obvious gully. Climb 3 meters up a corner to a traverse leading right. At the end of the traverse, climb a chimney to reach a low-angled gully. Scramble up the gully for about 100 meters to another chimney, which is climbed by its right side.

Above the chimney, easy ledges lead to a dike, which is followed into the main gully. Climb up and right to a ledge. Continue up and right to a large corner, which is followed for 50 meters to the lower end of the huge Lower Amphitheater, which is filled with loose blocks. Climb up the left side of the amphitheater to its top, where an obvious ledge sits below a crack with old pitons, the Piton Crack.

Aid up the crack for 12 meters (A1) to a stance, then traverse left for a few meters to the base of an arête. Climb the arête (Grade V), then a short crack that leads to a chimney. Climb the chimney to the Upper Amphitheater, then scramble up to the west ridge. Scrambling leads to the summit of Batian (5,199 meters / 17,058 feet).

This route requires 1–2 days.

15. NORTHEAST PILLAR OF NELION (GRADE V, A1 OR GRADE VI+)

This, the first route on Mount Kenya's east face, was first climbed by Barry Cliff and Denis Rutowitz on August 2–4, 1963.

East face of Mount Kenya with Routes 13–15 and 26 marked

The climb starts at the base of Nelion's northeast prow, which lies just left of the huge couloir that splits the mountain and divides Batian from Nelion. Set into the Krapf Glacier—which lies between the rounded Krapf Rognon and Nelion itself—is a large block, 15 meters away from the foot of the prow and near the start of the route, which follows a prominent crack, the Hourglass Crack.

Climb the face left of the crack and join it at a height of about 25 meters. Climb the crack until overhangs bar further upward progress, then move up and left to join the crest of a ridge. Climb 15 meters up the ridge to join a ramp, which is followed for 120 meters to the foot of the enormous Grey Pillar, a huge, square-shaped buttress. Traverse up and right around the Grey Pillar to two cracks, the right one very obvious, the left one not so obvious. The route follows the left one, which is also called Sinister Crack.

To start, climb up and left on blocks to a stance. Then, climb up and left, gaining the crack itself before reaching a stance. Follow the crack on the right wall above the stance to another stance, next to a loose flake. Continue up for another 40 meters to another stance. Climb up 30 meters, then traverse left to the shoulder of the Grey Pillar.

Continue up and right to a steep corner that can be climbed on aid or free at Grade VI+ to reach good ledges. Above the corner, traverse left to a large, gray, featureless slab with a crack in it. Climb the crack to a fixed piton, then pendulum across the slab. Above the slab, a short crack leads to a stance below the final chimney. Climb the chimney and scramble up to the summit of Nelion (5,188 meters / 17,022 feet).

This ascent is usually done in 1 long day or 2 shorter days.

16. EASTERN GROOVE OF NELION (GRADE VI, A1)
This route was first climbed by Ian Howell and Iain Allan on June 2–3, 1978. A very fine route, with 600 meters of excellent rock, it has been free climbed.

The route starts 15 meters left of the Northeast Pillar of Nelion. Climb a very smooth, obvious slab, which leads to more slabs and a cave. Climb left, out of the cave, and climb up and right on slabs, then turn a corner to the right (Grade V). Continue up a few meters more to a recess. Climb the steep crack above the recess (one point of aid), then climb up a left-sloping ramp to a mantle. Scramble up to the base of an off-width crack, which is climbed (one point of aid) to easier ground and a large ledge. Traverse left along the ledge for 90 meters until you are 15 meters from the left-hand edge of the ledge. Above will be the Grey Corner; just left of the Grey Corner is the Eastern Groove, a wide, obvious crack with a rounded flake forming its left side.

Two pitches lead to the base of the Groove. Climb the Groove for four pitches of stemming, jamming, and liebacking. Some aid points are generally used. Climb a fifth pitch by liebacking (Grade V+) up to a phallus-shaped rock. Above this rock, climb slabs up to a steep corner with a crack. Avoid this crack by going left to an off-width crack around the corner. Climb the off-width (several aid points), then traverse back around to the right. Continue up for two pitches to a large ledge. Traverse right on the ledge for one pitch, to the base of a gully filled with loose blocks. Climb the gully to a chimney on the right. Climb the chimney and then scramble to the summit of Nelion (5,188 meters/17,022 feet).

This route is generally climbed in 2 days.

17. EAST FACE ROUTE (GRADE VI, A3)

This route follows a series of cracks that runs from the summit of Nelion down the east face to the Krapf Glacier. It was first climbed by Heinrich Klier, Siegfried Aerberli, and Barry Cliff on August 7, 1963.

From the Krapf Glacier, climb two pitches in an obvious corner, to a big stance. The third pitch (called the Inverted Staircase) is a series of overhangs and the crux of the route. Above the overhangs is another stance, above which the right wall is climbed for 15 meters, followed by a traverse to the left for 3 meters.

Climb up a series of blocks to the Raven's Nest, a bivouac site. From the Raven's Nest, climb up and right to a stance. Continue up and right to an overhang (Grade VI), then a difficult crack to a traverse left, around a corner to a stance. Climb above the stance for 5 meters, then move left into an overhang. Climb the overhang and the slab above to the bottom of a prominent gully.

Climb the gully for three pitches, then move to the gully's left side, which offers easier climbing. Above will be the Black Crack, a prominent chimney that leads to the summit. To reach the Black Crack, climb two pitches of cracks that lead up and right. The Black Crack starts as a chimney (Grade VI-) for 15 meters, then becomes overhanging for 10 meters (A3), before a ledge is gained on the left. One more pitch with a few aid moves leads to easy scrambling and the summit of Nelion (5,188 meters/17,022 feet).

Allow 1 long day or 2 short days for an ascent.

POINT MELHUISH

Point Melhuish is a rounded hump sitting on Nelion's south ridge, between the Normal Route on Nelion/Batian and Point John.

18. POINT MELHUISH, EAST SIDE (SCRAMBLE)

Point Melhuish (4,880 meters/16,010 feet) can be ascended by an easy scramble up its eastern edge. From Austrian Hut (4,800 meters), cross the Lewis Glacier to the southeast side of Point Melhuish and scramble up ledges on the right side of the formation.

POINT JOHN

After Point Lenana and Nelion, Point John (4,883 meters/16,020 feet) probably sees more traffic than any other summit on the Mount Kenya massif. Although small, it is a genuine spire, comparable to any of the world's most spectacular rock peaks.

19. POINT JOHN, SOUTHEAST GULLY (GRADE III)

This popular route—the standard route up Point John—was first climbed by Eric Shipton and Pat Russell on December 18, 1929.

Mount Kenya's Point John, Point John Minor, Point Melhuish, and Nelion, with Routes 3, 6, 18–20, and 22 marked

The route follows the wide, scoured gully on the southeast face, directly below the summit. There are five pitches, with multiple cruxes, but none are harder than about Grade III. Descent is made by rappeling the route. There are many rappel anchors.

20. POINT JOHN, SOUTH RIDGE (GRADE III)

From American Camp or Austrian Hut (4,800 meters), walk to the base of the southeast gully and traverse left. Climb up and left to an obvious white spot on the south ridge. Follow steep rock up and right for several pitches to the top of the first tower. Continue climbing diagonally up past more towers to reach the summit. This route is generally climbed in six to seven pitches.

21. POINT JOHN, POINT JOHN COULOIR (GRADE V)

The first ascent of this route was by Phil Snyder and D. Karinga, in May 1972.

When it's in condition, this is one of the finest ice routes on the mountain. It is in the huge south-face amphitheater that contains the Diamond Couloir and Ice Window Routes and is just downhill and right of those two routes. More specifically, it lies on the north side of the south ridge of Nelion, at the point where the south ridge joins Point John Minor. The ice is continuous for the entire 180 meters of the route. There are very few fixed anchors, and the route is in the best condition from December through March.

The best descent is to climb through the notch on the south ridge, then scramble and rappel down the south side of the ridge. (This descent is also the Original Route on Point John Minor.)

22. POINT JOHN MINOR, ORIGINAL ROUTE (GRADE V)

Point John Minor (4,875 meters/15,994 feet) is a subsidiary summit of Point John, lying on Point John's northeast side. The Original Route climbs the obvious long gully on the south ridge of Nelion, leading to a notch between Point John Minor and the jumbled rock outcrops south of Point Melhuish (right of the notch).

It's three and a half pitches of easy scrambling to the notch. At the notch, turn left, and climb straight up for 16 meters (Grade V). About 30 meters above the notch, on the left, is a steep, wide crack with chockstones. Climb it to the top. Bring rappel anchors. After two rappels, the southeast gully on Point John is met, and it's possible to rappel that route to the bottom of Point John.

The Original Route is best climbed from Austrian Hut (4,800 meters), from December through March, although there can be snow on the upper part of the route.

MIDGET PEAK

Midget Peak (4,700 meters/15,420 feet) lies just west of Point John, and is a small, oblong-shaped tower standing on its end.

23. MIDGET PEAK, SOUTH GULLY (GRADE IV)

The first ascent of this, the standard route, was made in August 1930 by Eric Shipton and Bill Tilman.

On the south face of Midget Peak is a big gully, the south gully. The first 25 meters follow an obvious crack. Above the crack, scramble up 18 meters to an area of columnar rock. Several short pitches lead to an obvious cave. Climb up the left side of the cave to a prominent ledge, then climb the right wall above the ledge, then traverse left on a sloping ledge to another wide ledge. Continue left, then climb a bulge via a 6-meter crack, followed by a sloping slab that puts one over the north face. Climb up and around several large blocks to reach the summit. The best descent is to climb down a few meters toward the col between Point John and Midget Peak, then rappel.

POINT PETER

Point Peter (4,757 meters / 15,607 feet) is the spectacular triangular spire just south of Hausberg Col and southwest of the Kami campsite.

24. POINT PETER, SOUTH RIDGE (GRADE V)

The first ascent of this route was made by Eric Shipton and Bill Tilman in July 1930.

From the Kami campsite (4,400 meters), climb up to the col between Point Peter and Point Pigott. Turn right to face Point Peter. The first pitch follows the arête for about 18 meters, then traverses right on big, loose-looking holds

Point Peter, Mount Kenya, with Route 24 marked

to a belay. A strenuous move off the ledge (Grade V) leads to nice, steep face climbing, followed by an easy ridge leading to the summit.

The best descent is via the northeast ridge. Scramble down 16 meters to the northeast, to rappel slings. Two rappels (25 meters and 22 meters), followed by some third-class scrambling, put you on the talus below the peak.

Allow 2–3 hours for this route.

POINT DUTTON

Point Dutton (4,885 meters/16,207 feet) is the large peak immediately south of Point Peter and on the northwest side of the Northey Glacier.

25. POINT DUTTON, NORTHEAST FACE–EAST RIDGE (GRADE V)

This route was first climbed by S. Barusso and R. Metcalfe in August 1966.

From the Kami campsite (4,400 meters), approach the center of the northeast face. Scramble up the center of the northeast face for 60 meters, until a rope-up spot is reached. Two pitches of steep climbing with large holds lead above the Northey Glacier to an easy gully that goes back right to the base of an impressive finger. This marks the crux of the route. A few Grade V moves lead to easier climbing up steep cracks that end on the north summit. Three pitches along a spectacular exposed arête lead south to the actual high point. The best descent is down the steep north ridge (Class 3).

The climb takes 6 hours.

KRAPF ROGNON

The Krapf Rognon (4,800 meters/15,748 feet) is a rounded hump of rock—similar to Point Melhuish—sitting below the northeast face of Nelion.

26. KRAPF ROGNON, SOUTHEAST SIDE (SCRAMBLE)

The Krapf Rognon can be ascended by an easy scramble up the southeastern edge. Crampons are highly recommended. The summit offers excellent views of the east-face routes on Mount Kenya.

POINT THOMSON

Point Thomson (4,995 meters/16,388 feet) is Point Lenana's sister peak, and lies just west of the latter by a few hundred meters.

27. POINT THOMSON, EAST RIDGE (SCRAMBLE)

This climb is similar to Point Lenana's southwest ridge except that it involves serious glacier travel. Parties need crampons and ice axes, and should be roped because of crevasses on the upper Lewis Glacier.

The route is straightforward. Walk up the Lewis Glacier to the ridge between Point Lenana and Point Thomson, and scramble up the east ridge to the summit. Allow a half day from the Austrian Hut (4,800 meters).

THOMSON'S FLAKE

Thomson's Flake is the improbable spire between Point Thomson and Nelion's southeast face. It is rarely climbed.

28. THOMSON'S FLAKE, NORTH FACE (GRADE VI)

This route was first climbed by Leo Herncarek, Walter Welsch, and Barry Cliff in September 1962.

Start on the col (4,830 meters) between Point Thomson and Thomson's Flake, and climb up to the base of a chimney. Climb the corner on the left side to a ramp, traverse left along it to another corner. Climb this corner to reach a belay ledge. Climb the wall above the ledge to another ramp, then traverse right around a corner. Ascend the overhang above, then move up and right to the summit ridge. Scramble to the top. The best descent is to rappel the south face.

Allow half a day for this climb.

KASESE AREA IN UGANDA

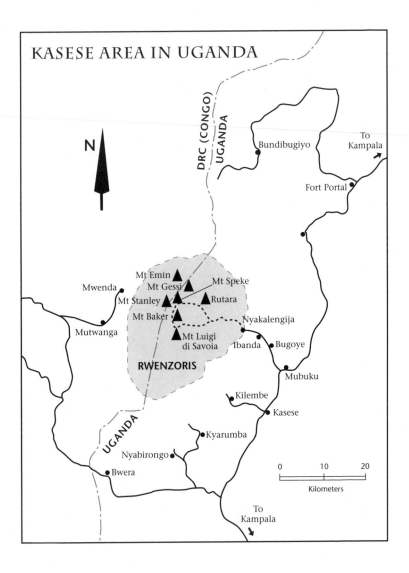

Chapter 7

RWENZORIS

You may be familiar with the Alps and the Caucasus, the Himalayas and the Rockies, but if you have not explored Rwenzori, you still have something wonderful to see.

—Douglas Freshfield, 1906

The Mountains of the Moon.

Almost no geographical title conjures up as much mystery and awe as this simple cognomen. It has been used for at least two thousand years; some say longer. Simply put, if you're a mountaineer, the Rwenzoris are *it* when it comes to East African climbing. Situated on the edge of the extremely humid Congo Basin (from whence it derives its perpetual mists) and being a block/fault type mountain range (not a volcano like Kili, Meru, and Mount Kenya), the Rwenzoris are an adventurer's range, with peaks approaching the 5,150-meter mark, perpetual ice and snow (though sitting on the equator), and the possibility for climbs of every kind, length, and difficulty imaginable—certainly, one of my favorite ranges in all the world.

Sadly—or perhaps luckily—the Rwenzoris are smack dab in one of the most troubled parts of Africa. In the 1970s and '80s, Uganda was as treacherous as any global hotspot, and tourists stayed away. Then, in the 1990s, rebels destabilized much of western Uganda by attacking the Ugandan army from hideouts in the Rwenzoris (the small city of Kasese at the foot of the range went from 70,000 people to 30,000 within a few years in the 1990s). The rebels' landmines are still commonly found in the southwestern part of the range. Compared to the highly regulated treadmill on Kilimanjaro (a multimillion dollar injection into northern Tanzania's economy), the Rwenzoris are still a wild frontier. Ironically, Idi Amin and other African despots did, however, do mountaineers heading to the Rwenzoris a favor—by turning the whole world off. That's why the place is so special.

In 1997, when (I'm told) the park was getting about 1,600 visits a year, Rwenzori National Park closed as a result of domestic and international fighting in the region. It finally reopened in July 2001, during massive efforts by the Ugandan government—aware of the lost tourism dollars across the country—to offer greater security for tourists, and the park began receiving about 400 visitors per year (with a goal of boosting that to 1,800 by the end of 2005). Today, the most common visitors are Britons, Norwegians, Germans, and Italians, whose pride in the Duke of Abruzzi seems to bring them to these exotic mountains.

These days, trekking and climbing in the Rwenzoris—as well as travel in the region—seems to be relatively safe, and the joys of a trip here, to my mind, outweigh by far the possible problems.

GEOGRAPHY

Geographically, the Rwenzoris are simultaneously one of the toughest and easiest ranges to understand in terms of geography. When you're on top of a tall peak, like Mount Baker for example, and the weather is clear, the range is like most other mountain ranges its size—easy to figure out. But when you're wandering around in, say, a vast bog, with mist descending between you and the porter a few meters in front of you, it's nearly impossible to guess where you are.

Essentially, the Rwenzoris lie in a north-northeast / south-southwest orientation. The three major peaks of the range—Mounts Speke, Stanley, and Baker are scattered along this main north-south line, which roughly approximates the Uganda-Congo border. Baker is to the southeast of the other two, Stanley is on the west, and Speke is to the north. High peaks (like Mounts Gessi, Emin, and Luigi di Savoia) are found north of Speke and south of Baker, however.

Stanley, Speke, and Baker aren't solitary summits, though. Indeed, each of them is a huge mountain massif in its own right, and all three boast dozens of subsidiary summits. The highest of these are Margherita (5,109 meters / 16,757 feet) on Stanley; Vittorio Emanuele (4,890 meters / 16,039 feet) on Speke; and Edward (4,843 meters / 15,885 feet) on Baker. In line with their heights, reaching these three highpoints requires increasing knowledge of various mountaineering skills. On Baker, only scrambling and routefinding are required. On Speke, some knowledge of glacier travel is helpful (although for much of the summit climb you can skirt the edge of the ice). And on Stanley, knowledge of and experience with glacier travel and minimal rock climbing skills are required. That said, all three are regularly climbed by trekkers who've never used crampons or a rope until they get to the Rwenzoris.

BUJUKU–MUBUKU CIRCUIT

There is one standard trekking route in the Rwenzoris, which goes by several names (the Summit Circuit; Rwenzori Loop Trail; and the Bujuku–Mubuku Circuit—after the rivers it follows), but which I'll refer to as the Bujuku–Mubuku Circuit. This trek, circumnavigating Mount Baker and other, lesser, peaks, is about 47 kilometers long and generally takes 7 days (although side trips up the mountains themselves must be added on to any itinerary). This is the Rwenzori experience most tourists want, and they are well rewarded by a trek here. Also described in this section are several side trips (the climbs to the summits of the three major peaks), as well as the approaches to those climbs (the track to Elena Hut on Mount Stanley, for example).

The Bujuku–Mubuku Circuit starts at the village of Nyakalengija, on the eastern side of the mountains. To reach Nyakalengija, drive north from Kasese on the main, sealed road. There is only one road out of Kasese, and it should be obvious on the northeastern edge of the small downtown area—if not, ask a local. Drive north for roughly 12 kilometers, then turn left, onto a dirt road (well-marked) that leads another 12 kilometers to Nyakalengija. If you are traveling by bus, you can easily catch one from Kasese to Fort Portal (on the northeastern side of the Rwenzoris) and ask to be let off at the intersection of the main road and the dirt road to Nyakalengija; from there, it's a nice day's walk, or you can try and bum a lift with a passing vehicle.

BUJUKU–MUBUKU CIRCUIT: NYAKALENGIJA TO NYABITABA HUT / DAY 1

Ascent: 1,020 meters to 2,650 meters
Distance: 9 kilometers
Time: 4 to 5 hours

This trek starts in the village of Nyakalengija, where the national park offices and offices of Rwenzori Mountaineering Services (RMS) are located. After the business of porters, guides, and park fees has been sorted out at the park offices, you begin the hike, which for about 1.6 kilometers or so follows the dirt road west out of the village[93] while paralleling the Mubuku River and a massive aqueduct. After 1.6 kilometers, you'll reach the even smaller village of Nyabitaba and the park "gate" (although there's not really a gate here).

From the gate (at 1,500 meters), the trail heads into the jungle. Entering the park requires signing in at a small hut staffed by park officials. From here, the easily walked trail goes about 1.6 kilometers along the Bujuku River valley bottom, then begins a gradual climb. The trail steepens considerably (maybe 30 degrees or so) for at least 1.6 kilometers, which yields to easier hiking and, eventually, gains a ridge, where you'll find Nyabitaba Hut.

There are actually two huts here: a tin hut for tourists, which sleeps about twenty, and a big wooden structure that the porters and guides sleep in. There are also several (small) tent sites. There's a large cistern too (a big concrete box), into which clean water drains from higher in the mountains.[94]

If the weather clears, there are some stunning views to the north of Rutara, one of the "Portal Peaks."

BUJUKU–MUBUKU CIRCUIT: NYABITABA HUT TO JOHN MATTE HUT OR BIGO HUT / DAY 2

Ascent: 2,650 meters to 3,360 meters (John Matte Hut) or to 3,350 meters (Bigo Hut)
Distance: 7 kilometers (John Matte Hut) or 9 kilometers (Bigo Hut)
Time: 4.5 hours (John Matte Hut) or 6 hours (Bigo Hut)

From Nyabitaba Hut, the trail continues up the ridge for a short distance (500 meters), where it meets the junction from the return of the loop trail (the route to Guy Yoeman Hut, etc.). From here, the trail descends steeply about 1.2 kilometers to a bridge across the Bujuku River (just below its confluence with the Mubuku River). Across the bridge begins a long, extremely hard trail that follows the river valley bottom for about 3.2 kilometers. It's very rocky, very muddy, and very difficult to walk (arguably the hardest stretch of this trek, and one of the roughest stretches of trail I've done anywhere).

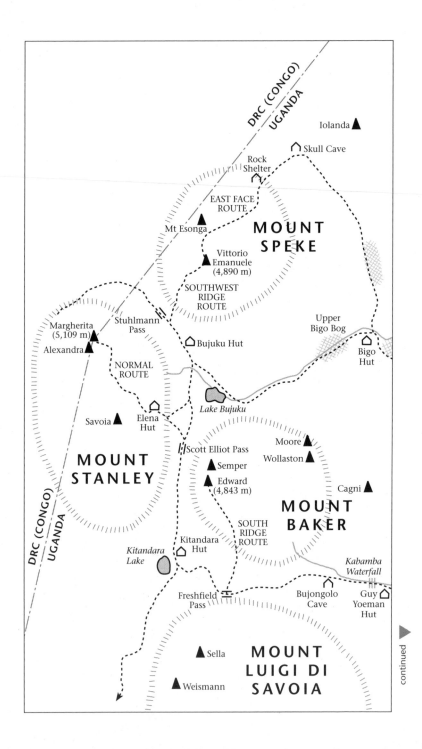

Iolanda ▲

⌂ Skull Cave

Rock
Shelter

EAST FACE
ROUTE

Mt Esonga ▲

**MOUNT
SPEKE**

Vittorio
Emanuele ▲
(4,890 m)

SOUTHWEST
RIDGE
ROUTE

Margherita ▲
(5,109 m)

Stuhlmann
Pass

Alexandra ▲

⌂ Bujuku Hut

Upper
Bigo Bog

⌂ Bigo
Hut

NORMAL
ROUTE

Savoia ▲

⌂ Elena
Hut

Lake Bujuku

**MOUNT
STANLEY**

│Scott Elliot Pass

Moore ▲

Wollaston ▲

▲ Semper

Cagni ▲

▲ Edward
(4,843 m)

**MOUNT
BAKER**

SOUTH
RIDGE
ROUTE

*Kitandara
Lake*

Kitandara
⌂ Hut

*Kabamba
Waterfall*

Freshfield
Pass

Bujongolo
Cave

Guy ⌂
Yoeman
Hut

DRC (CONGO)
UGANDA

▲ Sella

**MOUNT
LUIGI DI
SAVOIA**

▲ Weismann

DRC (CONGO)
UGANDA

continued ▶

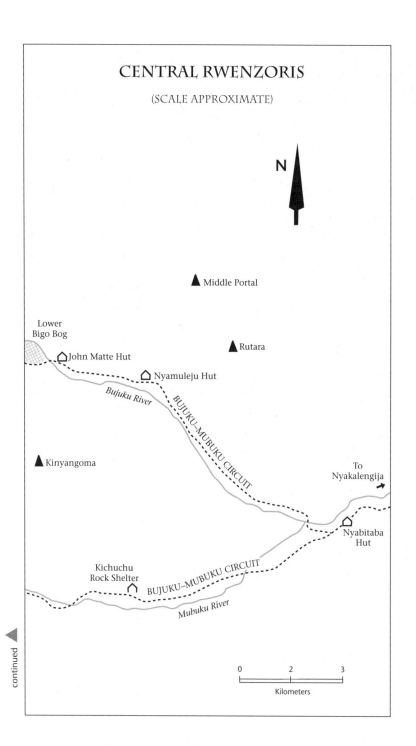

CENTRAL RWENZORIS

(SCALE APPROXIMATE)

N

▲ Middle Portal

Lower
Bigo Bog

⌂ John Matte Hut

▲ Rutara

⌂ Nyamuleju Hut

Bujuku River

BUJUKU–MUBUKU CIRCUIT

▲ Kinyangoma

To
Nyakalengija
➤

⌂
Nyabitaba
Hut

Kichuchu
Rock Shelter

⌂ BUJUKU–MUBUKU CIRCUIT

Mubuku River

continued ◀

0   2   3
Kilometers

Day 2 on the Bujuku–Mubuku Circuit

At about 6.4 kilometers from Nyabitaba, you reach an old, now-unused hut (Nyamuleju Hut) with nearby cave, which your porters will linger in. Then, after another 1.6 kilometers through exceedingly weird and boggy forest terrain (it takes about an hour), you reach John Matte Hut (and its outbuildings at 3,360 meters), a wonderful wooden structure with great views and lots of room. There's water in the nearby Bujuku River. Most parties will stay here a night, though some might prefer to go on to Bigo Hut, especially if pressed for time.[95]

From John Matte Hut, the trail continues through some of the strangest landscape you might ever experience—huge giant heather and weird trees with massive carpets of mosses growing on everything and boggier ground than most places on the planet. This section of the "trail" leads to a huge "alpine" valley (both relative terms in this part of the world)—the notorious Lower Bigo Bog—at about 3,350 meters, with a pretty substantial section of the Bujuku River running through it. Cross the river. Traversing around the left-hand edge of this Lower Bigo Bog is one of the world's more surreal experiences.

At the "upper" end of the Lower Bigo Bog, just uphill and southwest from the bog, is Bigo Hut (3,350 meters), a small, round, metal hut that could likely sleep eight at most. Water is available at several nearby streams (if you don't, literally, step in the streams and can't find them, ask the porters).

From Bigo Hut you can add 2 days to the circuit by taking a side trip around and over the summit of Mount Speke. See the Mount Speke Side Trip.

MOUNT SPEKE SIDE TRIP: JOHN MATTE HUT OR BIGO HUT TO SKULL CAVE / DAY 1

Ascent: 3,360 meters (John Matte Hut) or 3,350 meters (Bigo Hut) to 3,950 meters

Distance: 6 kilometers (from John Matte Hut) or 4 kilometers (from Bigo Hut)

Time: 4 (from Bigo Hut) to 5 hours (from John Matte Hut)

A traverse of Mount Speke—up the East Face Route and down Speke's Southwest Ridge Route—is a wonderful side trip, but it requires leaving the regular circuit just beyond Bigo Hut, ascending the Mugusu River valley toward Cavelli and Rocatti Passes, stopping overnight at Skull Cave (3,950 meters) and then at the Rock Shelter before continuing over Mount Speke the following day to Bujuku Hut.

This takes 3 days—or 2 days more than the straightforward circuit trek from John Matte/Bigo Huts to Bujuku Hut—but is well worth it for mountaineers wanting to do all three big Rwenzori peaks. A tent is a requirement; there are no huts. Crampons and an ice ax are also recommended. Ropes and technical gear are unnecessary, unless you are traveling with inexperienced climbers. Also, you'll need to negotiate this side trip with RMS, as a full day's portering from the high camp (the Rock Shelter) with your gear around to Bujuku Hut will add to the expense.

The trail from the John Matte/Bigo Huts up to Skull Cave is horrendously boggy and difficult to follow (luckily, a guide is required). From Bigo Hut, hike north out of the clearing and follow the trail through the woods. A large valley

Benny Bach crossing the Bujuku River between John Matte and Bigo Huts

will open up on the north side of the Bujuku Valley. Follow this valley for about 2 kilometers as it narrows and gets even boggier (and any semblance of a trail disappears). Here, you'll be among snow-covered rock towers.

Head to the western side of the valley, up to the rocky edges, and eventually you'll reach a fairly level spot with an exposed rock wall (at the base of which sits a human skull), improbably called Skull Cave. You don't sleep in Skull Cave (your porters will)—you camp near it. No one seems to know the origin of the skull itself, but it has been mentioned on maps back at least to the late 1980s.[96]

MOUNT SPEKE SIDE TRIP: SKULL CAVE TO ROCK SHELTER / DAY 2

Ascent: 3,950 meters to 4,271 meters
Distance: 4 kilometers
Time: 4 to 5 hours

From Skull Cave, continue up the valley until you reach a huge amphitheater that forms the northeast side of the mountain. In it, there's an enormous right-angling ramp that will become obvious. Climb the ramp (it's 1.5 kilometers in length) to roughly the halfway point, where there are several campsites at the base of the east face of Mount Speke.

Look for an exposed area of white rock—the Rock Shelter is about 500 meters down and left of that. The shelter isn't really a shelter; rather, it's a bit of an outcrop that has enough space below it for porters to sleep and stay dry. The best tent sites are, literally, built atop hacked-down groundsels and their leaves.

MOUNT SPEKE SIDE TRIP: ROCK SHELTER TO BUJUKU HUT / DAY 3

Ascent / descent: 4,271 meters to 4,890 meters (Vittorio Emanuele)
    to 3,915 meters
Distance: 8 to 9 kilometers
Time: 6 to 7 hours

This third day of the Speke side trip follows the East Face Route (Grade III) and the Southwest Ridge Route (Grade II), which are fully detailed later in the chapter, in the Mount Speke description. This is the east-west traverse of the Speke massif via the summit, Vittorio Emanuele (4,890 meters / 16,039 feet).

BUJUKU–MUBUKU CIRCUIT: JOHN MATTE HUT OR BIGO HUT TO BUJUKU HUT / DAY 3

Ascent: 3,360 meters (John Matte Hut) or 3,350 meters (Bigo Hut) to 3,915
    meters
Distance: 6 kilometers (from John Matte Hut) or 4 kilometers (from Bigo
    Hut)
Time: 5 hours (from Bigo Hut) to 6 hours (from John Matte Hut)

From John Matte Hut, the trail continues around the left-hand side of the Lower Bigo Bog. Traverse around the left-hand edge of the bog (on tussocks and mud), on the Bujuku River's south side. At the "upper" end of the Lower Bigo Bog, just uphill and southwest from the bog, is Bigo Hut (3,350 meters), a small, round, metal hut.

From here, the trail enters thick woods as it climbs the narrow Bujuku Valley, gaining, after about an hour, the Upper Bigo Bog, which has a wooden walkway across it. After the bog, the trail steepens and climbs to the beautiful Lake Bujuku, at about 4,000 meters. Wander around the lake on its right-hand side. Mount Stanley's various summits will be visible off to the southwest.

After the lake, it takes another half hour or so to reach Bujuku Hut (3,915 meters), at the base of the southern side of the Speke massif. There are several buildings here, but despite much accommodation space it's often crowded. If the huts are full, there are many campsites to the south, across the stream that flows near the huts.

If the altitude is hampering your trip, this is a good place to turn around. The trail from here to Elena Hut or up over Scott Elliot Pass is fairly steep and demanding, which can only add to the effects of altitude. The trail running west, up the valley, leads to Stuhlmann Pass and the Congo. Along this trail, about 20 minutes from the huts, is the start of the Southwest Ridge Route on Mount Speke.

BUJUKU–MUBUKU CIRCUIT: BUJUKU HUT TO KITANDARA HUT / DAY 4

Ascent / descent: 3,915 meters to 4,370 meters (Scott Elliot Pass) to 4,027 meters

Distance: 5 kilometers

Time: 3 to 4 hours

From Bujuku Hut, the Bujuku–Mubuku Circuit heads southwest, then south-southeast, toward the bulk of Mount Baker. The trail gets continually steeper, until, at one point, you are even required to climb a huge metal ladder, at the top of which is a lovely lookout over Lake Bujuku.

A little while after this, the trail splits, and the trail to Kitandara Hut heads left (southeast) and over Scott Elliot Pass, at 4,370 meters the lowest point between the Baker and Stanley massifs. The trail to Elena Hut (and climbing the Normal Route on Mount Stanley) heads up a large, rocky wall, to the right (see the Elena Hut Side Trip). If you're going straight to Kitandara Hut, take the left path.

The trail over Scott Elliot Pass steepens and gets fairly rocky. Once you have crested the pass the trail descends rapidly into one of the deepest, most spectacular valleys in East Africa, with the 600- to 900-meter flanks of Mount Baker on the left and the huge ramparts of Mount Stanley on the right. The trail down this valley is a straightforward hike, all the way to Kitandara Lake.

You'll see the lake before the huts, which are scattered along the trail near some steep sections of path. The porters hut is met first, then, 100 meters later, the trekkers hut, which is a fabulous wooden structure with a loft. This is one of the prettiest hut sites in all East Africa.[97]

ELENA HUT SIDE TRIP: BUJUKU HUT TO ELENA HUT TO KITANDARA HUT / ALTERNATE DAY 4 OF CIRCUIT

Ascent / descent: 3,915 meters to 4,550 meters (Elena Hut) to 4,027 meters (Kitandara Hut)

Distance: 6 kilometers

Time: 4 hours

Elena Hut is approached via a spur trail off the Bujuku Hut–Kitandara Hut trail. Follow the Bujuku Hut–Kitandara Hut trail described above to the Bujuku Lake overlook, then the trail splits. Go right.

The trail to Elena Hut heads improbably up a large, rocky wall, via a big right-trending ramp, then skirts left around it and over a rib. Once over this rib, Stanley's minor southern summits come into view, and after crossing about 500 meters of angling rock ribs, you'll reach Elena Hut (4,550 meters). There are cairns and markers all the way.

Elena is a nice, A-frame hut on the rocky slopes of the east side of the Stanley massif. There are actually three huts here (the other two being porters/guides huts), and an outhouse, nestled among the boulders.

If you're planning to climb the Normal Route on Mount Stanley to its summit (Margherita), you'll want to spend at least one night here (see the Mount Stanley description, below).

Rough approximation of the trail to Elena Hut, up the right-trending ramp described in the Elena Hut Side Trip

After an ascent of Stanley, the descent to the trail between Bujuku and Kitandara Huts is short and fairly straightforward, over rocky scree and down to the Bujuku Hut–Kitandara Hut trail near Scott Elliot Pass. From here, it's a straightforward hike down to Kitandara Lake. From Elena Hut to Kitandara Hut takes about 2.5 hours.

BUJUKU–MUBUKU CIRCUIT: KITANDARA HUT TO GUY YOEMAN HUT / DAY 5

Ascent / descent: 4,027 meters to 4,282 meters (Freshfield Pass) to 3,530 meters
Distance: 5 kilometers
Time: 5 to 6 hours

From Kitandara Hut, the Bujuku–Mubuku Circuit heads in an unlikely direction. You might think you're going to wander down the obvious Batawu River drainage to the south, but the trail goes directly east from the huts, straight up onto the flanks of the Mount Baker massif (the trail is tough to find on your own, but your guide will know where it is).

The trail winds through rocky, tree-strewn terrain (by far, some of the toughest hiking on this circuit) for about an hour—at times you'll be pulling yourself up on branches. As with everything else in the Rwenzoris, in the rain, it's a bit of a nightmare. Eventually, the trail flattens considerably and crests Freshfield Pass (4,282 meters); the South Ridge Route on Mount Baker starts from the pass, going left (north). See the Mount Baker description, below.

From Freshfield Pass, descend into the Mubuku River valley, to the east. The hiking is on typical high-altitude Rwenzori trail (mud and rocks), which yields to typical lower-elevation Rwenzori trail (mud and tussocks) before reaching Bujongolo Cave. The cave is a pretty interesting place, as it was used extensively by the Duke of Abruzzi's expedition in 1906. Filippo de Filippi, the expedition's chronicler, described the cave as "a heap of blocks, surrounded by tree heaths,...overhung by a high rock which forms a shelter...the place is rough and wild."

From the cave, the trail continues down the valley through a forest of giant heather, past the Kabamba Waterfall on the right (south), to Guy Yoeman Hut (3,530 meters). It's about an hour from Bujongolo Cave to Guy Yoeman Hut.

BUJUKU–MUBUKU CIRCUIT: GUY YOEMAN HUT TO NYABITABA HUT / DAY 6

Descent: 3,530 meters to 2,650 meters
Distance: 6 kilometers
Time: 5 hours

From Guy Yoeman Hut, the Bujuku–Mubuku Circuit continues down boggy terrain along, at first, the right (south) side of the Mubuku River, then after 20 minutes' hiking, it crosses to the north side of the river.

After 2 hours' walk, the trail descends steeply, on rocky, slippery, exposed terrain. Many trekkers describe this as the trickiest part of the circuit, as the descent requires balance, calm, and attention to footing. Any rock climber will find it easy, but trekkers with limited scrambling experience should follow their guide's lead.[98]

At the base of this steep section is the historic Kichuchu Rock Shelter, near where a stream draining Mount Cagni enters the Mubuku Valley from the northwest, amid a series of rocky platforms. There are several tent sites here, and water is available from the stream. Below Kichuchu, the trail rejoins the Mubuku River (and crosses it) and descends the valley, where several paths join the main path—including the main circuit loop trail from the left—shortly before Nyabitaba Hut (2,650 meters).

Whether you stay at Nyabitaba Hut on your last night (making it a 7-day instead of a 6-day trek) is up to several factors: how tired you and your companions are, time of day, and schedule. If you descend to Nyakalengija, the 9 kilometers from Nyabitaba Hut takes about 3 hours and is fairly straightforward (see the circuit's Day 1 description).

MOUNT SPEKE

After Mount Stanley and Mount Baker, Mount Speke (4,890 meters / 16,039 feet) is probably the most climbed mountain in the Rwenzoris. Mount Speke is a beautiful, big, and geographically complex mountain. While the huge glaciers that used to cover the east side of the mountain have disappeared in recent decades, there are still some beautiful glaciers to see on the southwestern side of the mountain.

There are two standard climbs done by most people who visit Mount Speke, the east face and the southwest ridge. The Southwest Ridge Route is done much more commonly, as it's easily accessed from Bujuku Hut (to reach the hut, see Days 1–4 of the Bujuku–Mubuku Circuit, above). Doing the East Face Route (generally) requires an overnight at Skull Cave, north and west of Bigo Hut (see the Mount Speke Side Trip, earlier this chapter).

1. EAST FACE ROUTE (GRADE III)

This route is typically done as part of an east-west traverse of the Mount Speke massif via the summit, Vittorio Emanuele (4,890 meters / 16,039 feet), from the Rock Shelter to Bujuku Hut (this is Day 3 of the Mount Speke Side Trip).

From the Rock Shelter, go straight up the gentle slopes above it toward a huge rock boss. It takes an hour or so to reach this feature. Before global warming began its recent acceleration, a glacier filled the east face to near the base of this rock boss. Now, that glacier is entirely gone.[99]

Skirt right of the boss and continue up a huge trough that runs from the lower left-hand edge of the east face all the way, nearly, to the ridge between Esonga (a subsidiary peak on Speke, off to the right (west)) and the main summit itself, which will be off to your left. Take any one of many couloirs (many variations—easy snow climbs rated, perhaps, AI 2 at most) up and left to the ridge proper, then traverse southeast for about 800 meters along the ridge to the summit of Speke, Vittorio Emanuele.

This ridge traverse gets a little bit tricky in places (there is some fourth-class scrambling) and your Ugandan guides might want you to give them a belay

Mount Speke from low on the East Face Route (Route 1). The summit is behind the large rock boss.

(if you have a rope). For the most part, the ascent requires staying almost on the crest of the ridge itself. However, near the summit it is necessary to cross to the southwest (right) side of the ridge to gain the summit. Reaching the summit takes about 4–5 hours from the Rock Shelter (for a middle-aged, fairly fit party).

The descent can be back down to the Rock Shelter below the East Face. Or to make the east-west traverse over Speke (which is recommended—because it takes less time, a major consideration if you are going to continue around the Bujuku–Mubuku Circuit), descend Speke's Southwest Ridge Route to Bujuku Hut.

From the summit, head southwest, winding your way down the last 100 meters of the ascent route, then leave the rocks for the Speke Glacier, which will be obvious below, to the southwest. Skirt the right-hand edge of the glacier—walking down the ice (with crampons) is easiest—until it steepens considerably, then break out right onto the rock buttress to the right and follow cairns down through the very rocky terrain (this is the Southwest Ridge Route) until the route becomes a muddy trail. This is the trickiest part of the descent; there are cairns all the way, but watch the drop-offs to the right. When they get really big, you've gone too far right (west).

This trail continues down into the Stuhlmann Pass area and joins the Bujuku Hut–Stuhlmann Pass trail, about 20 minutes west of Bujuku Hut. Turn left, and you'll soon be at the hut.

The only reason the East Face Route gets a Grade III is because of the traverse along the summit ridge, which—unless you really are willing to make all sorts of lengthy detours around gendarmes—can get into the Grade III range (in U.S. standards, 5.3–5.4; in UK, difficult to very difficult; and in French, AD, or *assez difficile*).

2. SOUTHWEST RIDGE ROUTE (GRADE II)

This—the Normal Route up Mount Speke—was first climbed by Eric Shipton and Bill Tilman on January 23, 1932.

The route is best done in a long day from Bujuku Hut (3,915 meters), which sits on the southern side of the Speke massif. It's a wonderful, though grueling, hike and takes you up past some of the most spectacular glaciers left in the Rwenzoris (those on the southwest side of the Mount Speke massif).

Mount Speke from the south, with Route 2 marked

From Bujuku Hut, head west on the obvious trail, toward Stuhlmann Pass. The trail winds along the edge of the remains of the Bujuku River (a stream here), until an obvious trail branches off straight up the hill to the right. This trail is wildly steep, slippery, rocky, and muddy (not the kind of bog mud you've experienced at lower elevations; this is slick, steep-trail mud).

The trail is very obvious until it steepens and starts crossing mossy slabs. There are cairns all the way (and many variations), but it soon gains a long rock rib that leads upward. Near the top of this ridge, most parties move out right (northeast) onto the Speke Glacier itself, as it's easier to travel. Follow the left-hand edge of the glacier to the base of the final ridge (the summit will be directly ahead of you), then wander up broken ledges to the summit (Vittorio Emanuele, 4,890 meters / 16,039 feet).

Descent follows the same route. Crampons and an ice ax are highly recommended, although the more you stay left on the rock rib, the less necessary they become on the ascent. Crampons are, however, very useful on the final ledges that gain the summit and are definitely recommended for the descent, as wandering gently down the glacier is much easier than scrambling down the rocks.

The entire round trip takes a full day, as long as you're moderately fit.

MOUNT STANLEY

While Mounts Speke and Baker are big and complex, Mount Stanley is even more so. It is one of the biggest mountain massifs in Africa. Although there are dozens of routes and variations on Stanley, most climbers simply wanting to bag the peak's highest point, Margherita (5,109 meters / 16,763 feet), will do so via the Normal Route starting at Elena Hut (see the Elena Hut Side Trip, above).

3. NORMAL ROUTE (GRADE III)

The historic title for the Normal Route (in Osmaston and Pasteur's Rwenzori guidebook) was "Margherita from Stanley Plateau via Margherita Glacier and Upper Part of East Ridge," which, though wordy, accurately describes where the heck the route used to go. The modern version of the Normal Route, described here, appears to be a variation of the first-ascent route, which was done by the Duke of Abruzzi, J. Petigax, C. Ollier, and Joseph Brocherel on June 18, 1906 (the last two men had also made the first ascent of Mount Kenya, with Halford Mackinder).

From Elena Hut (4,550 meters), the trail wanders west, through the rocks surrounding the camp, and gains a series of rock ridges running northwest-southeast. Ascend these ribs for several hundred meters until the trail crests a rock rib north of the hut.

The trail then wanders west (follow the cairns) over rocks to the edge of the East Stanley Glacier and the eastern edge of the Stanley Plateau, a wide icefield that fills the area between the southern Stanley peaks (Moebius, Elena, Savoia, etc.) to the south and Alexandra (Stanley's second highest summit) to

Mounts Stanley, Speke, and Baker, with Routes 2–4 marked

Mount Stanley

Mount Baker

Summit

Normal
Route

Elena Hut
(approx. location,
behind ridge)

South Ridge
Route

Mount Speke

③

②

④

Normal Route (Route 3) from Elena Hut, Mount Stanley, photographed in the 1970s
(Photo © John Cleare)

the north. Margherita is behind (north of) Alexandra and not visible at this point. Where the rocks yield to ice, there are many flat and obvious places to rope up and don crampons.[100]

From the rock-glacier junction, head north, following the right-hand (eastern) edge of the glacier to another rock rib (a good resting point) about 800 meters away, then drop down 100 meters and skirt the eastern edge of the long east rib of Alexandra. From here, the plateau between Alexandra and Margherita (filled by the Margherita Glacier) can be gained via a fairly straightforward hike east-northeast. This is the most aerobic part of the ascent, and if you're going to feel the altitude anywhere, it'll likely be on this long uphill slog. There are numerous crevasses—some wider than one might imagine—but most are easily stepped over or jumped across. Staying roped up is essential.

After nearly 800 meters of uphill hiking, which gets more and more gentle in angle, you reach the "saddle" between Alexandra and Margherita; Margherita is on your right (north). Hike up steep snow to the base of the south-facing rock wall on Margherita, and look for a long, steep, gully and ledge system that ascends the rock face. You'll usually find a fixed rope dangling down it.

The route climbs this wall (Grade III, or about U.S. 5.5), going over several steep bulges. The ubiquitous fixed ropes here are not recommended, although any East Africans climbing with you will happily tug away. After a couple of steep sections—the tricky bits are only found in the first 15 or 20 meters—the climbing gets easier, moving out right on edges and finally cresting the east ridge of Margherita itself. Turn left and scramble the last 100 meters to the 5,109-meter (16,763-foot) summit.

Charlie French on the final section of Margherita, Mount Stanley

Descent is via the route of ascent. The entire round trip takes a full day, depending on your fitness level.

MOUNT BAKER

Mount Baker is also a vast and complex massif, and the standard route, although requiring nothing more than scrambling ability, is one of the most difficult to follow routes on the Rwenzoris' main peaks—especially in the mist. It winds around (all over the place) on the western side of a huge sloping ridge, the south ridge. Not only is the hiking on Baker circuitous, the south ridge is a very long (and tiring) ascent.

Access the South Ridge Route from Freshfield Pass, between Kitandara Hut and Guy Yeoman Hut on the Bujuku–Mubuku Circuit (see the description for Day 5 of the Bujuku–Mubuku Circuit, earlier this chapter). At Freshfield Pass, the trail levels off and there is a large flat area. A sign announces the pass and points left (north) toward Mount Baker. This is the start of the route.

4. SOUTH RIDGE ROUTE (GRADE II)

This, the Normal Route to Mount Baker's highest summit, Edward (4,843 meters/15,885 feet), was first climbed during the Duke of Abruzzi's 1906 expedition to the Rwenzoris. It was climbed on July 2, 1906, by Vittorio Sella (of photography fame), J. Brocherel, and E. Botta.

Although many guidebooks refer to the "summit" routes in the Rwenzoris as being "technical" mountaineering objectives, the Edward summit of Baker via the south ridge is not. There is some exposed scrambling, much trailfinding, and huge distances across rocky terrain, but there is nothing "technical" about it (by U.S. standards, it's Class 3). Ropes, crampons, rock gear, and an ice ax are all unnecessary.[101] That said, if you're not comfortable with extensive and sometimes exposed scrambling, then don't try this route—especially in bad weather.

From Freshfield Pass (4,282 meters), head north-northeast, across moss-covered rock interspersed with muddy sections of track, toward a rock boss. Below the boss, the trail begins up low-angled mossy rock slabs (maybe 35 degrees) that are cut horizontally with small ledges. At the base of the boss, go left, up a steep rock gully left of it. This is one of two cruxes of the climb, and when it's running with water, it can be tricky.

At the top of the gully, the route stops at a notch, with the south ridge proper 100 meters away to the right. Here the "trail" begins a wildly circuitous traverse up and left (north-northwest) across boulders, up and down ledges, and across a number of flat stretches between them, for 1.5 kilometers (it feels more like several, but according to various maps, is much less). This route roughly follows the line of the south ridge, but goes up and down because the terrain requires skirting cliffs and gendarmes.

One of the two cruxes on Mount Baker;
this one is the ledge traverse near the summit.

After about 1.5 kilometers, the Edward Glacier will come into view, down and to the left (it's actually visible from the Freshfield Pass area, though not in fog). Once the glacier is reached, the trail begins heading up and right, toward the south ridge itself, and finally culminates in a large rock drop-off to the north. There is a narrow, short but steep chimney/ledge system here that must be downclimbed.

At the bottom of the chimney is a wide, rock-strewn talus slope, sloping steeply downhill to the left (west). The summit of Edward is barely visible up the talus slope to the right. There is a well-worn trail heading east, up the talus slope to the summit, about 550 meters away. Climb this to reach Edward (4,843 meters/15,885 feet) and the top of the mountain.

The descent is via the same route. The entire round trip takes a full day, depending on your fitness level.

Appendix A

EMBASSIES

In these appendixes I've tried to make the phone and fax numbers consistent and easy to use. The + symbol before a number signifies a country code. A caller needs to add his international access number (in the United States and Canada, for example, that would be 011; in the UK, 00; in Australia, 0011) before the + symbol, which is then followed by the country code (254, 255, and 256 for Kenya, Tanzania, and Uganda, respectively) and the rest of the phone number. When dialing within a country (say, Tanzania), it's necessary to replace the country code with a zero. And, when dialing locally, drop the zero. For example, if you dial a business from the United States, after the international access code you'd dial 255-12-1234567. If you dial within East (or all) Africa, it would also be 255-12-1234567. If you dial within Tanzania, you would dial 027-12-1234567. And if you dial within Moshi, it would be simply 1234567. A great resource for making these calls is *www.countrycallingcodes.com*, but your long-distance carrier should also be able to help as well.

TANZANIAN EMBASSIES ABROAD
In addition to the embassies below, other Tanzania embassies abroad are listed at *www.tanzania-online.gov.uk/visa/envoys.html*.

Belgium
   72 Avenue Franklin Roosevelt, 1050 Brussels
   Tel: +32-2-640-6500/6527
   Fax: +32-2-646-8026
   Email: tanzania@skynet.be
Canada
   50 Range Road, Ottawa, Ontario K1N 8J4
   Tel: +1-613-232-1500/1509
   Fax: +1-613-232-5184
   Email: tzottawa@synapse.net
   www.tanzaniahighcommission.ca
China
   No. 53, Dong Liu Jie, San Li Tun, Chaoyang District, Beijing 100600
   Tel: +86-10-65321491/08
   Fax: +86-10-65324351
   Email: tzrepbj@sina.com

France

13 Avenue Raymond Poincaré, 75116 Paris
Tel: +33-1-53-70-63-66
Fax: +33-1-47-55-05-46
Email: info@amb-tanzanie.fr
www.amb-tanzanie.fr

Germany

Eschenallee 11, 14050 Berlin (Charlottenburg, Westend)
Tel: +49-30-303-0800
Fax: +49-30-303-08020
Email: info@tanzania-gov.de, tzberlin.habari@gmx.de
www.tanzania-gov.de

Italy

Villa Tanzania, Viale Cortina D'ampezzo 185, 00135 Rome
Tel: +39-06-334-85801/02/04
Fax: +39-06-334-85828
Email: info@embassyoftanzania.it, info@tanzania-gov.it
www.tanzania-gov.it

Japan

4-21-9, Kamiyoga, Setagaya-ku, Tokyo 158-0098
Tel: +81-3-3425-4531
Fax: +81-3-3425-7844
Email: tzrepjp@tanzaniaembassy.or.jp, visa@tanzaniaembassy.or.jp
www.tanzaniaembassy.or.jp

Kenya

Continental House, 4th Floor, PO Box 47790, Nairobi
Tel:+254-2-331056/057/104
Fax: +254-2-721874
Email: tanzania@user.africaonline.co.ke

Russia

Pyatnitskaya, U Litsa 33, Moscow
Tel: +7-095-231-5431
Fax: +7-095-230-2968
Email: tanmos@wm.west-call.com

Saudi Arabia

PO Box 94320, Riyadh 11693
Tel: +966-1-0-4542839/4542833
Fax: +966-1-4549660
Email: tzriyad@deltasa.com

South Africa

822 George Avenue, Arcadia, 0083, or PO Box 56572, Acardia, 0007
Tel: +27-12-342-4371/93
Fax: +27-12-430-4383
Email: thc@tanzania.org.za, diplomat@cyberhost.co.za
www.tanzania.org.za

Sweden
Wallingatan 11, Box 7255, 111 60 Stockholm
Tel: +46-8-503-206-00/1
Fax: +46-8-503-206-02
Email: mailbox@tanemb.se
www.tanemb.se

Uganda
6 Kagera Road, PO Box 5750, Kampala
Tel: +256-41-256272
Email: tzrepkla@imul.com

United Arab Emirates
No. S6A1 Nasr Street Khalidiyah, PO Box 43714, Abu Dhabi
Tel: +971-2-6650226
Fax: +971-2-6661613
Email: tanrep@emirates.net.ae

United Kingdom
3 Stratford Place, London W1C 1AS (opposite Bond Street tube station)
Tel: +44-207-569-1470
Fax: +44-207-491-3710
Email: balozi@tanzania-online.gov.uk, balozi@tanzania-online.gov.uk
www.tanzania-online.gov.uk (this website takes a long time to load)

United States
2139 R Street, NW, Washington DC 20008
Tel: +1-202-939-6123/5/7
Fax: +1-202-797-7408
Email: balozi@tanzaniaembassy-us.org
www.tanzaniaembassy-us.org

KENYAN EMBASSIES ABROAD

Australia
6th Floor, Q.B.E Building, 33–35 Ainslie Ave, GPO Box 1990, Canberra,
ACT 2601
Tel: +61-2-6247-4788/4722/4688/4311
Fax: +61-2-6257-6613
Email: kenrep@austarmetro.com, kenrep@dynamite.com.au

Belgium
Avenue Winston Churchill 208, 1180 Brussels
Tel: +32-2-340-1040/230-3065
Fax: +32-2-340-1050
Email: info@kenyabrussels.com
www.kenyabrussels.com

Canada

415 Laurier Avenue East, Ottawa, Ontario, KIN 6R4
Tel: +1-613-563-1773/4/6
Fax: +1-613-233-6599
Email: kenyahighcommission@rogers.com,
    webmaster@kenyahighcommission.ca
www.kenyahighcommission.ca

France

3 Rue, Freycinet, 75116 Paris
Tel: +33-1-566-22525
Fax: +33-1-472-04441
Email: paris@amb-kenya.fr
www.kenyaembassyparis.org

Germany

Mark Graf En Strasse 63, Berlin 10969
Tel: +49-30-259-2660
Fax: +49-30-259-26650
Email: office@embassy-of-kenya.de

Italy

Via Archimede 164, 00197, Rome
Tel: +39-06-8082717/8
Fax: +39-06-8082707
Email: info@embassyofkenya.it
www.embassyofkenya.it

Japan

No. 24-3 Yakumo, 3-Chome, Meguro-Ku, Tokyo 152
Tel: +81-3-37234006/7
Fax: +81-3-37234488
Email: info@kenyarep-jp.com
www.kenyarep-jp.com

Netherlands

Nieuwe Parklaan 21, 2597 LA The Hague
Tel: +31-70-3504215
Fax: +31-70-3553594
Email: info@kenya-embassy.nl

Russia

Bolshaya Ordinka, Dom. 70, Moscow
Telephone: +7-095-237-4702/3462/4541
Fax: +7-095-230-2340

Saudi Arabia

PO Box 94358, Riyadh 11693
Tel: +966-1-4881238
Fax: +966-1-4882629

South Africa

302 Brooks Street Menlo Park, 0081, Pretoria

Tel: +27-12-362-2249/2250/2251

Fax: +27-12-362-2252

Email: kenep@mweb.co.za

Sweden

Birger Jarl Gatan 37, 2nd Floor, PO Box 7694, 10395 Stockholm

Tel: +46-8-218300/4/9

Fax: +46-8-209261

Email: kenya.embassy@telia.com

Switzerland

1–3 Avenue de la Paix, 1202 Geneva

Tel: +41-22-9064050

Fax: +41-22-7312905

Email: commissionkenya@ties.itu.int

Tanzania

14th floor, N.I.C Investment House, Samora Avenue, PO Box 5231,
    Dar es Salaam

Tel: +255-22-2112-955/56

Fax: +255-22-2113-098

Uganda

Plot No. 41, Nakasero Road, PO Box 5220, Kampala

Tel: +256-41-258235/6

Fax: +256-41-258239

United Kingdom

45 Portland Place, London, W1B 1AS

Tel: +44-207-6362371/5

Fax: +44-207-3236717

Email: kcomm45@aol.com

www.kenyahighcommission.com

United States

2249 R Street, NW, Washington DC 20008

Tel: +1-202-387-6101

Fax: +1-202-462-3829

Email: information@kenyaembassy.com

www.kenyaembassy.com

and

Park Mile Plaza, Mezzanine Floor, 4801 Wilshire Boulevard, Los Angeles,
    CA 90010

Tel: +1-323-939-2408

Fax: +1-323-939-2412

Email: losangeles@kenyaembassy.com

UGANDAN EMBASSIES ABROAD

Australia

7 Dunoon Street, O'Malley ACT 2606, or PO Box 2205, Canberra
ACT 2601

Tel: +61-2-6286-1234 / 6290-7300 / 6290-7301 / 6290-7303

Fax: +61-2-6286-1243

Email: ugacnbr@bigpond.net.au

Belgium

Avenue De Tervuren 317, 1150 Brussels

Tel: +32-2-792-5825

Fax: +32-2-763-0438

Email: ugembrus@brutele.be

Canada

231 Cobourg Street, Ottowa, Ontario

Tel: +1-613-233-7797

Fax: +1-613-232-6689

Email: ugandahighcomm@bell.net.ca

www.ugandahighcommission.ca

China

5 San li tun Dong jie, Beijing 100600

Tel: +86-10-6532-1708 / 2370 / 2242

Fax: +86-10-6532-2242

Email: info@ugandaembassycn.org, idrophil@yahoo.com

www.ugandaembassycn.org

Denmark

Sofievej 15, Copenhagen 2900 Hellerup

Tel: +45-39620966

Fax: +45-39610148

Email: ugandaembassy@mail.dk

www.ugandaembassy.dk

Egypt

9 Midan al-Missaha, Dokki, Cairo

Tel: +20-2-248-5975

Fax: +20-2-48-5980

France

13, Avenue Raymond Poincaré, Paris 75116

Tel: +33-1-53-70-62-70

Fax: +33-1-53-70-85-15

Email: Uganda.embassy@club-internet.fr

Germany

Axel-Springer-Straße 54a, Berlin 10117

Tel: 030-24-04-75-56

Fax: 030-24-04-75-57

Email: ugembassy@yahoo.de, mail@uganda.de

www.uganda.de

India

B-3/26,Vasant Vihar, New Delhi 110 057

Tel: +91-11-2614-4413/5817

Fax: +91-11-2614-4405

Email: ughcom@vsnl.net.in

Italy

Lungotevere dei Mellini, 44, Scala Valadier, int B, 00193 Rome

Tel: +39-06-3225220/3207232

Fax: +39-06-3213688

Email: ugandaembassyrome@hotmail.com

Japan

4-15-3, Shimomeguro, Meguro-ku, Tokyo 153-0064

Tel: +81-3-5773-0481/2

Fax: +81-3-5725-3720

E-mail: info@ugandaembassy.jp

www.uganda-embassy.jp

Kenya

Riverside Paddocks, off Riverside Drive, PO Box 60853, Nairobi

Tel: +254-20-4445420/4449096

Fax: +254-20-4443772

Email: ugacomnrb@todays.co.ke, ugahicom@todaysonline.com

www.ugandahighcommission.co.ke

Russia

Korovy Val 7, Flat No. 3, 119049 Moscow

Tel: +7-095-230-2276

Fax: +7-095-230-2131

Email: ugaembassymoscow2003@yahoo.co.uk

Saudi Arabia

11, Hassan Bin Al-Numaman Street, west of Salahddin Hotel, Al Worood
Quarter, PO Box 94344, Riyadh 11693 K.S.A

Tel: +966-1-454-4910

Fax: +966-1-454-9264

Email: ugariyadh@hotmail.com

South Africa

Trafalgar Court, Apartment 35B, 634 Park Street, Arcadia 0083, Pretoria

Tel: +27-12-3426031/34

Fax: +27-12-3426206

Email: ugacomer@mweb.co.za

Tanzania

Extelcom Building, Floor 7, Samora Avenue, PO Box 6237, Dar es Salaam

Tel: +255-7-222-667391

Fax: +255-7-222-667224

Email: ugadar@intafrica.com

United Kingdom
  Uganda House, 58–59 Trafalgar Square, London WD2N 5DX
  Tel: +44-20-7839-5783
  Fax: +44-20-7839-8925
  Email: info@ugandahighcommission.co.uk
  www.ugandahighcommission.co.uk
United States
  5911 16th Street, NW, Washington DC 20011
  Tel: +1-202-726-7100
  Fax: +1-202-726-1727
  Email: info@ugembassy.com, ugembassy@aol.com
  www.ugandaembassy.com

FOREIGN EMBASSIES IN TANZANIA
Belgium
  Ocean Road 5, Dar es Salaam
  Tel: +255-22-602291
  Fax: +255-22-117621
Canada
  38 Mirambo Street / Garden Avenue, Dar es Salaam
  Tel: +255-22-211-2831
  Fax: +255-22-211-6897
  Email: dslam@dfait-maeci.gc.ca
  www.dfait-maeci.gc.ca/tanzania/menu-en.asp
  This embassy also serves Australians.
Denmark
  Ghana Avenue, PO Box 9171, Dar es Salaam
  Tel: +255-22-211-3887
  Fax: +255-22-211-6433
  Email: daramb@um.dk
Finland
  Mirambo Street / Garden Avenue, PO Box 2455, Dar es Salaam
  Tel: +255-22-219-6565
  Fax: +255-22-219-6573
  Email: sanomat.dar@formin.fi
  www.finland.or.tz
France
  Junction Ali Hassan Mwinyi Road and Kilimani Road, PO Box 2349, Dar
    es Salaam
  Tel: +255-22-266-6021 / 3
  Fax: +255-22-266-8435
  Email: ambafrance@ctvsatcom.net
  www.ambafrance-tz.org

Germany

Umoja House, Mirambo Street, Dar es Salaam
Tel: +255-22-211-7409/15
Fax: +255-22-211-2944
Email: german.embassy@bol.co.tz
www.daressalam.diplo.de/de/Startseite.html

India

82 Kinondoni Road, PO Box 2684, Dar es Salaam
Tel: +255-22-266-9040/1/2
Fax: +255-22-266-9043/9050
Email: hci@hcindiatz.org
www.hcindiatz.org

Ireland

No. 1131 Msasani Road, Oysterbay, PO Box 9612, Dar es Salaam
Tel: +255-22-260-2355/2356/2361
Fax: +255-22-260-2362/2367
Email: iremb@raha.com

Italy

316, Lugalo Road, Dar es Salaam
Tel: +255-22-211-5935
Fax: +255-22-211-5938
Email: italdipl@raha.com
www.italdipl-dar.org

Netherlands

Umoja House, 4th Floor, Corner Mirambo Street/Garden Avenue, PO Box
9534, Dar es Salaam
Tel: +255-22-211-0000
Fax: +255-22-211-0044
Email: nlgovdar@intafrica.com
www.netherlands-embassy.go.tz

United Kingdom

Umoja House, Garden Avenue, PO Box 9200, Dar es Salaam
Tel: +255-22-211-0101; 744-242-242 (emergencies only)
Fax: +255-22-211-0102
Email: bhc.dar@fco.gov.uk
www.britishhighcommission.gov.uk/tanzania

United States

686 Old Bagamoyo Road, Msasani, PO Box 9123, Dar es Salaam
Tel: +255-22-266-8001
Fax: +255-22-266-8238/8373
Email: embassyd@state.gov
http://tanzania.usembassy.gov

FOREIGN EMBASSIES IN KENYA

Australia

Riverside Drive (400 meters off Chiromo Road), PO Box 39341, Nairobi
Tel: +254-20-444-5034-9
Fax: +254-20-444-4718
www.embassy.gov.au/ke.html

Austria

City House Wabere Street, Nairobi
Tel: +254-333272/228281/228282
Fax: +254-331792

Canada

Limuru Road, Gigiri, PO Box 1013, 00621 Nairobi
Tel: +254-20-366-3000
Fax: +254-20-366-3900
Email: nrobi@dfait-maeci.gc.ca
www.dfait-maeci.gc.ca/nairobi/menu-en.asp

Denmark

Cassia House, Westlands Office Park (off Waiyaki Way), Westlands, PO
    Box 40412, Nairobi
Tel: +254-020-445-1460-3
Fax: +254-020-445-1474
Email: nboamb@um.dk

Finland

International House, 2nd floor, Mama Ngina Street, PO Box 30379,
    Nairobi
Tel: +254 20-318575/340681
Fax: +254 20-342927
Email: sanomat.nai@formin.fi

France

Barclay's Plaza, 9th Floor, PO Box 41784, Loita Street, Nairobi
Tel: +254-20-316363
Fax: +254-20-217013/211735
Email: ambafr@accesskenya.com
www.ambafrance-ke.org

Germany

Riverside Drive 113, Ludwig Krapf House, PO Box 30180, Nairobi
Tel: +254-20-426-2100
Fax: +254-20-426-2129
Email: info@nairobi.diplo.de

Greece

Nation Tower, 13th Floor, Kimathi Street, PO Box 30543, Nairobi
Tel: +254-2-340722/340744/228473
Fax: +254-2-216044
Email: embgr@kenyaweb.com

Italy
International House, 9th floor, Mama Ngina Street, PO Box 30107, Nairobi
Tel: +254-2-337356
Fax: +254-2-337056
Email: ambnair@swiftkenya.org

Japan
Ground Floor, ICEA Building, Kenyatta Avenue, PO Box 60202, Nairobi
Tel: +254-20-315850/52/55
Fax: +254-20-216530
Email: jinfocul@eojkenya.org
www.ke.emb-japan.go.jp

Netherlands
Riverside Lane, PO Box 41537, Nairobi
Tel: +254-20-445-0129
Fax: +254-20-444-7416
Email: nlgovnai@africaonline.co.ke
www.netherlands-embassy.or.ke

Norway
Lion Place, Waiyaki Way, Westlands, PO Box 46363-00100, Nairobi
Tel: +254-20-445-1510-6
www.norway.or.ke/info/embassy.htm

Tanzania
Continental House, 4th floor, PO Box 47790, Nairobi
Tel: 02-331056-7
Email: tancon@users.africaonline.co.ke

United Kingdom
Upper Hill Road, PO Box 30465-00100, Nairobi
Tel: +254-20-284-4000
Fax: +254-20-284-4111
Email: ConsularSection.nairobi@fco.gov.uk, VisaSection.nairobi@fco.gov.uk
www.britishhighcommission.gov.uk/kenya

United States
United Nations Avenue, PO Box 606, Village Market, 00621 Nairobi
Tel: +254-2-240290
http://usembassy.state.gov/nairobi/

FOREIGN EMBASSIES IN UGANDA

Canada
IPS Building, Plot 14, Parliament Avenue, PO Box 20115, Kampala
Tel: +256-11-258141
Fax: +256-11-349484
Email: canada.consulate@utlonline.co.ug
www.dfait-maeci.gc.ca/nairobi/uganda_office-en.asp

Denmark
Plot 3, Lumumba Avenue, PO Box 11243, Kampala
Tel: +256-41-256783
Fax: +256-41-254979
Email: kmtamb@um.dk
www.danishembassyuganda.co.ug

Germany
15 Philip Road, Kalolo, Kampala
Tel: +256-41-501111
Fax: +256-41-501115
Email: Germemb@africaonline.co.ug

Italy
Plot No. 10 Lourdel Road, Nakasero, or PO Box 4646, Kampala
Tel: +256-41-250450
Fax: +256-41-250448
Email: ambkamp@imul.com
www.imul.com/embitaly

Tanzania
6 Kagera Road, PO 5750, Kampala
Tel: +256-41-257357/242815/256272
Fax: +256-41-242890
Email: tzrepkla@imul.com

United Kingdom
4 Windsor Loop, PO Box 7070, Kampala
Tel: +256-31-312000
Fax: +256-41-257304 (general inquiries)
Email: bhcinfo@starcom.co.ug, ConsularVisa.Kampala@fco.gov.uk
www.britain.or.ug

United States
Plot 1577 Ggaba Road, PO Box 7007, Kampala
Tel: +256-41-259791/2/3/5
Fax: +256-41-259794
http://kampala.usembassy.gov

Appendix B

NATIONAL PARKS

TANZANIA
Tanzania National Parks
PO Box 3134, Arusha
Tel: +255-27-2503471/2504082
Fax: +255-27-2508216
Email: info@tanzaniaparks.com
www.tanzaniaparks.com
Kilimanjaro National Park (KINAPA)
PO Box 96, Marangu
Tel: 50, in Tanzania
Arusha National Park (Mount Meru)
PO Box 3134, Arusha
Tel: +255-27-2501930/1-9
Fax: +255-27-2548216
Email: tanapa@habari.co.tz

KENYA
Kenya Wildlife Service (KWS)
PO Box 40241, Nairobi
Tel: +254-20-600800
Fax: +254-20-603792
Email: kws@kws.org
www.kws.org
Administers all Kenyan parks.
Mount Kenya National Park
PO Box 69, Naro Moru
No telephone listed.

The Kenya Wildlife Service's website also lists an address in Nyeri for the
park warden:
PO Box 753, Nyeri
Tel: +254-61-55645/55201
Email: adwildlife@kws.org
www.kws.org/mt-kenya.html

UGANDA

Uganda Wildlife Authority
Plot 7 Kira Road, Kamwokya, PO Box 3530, Kampala
Tel: +256-41-346287/346288/355000
Fax:+256-41-346291
Email: uwa@uwa.or.ug
www.uwa.or.ug/rwenzori.html

Appendix C

TRANSPORTATION

The larger airlines in this appendix have many offices, which can be located using each airline's website; hence, only websites for those airlines are listed.

GENERAL
These are excellent resources for planning travel:

East Africa Shuttles
   www.eastafricashuttles.com

Tanzania Online Information Center
   www.tzonline.org/Transportation.htm

AIRLINES AND AIRPORTS

Kilimanjaro International Airport (KIA)
   64 kilometers west of Moshi and about 40 kilometers from Arusha, in Tanzania
   www.kilimanjaroairport.co.tz (this website doesn't open in all web browsers)

EUROPEAN AIRLINES

British Airways
   www.britishairways.com

KLM
   www.klm.com

Lufthansa
   www.lufthansa.com

AIRLINES IN EAST AFRICA

African Safari Airways
   African Safari Club, Imperial House, 21–25 North Street, Bromley, Kent, BR1 1SD UK
   Tel: +44-845-345-0014
   Fax +44-20-8466-0020
   Email: info@africansafariclub.com
   www.africansafariclub.com
   Flies between the United Kingdom and several other European cities (including Vienna, Basel, Frankfurt, and Malpensa) to/from Mombasa several times a week.

Air Tanzania

www.airtanzania.com

Flies between major Tanzanian destinations (including Kilimanjaro
International Airport) and to/from numerous other African countries.

Eagle Air

Adam House, Plot 11 Portal Avenue, PO Box 7392, Kampala, Uganda

Tel: +256-(0)41-344292/232185

Mobile: +256-(0)77-777334/(0)75-793860

Fax: +256-41344501

Email: marketing@eagleuganda.com, admin@eagleuganda.com

www.flyeagleuganda.com

Flies between Entebbe and Kasese, in Uganda.

Ethiopian Airlines

www.flyethiopian.com

Kenya Airways

www.kenya-airways.com

Mission Aviation Fellowship

PO Box 1, Kampala, Uganda

Tel: +256-41-267462/268388/039-777402/075-777402; 077-777208
(emergencies only)

Email: MAF-UG-OPSMGR@maf.or.ug, maf-us@maf.org

Flies between Entebbe and Kasese, in Uganda.

Precision Air

www.precisionairtz.com

Flies from Nairobi to several East African destinations, including
Kilimanjaro International Airport.

South African Airlines

www.flysaa.com

SHUTTLE AND BUS OPERATORS
Tanzania
Davanu Car Hire and Tours

Adventure Centre, Gollondoi Road, Arusha

Tel: +255-578142

Fax: +255-574311

Impala Shuttles

Impala Hotel, Old Moshi Road, Kijenge

Tel: +255-2-751786

Email: impala@kilinet.co.tz

Riverside Shuttles

PO Box 1734, Arusha

Tel: +255-572-2639/3916

www.riverside-shuttle.com

Scandinavia Express Services
Msimbazi Road, corner of Nyerere Road, Dar es Salaam
Tel: +255-22-218-4833 or 0748-218484/5
Email: md@scandinaviagroup.com, gm@scandinaviagroup.com
Kituoni Street, PO Box 12340, Arusha
Tel: +255-027-250-0153
Mawenzi Street, PO Box 2145, Moshi
Tel: +255-027-275-1387
www.scandinaviagroup.com

Kenya
Davanu Car Hire and Tours
4th Floor, Windsor House, University Way, PO Box 9081, Nairobi
No working telephone number as of publication.
Operators of the Davanu shuttle between Nairobi and Moshi.
Riverside Shuttles
Pan Africa Insurance House, Kenyatta Avenue, 3rd Floor, Room 1, PO Box
62997, Nairobi
Tel: +254-229618/241032
www.riverside-shuttle.com
Scandinavia Express Services
River Road, PO Box 3663, Nairobi
Tel: +254-020-242523
www.scandinaviagroup.com

Uganda
Scandinavia Express Services
Neota Cinema Building, Colville Street, PO Box 7233, Kampala
Tel: +256-41-348895
Email: kampala@scandinaviagroup.com
www.scandinaviagroup.com

Appendix D

OUTFITTERS

KILIMANJARO AND MOUNT MERU

The following outfitters have been recommended by Kilimanjaro National Park officials or by other travelers.

Hoopoe Safaris

India Street, Arusha, Tanzania

Tel: +255-27-250-7011; 800-408-3100 in the U.S.; +44-(0)1923-255462 in the UK

Fax: +255-27-254-8226

Email: hoopoe@kirurumu.com; for the Americas, inquiry@HoopoeUSA.com; for the United Kingdom and Europe, HoopoeUK@aol.com

Hoopoe won *Conde Nasté Traveler* magazine's "Best Ecotourism Company in the World" award in 2004.

Kinoynoga Tours & Safaris

PO Box 170, Moshi, Tanzania

Tel: +255-27-275-8551

Mobile: +255-744-282037

Email: info@kinoynogasafaris.com

www.kinoynogasafaris.com

Marangu Hotel

PO Box 40, Moshi, Tanzania

Tel: +255-27-275-6594/6361

Fax: +255-27-275-6591

Email: info@maranguhotel.com

www.maranguhotel.com

MEM Tours and Safaris

Moshi, Tanzania

Tel: +255-27-275-4234

Mobile: +255-744-482791

Fax: +255-27-275-4788

Email: mohammed@memtours.com

www.memtours.com

MJ Safaris International

PO Box 558, Moshi, Tanzania

Tel: +255-55-52017/51241

Fax: +255-55-50096

www.habari.co.tz/mjsafaris

Shah Tours and Travel, Ltd.
 PO Box 1821, Moshi, Tanzania
 Tel: +255-27-275-2370
 Email: kilimanjaro@eoltz.com, kilimanjaro@kilinet.co.tz
 www.kilimanjaro-shah.com
 Shah Tours and Travel has an office located on Mawenzi Road, in Moshi.
Zara Tanzania Adventures
 Ghalla Street, PO Box 1990, Moshi, Tanzania
 Tel: +255-27-27-50011
 Mobile: +255-744-451000
 Fax: +255-27-27-53105
 Email: zara@kilinet.co.tz
 www.kilimanjaro.co.tz

MOUNT KENYA
Kenya's Mountain Scene Club
 PO Box 461, Chogoria, Kenya
 Tel: +254-1622204
Mountain Rock Lodge
 PO Box 333
 Tel: +254-17662625
 Email: info@mountainrockkenya.com, base@mountainrockkenya.com
 www.mountainrockkenya.com/mountain_rock_lodge.htm
 About 180 kilometers north of Nairobi and 1 kilometer from the main road.
Mount Kenya Chogoria Porters and Guides Association
 PO Box 338, Chogoria, Kenya
 Email: mbogori2000@yahoo.com, carruufas@yahoo.com
 This club is based out of the Marimebu Lodge, up the Chogoria road, past
   the Transit Motel, about 1 kilometer before the park gate.
Mount Kenya Guides & Porters
 PO Box 128, Naro Moru, Kenya
 Tel: +254-62-62015
Mount Kenya Muthambi Guides and Porters Club
 PO Box 73, Chogoria, Kenya
Naro Moru River Lodge
 PO Box 18, Naro Moru, Kenya
 Tel: +254-62-62023/62201/62212
 Fax: +254-62-62211
 Email: mt.kenya@africaonline.co.ke
 www.alliancehotels.com/naromoru-br.html
Naro Moru Safari Camp Guides
 PO Box 145, Naro Moru, Kenya
Old Moses Porters and Guides Club
 PO Box 333, Nanyuki, Kenya
Tourist Safari Guides and Porters Club
 PO Box 56, Naro Moru, Kenya

RWENZORIS

Rwenzori Mountaineering Services (RMS)
PO Box 33, Saad House, Kasese, Uganda
Tel: +256-(0)483-44936
Mobile: (0)75-598461 (reservations office), (0)78-325431 (director)
Email: rwenzorims@yahoo.co.uk
www.traveluganda.co.ug/rwenzorimountaineeringservices

RMS also has an office in Nayakalengija:
PO Box 33, Nyakalengija, Uganda
Mobile: +256-7-598461

Appendix E

HOTELS AND HUT RESERVATIONS

The following hotel list is pretty random, but I have heard mostly good things about the hotels listed herein, or have stayed at them (at my own expense). Unless otherwise noted, starting prices listed are for single rooms.

ARUSHA HOTELS
Impala Hotel
Old Moshi Road, Kijenge
US$72–83 per night.
L'Oasis Lodge
Lot 734, Sekei
US$70–75 per night.

DAR ES SALAAM HOTELS
Harbour View Suites
JM Mall Centre, Samora Avenue, PO Box 9163
Tel: +255-22-212-4040
Mobile: +255-0748-564848
Fax: +255-22-212-0333
Email: reservation@harbourview-suites.com
www.harbourview-suites.com
Keys Hotel
13 Uhuru Street
Tel: +255-22-218-3033/2801
Fax: +255-22-218-3086
www.keys-hotels.com/dar.htm
At around US$8 per night, great for budget travelers.
Kilimanjaro Hotel Kempinski
Kivukoni Street, PO Box 9574
Tel: +255-22-213-1111
Fax: +255-22-212-0777
Email: reservations.kilimanjaro@kempinski.com
www.kempinski.com
At about US$270 per night (and up to US$900!), a swanky place (which the author is never likely to afford), but it is in the center of town and on the Indian Ocean.

Kipepeo Beach & Village

PO Box 1520

Tel: +255-22-282-0877

Mobile: +255-744-276178

Email: info@kipepeocamp.com, info@kipepeovillage.com

www.kipepeocamp.com, www.kipepeovillage.com

Kipepeo Beach is south of Dar es Salaam. Take the Kigamboni ferry (next to the fish market) for the 10-minute crossing from the harbor mouth to the south coast. Drive 8 kilometers south along the tarmac road, and you'll see a sign ("Kipepeo Beach") and a left turn onto a sandy road. Follow this road for another 800 meters to the resort. Campsite rates are US$4 per person per night. Simple beach *bandas* are US$13 for a single, US$20 for a double, and US$28 for a triple per night. They also offer self-contained, elevated chalets starting at US$50 for a single.

Mediterraneo Hotel

Off Kawe Road, PO Box 36110

Tel/fax: +255-22-261835

Mobile: +255-744-812567

Email: info@mediterraneotz.com, reservations@mediterraneotz.com

www.mediterraneotz.com

Singles start at about US$60.

Nyumbani Heritage

Plot 304, Mikocheni district, just off Old Bagamoyo Road, PO Box 32665

Tel: +255-744-695443

Email: nyumbani_heritage@yahoo.co.uk

www.homestead.com/nyumbani

Nyumbani Heritage is not a hotel in the usual sense; rather, it's a serviced self-catering accommodation (which is quite unusual in Tanzania). Charges (high season) start at around US$100 per night for up to four people.

Palm Beach Hotel

305 Ali Hassan Mwinyi Road, Upanga, or PO Box 1520, Dar es Salaam

Tel: +255-22-213-0985/212-2931/741-222299

Fax: +255-22-211-9272/260-0151

Email: info@pbhtz.com

www.pbhtz.com

Located near the ocean but within easy reach of the town center. Prices per room are US$55 for a single, US$80 for a double/twin, and US$90 for a triple.

Peacock Hotel

Bibi Titi Mohamed Road, in the center of Dar

Tel: +255-22-212-0334/14071

Fax: +255-22-211-7962

Email: info@peacock-hotel.co.tz; reservation@peacock-hotel.co.tz

www.peacock-hotel.co.tz

Singles start at about US$70.

Q-Bar & Guesthouse
Off Haile Selassie Road, behind Morogoro Stores, PO Box 4594
Tel: +255-722-282474
Fax: +255-22-211-2667
Email: qbar@cats-net.com
About US$45 per night. Fun place—reggae bands play here regularly.

Sleep Inn Hotel
Lumumba Road at Mahiwa Street, PO Box 88
Tel: +255-22-2183100/101/103
Fax +255-22-2183102/113
Email: sleepinn@cats-net.com
www.sleepinnhoteltz.com
Singles start at US$30; executive suites are US$75.

MOSHI HOTELS

Hotel Da Costa
Mawenzi Road
Tel: +255-74-481-7615
Email: hoteldacosta@yahoo.com
About US$5 per night for a single. Very basic, but affordable.

Keys Hotel
Uru Road, PO Box 933
Tel: +255-27-27-52250/51875
Fax: +255-27-27-50073
Email: reception@keys-hotels.com
www.keys-hotels.com/moshi.htm
About US$30 per person, bed and breakfast. Located on the northeast side
of Moshi, this hotel is nevertheless a base for budget climbers.

Kilimanjaro Crane Hotels, Ltd.
Kaunda Street, PO Box 1496
Tel: +255-27-27-51114/53037
Fax: +255-27-27-54876
Email: kilicrane@eoltz.com
www.kilimanjarocranehotels.com
Prices start at about US$40 for a single; suites are US$90. Gets relatively
good reviews from travelers.

Kilimanjaro Tourist Inn
Lema Road, PO Box 1993
Tel: +255-27-27-53252
Fax: +255-27-27-52748

Kindoroko Hotel
Mawenzi Road, PO Box 1341
Tel: +255-27-54054/50082
Email: kindoroko@kilionline.com
www.kindoroko.com
About US$15 per night. A pretty nice place (on the inside) for the price,
with a great bar and restaurant.

Moshi Leopard Hotel

Market Street, PO Box 232

Tel: +255-27-27-55134

Fax: +255-27-27-51261

Email: leopardhotel@eoltz.com, email@leopardhotel.com

www.leopardhotel.com

Prices start at around US$35 for a single. Boasts clean and comfortable rooms, right in the center of Moshi.

Mountain Inn

6 kilometers east of Moshi on the road to Marangu / Dar

Tel: +255-27-275-2370 / 2998

Fax: +255-27-275-1449

Email: kilimanjaro@kilionline.com

www.kilimanjaro-shah.com/mountain_inn.htm

Owned by the same people that own Shah Tours and Travel. Prices start at around US$35.

New Livingstone Hotel

Rangua Street, PO Box 1819

Tel: +255-27-27-55212

Fax: +255-27-27-55212

Prices start around US$20 for a single.

Springlands Hotel

Pembo Road

Tel: +255-27-27-53581

Email: info@zaratravel.com

www.zaratravel.com/info/springlands.html

A gorgeous hotel and grounds located on the southeastern side of Moshi. Owned by the same people who own Zara Tanzania Adventures. Prices starts at US$50. The hotel is for (trekking, safari, etc.) clients of Zara Tanzania Adventures only.

Uhuru Tourism & Conference Centre

Sekou Toure Way, PO Box 1320

Tel: +255-27-27-54084

Email: uhuru@elct.orgwww.uhuruhostel.org

About US$14–45 per night for a single. An excellent place to stay. It's a Christian retreat serving only soft drinks; alcohol is strictly prohibited. I spent several nights here in 1997 and it was very clean.

NAIROBI HOTELS

A good resource for Nairobi hotels is East Africa Shuttles at *www.eastafricashuttles. com/hotels*.

Boulevard Hotel

Harry Thuku Road

Tel: +254-20-227567

Fax: +254-20-334071

Email: hotel@hotelboulevard.com

About US$70–120 per night.

Nairobi YMCA
State House Road
Tel: +254-20-2724116/7
Fax: +254-20-2728825
Email: info@kenya-ymca.org
www.kenya-ymca.org
About US$20 per night.

The New Stanley Hotel
Corner of Kimathi Street and Kenyatta Avenue
Tel: +254-020-228830
Fax: +254-020-229388
Email: reservations@thestanley.sarova.co.ke
www.sarovahotels.com
Right in the heart of the city. The hotel's famous Thorn Tree Cafe is one
of Ernest Hemingway's old haunts and is a great place to people-
watch. US$90–180 per night.

Norfolk Hotel
Harry Thuku Road
Tel: +254-20-250900
Fax: +254-20-336742
Email: norfolkreservation@lonrhohotels.co.ke
www.lonrhohotels.com/norfolk/introduction.html
About US$285 per night for a single. Staying here is a trip back in
history—wish I could afford it.

Oakwood Hotel
Kimathi Street and Kenyatta Avenue
Tel: +254-20-220592
Across Kimathi Street from the New Stanley. About US$60 per night.
Nairobi's largest concentration of taxi drivers seems to congregate just
outside the Oakwood, so it's a good place to arrange a taxi to Mount
Kenya.

Suncourt Inn
Windsor House, University Way
Tel: +254-20-221413
Fax: +254-20-217500
About US$50 per night for a double. The folks here were so friendly and
the rates so good, a friend and I stayed a week.

KAMPALA HOTELS

Antlers Inn
Bombo Road
Tel: +256-41-257120
About US$20 per night.

College Inn
Plot 359 Bombo Road
Tel: +256-41-533-835
About US$25 per night.

New Gloria Hotel
  William Street
  Tel: +256-41-257790
  About US$11 per night.

Speke Hotel
  Kimathi Avenue
  Tel: +256-2592221/235332/235335
  Fax: +256-41-235345
  Email: spekehotel.com@spekehotel.com
  www.spekehotel.com
  About US$120 per night. I split a room with two friends, so it ended up being a fabulous experience (think Victorian-era grand hotel) for about US$40 per night.

KASESE HOTELS

Margherita Hotel
  About 2 kilometers out of town on the Kilembe Road
  Tel: +256-483-44015
  Mobile: +256-77-695808
  Fax: +256-483-44380
  Email: info@hotel-margherita.com
  www.hotel-margherita.com
  About US$45 per night for a single. It feels a bit isolated, but you'll sleep well here.

Mt. Rwenzori Lodge
  Plot 39, Alexander Street
  Tel: +256-77-930265
  About US$5 per night. Basic but good.

New Saad Hotel
  Tel: +256-483-44139/077-499552
  Email: info@newsaadhotel.com

Rwenzori International Hotel
  Mbogo Road
  Tel: +256-483-44148
  Mobile: +256-77-904236
  Fax: +256-483-44147
  Email: rwenzoriinternationalkasese@yahoo.com
  Prices start at about US$15 per night.

Virina Garden
  Rwenzori Road, PO Box 90
  Tel: +256-483-44788
  Email: virinagarden@yahoo.com
  Excellent value (about US$20 per person or so). Self-contained round huts with hot water and very clean rooms. I stayed at several Kasese hotels in early 2005, and this was the best of the lot. The worst of those hotels is not listed—it was horrendous.

White House Hotel
  Kilmebe Road
  Tel: +256-483-44706
  US$8–11 per night. In the downtown area, offers basic accommodation
    and has a popular bar.

MOUNT KENYA HUT RESERVATIONS
  To reserve hut space on the Naro Moru Route (Meteorological Station and
    Mackinder's Camp), contact:
  Naro Moru River Lodge
  PO Box 18, Naro Moru, Kenya
  Tel: +254-20-4443357/8,
  Fax +254-20-4445309
  or
  Alliance Hotels
  College House
  PO Box 49839, Nairobi, Kenya
  Tel: +254-337501
  Email: mt.kenya@africaonline.co.ke
  www.alliancehotels.com/naromoru-br.html

  Their Nairobi agents are:
  Let's Go Travel
  PO Box 60342, ABC Place Waiyaki Way, Nairobi, Kenya
  Tel: +254-20-4447151

  To reserve hut space on the Sirimon Route (Old Moses and Shipton's
    Camp), contact:
  Mountain Rock Lodge
  PO Box 333, Nanyuki, Kenya
  Email: info@mountainrockkenya.com, base@mountainrockkenya.com
  www.mountainrockkenya.com/mountain_rock_lodge.htm

Appendix F

MAP AND GUIDEBOOK SOURCES

AFRICA
Hoopoe Safaris
India Street, Arusha, Tanzania
Tel: +255-27-250-7011; 800-408-3100 in the U.S.; +44-(0)1923-255462 in the UK
Fax: +255-27-254-8226
Email: hoopoe@kirurumu.com; for the Americas, inquiry@HoopoeUSA. com; for the United Kingdom and Europe, HoopoeUK@aol.com
Nature Discovery (for Kilimanjaro)
PO Box 10574, Arusha, Tanzania
Email: info@naturediscovery.com

CANADA
Map Connection, Ltd.
400 5th Avenue SW, Calgary, Alberta, T2P 0L6, Unit 100
Tel: +1-403-215-4058
Fax: +1-403-266-0935
Email: sales@mapconnection.com
www.mapconnection.com

UNITED KINGDOM
Cordee
3a DeMontfort Street, Leicester, LE1 7HD
Tel: +44-116-254-3579
Fax: +44-116-247-1176 (UK)
Email: info@cordee.co.uk, sales@cordee.co.uk
www.cordee.co.uk
EWP
Haulfryn, Cilycwm, Wales, SA20 0SP
Tel: +44-(0)-1550-721319
Fax: +44-(0)-1550-720053
Email: ewp@ewpnet.com
www.ewpnet.com/maps.htm

West Col Productions
Copse House, Goring Heath, Reading, Berkshire, RG8 7SA
Tel: +44-1491-681284

UNITED STATES

Adventurous Traveler Bookstore
PO Box 64769, Burlington, VT 05406-4769
Tel: 800-282-3963, +1-802-860-6776
Email: books@atbook.com
http://atb.away.com/index.html

Chessler Books
PO Box 4359, Evergreen, CO 80437
Tel: 800-654-8502, +1-303-670-0093
Fax: +1-303-670-9727
Email: orders@chesslerbooks.com
www.chesslerbooks.com

Appendix G

GLOSSARY OF LOCAL LANGUAGES

Nearly all Swahili words listed below are adaptations of English words. This is because the items being described were generally introduced by Europeans and never existed before. In most cases, an English term can be substituted for a Swahili term (e.g., crampons).

Meru is spoken on the eastern side of Mount Kenya, Kikuyu is spoken throughout Kenya, Chagga is spoken on the southeastern side of Kilimanjaro, and Bakonjo is spoken on the eastern side of the Rwenzoris.

ENGLISH	SWAHILI	MERU	KIKUYU	CHAGGA (MARANGU)[102]	BAKONJO
abseil (rappel)	temlemka, kwamawe kutokajuu	kuikuruka	guikuruka	rendemka	—
alpinist	mpandaji	mutuii	mutuii	mruomsari	amunyabitwa
altitude sickness	—	—	—	—	obuyiserugulike
to arrive (at the summit)	kufika	gukinya	gukinya	ishika	eriwisya
aspirin	aspirini	aspirini	aspirini	asipirinyi	ekinini
baggage	mizigo	murigo	murigo	msiko	omuheke
beer	pombe	nchobi	njohi	wari	obwabu
to belay	kuteremsha	guturemukia	kuharurukia	isotsa	eriboha omuhuka
bivouac	—	kurungaria	ngurunga	—	ekisaho ekyomuka
blizzard	dhoruba	kirorua	kiroruha	kiwiliwili	—
boots	buti	mbuti	mbuti	mabudi	ebutsi
carabiner	karabina	gwati	gwati	karapina	carabiner
campsite	kambi	kambi	kambi	kambi	—

218

English					
cliff	gebali	karima kanini	karima kanini	kingony	ekikuka
to climb	kupanda	gwitia	gutamba	iro	erihetuka
the climb	upandaji	kwambata	uhaichi	iroya	akiruka
the climber	mpandaji	mwitia	muhaichi	mruomsari	omusambi
cloud	mawingu	matu	matu	mapichi	ebitu
col	m'gongo	ntumbii	—	mongo	
cold	baridi	mpio	heho	mbeo	obuhuhirire
compass	dira	kabachi	kabathi	dira	—
crack	ufa	mwatuka	mwatuka	ngua	omughenyu
crampons	viatu ya barafu	iratu bia barubu	iratu cia barabu	kirampo	engeta ayamahwa awe
danger	hatari	ugwati	'uguati	atari	nzururu
dangerous	—	—	—	—	akabe
the descent	kuturemka	guteremka	kuharuruka	isoka	ekitsibo
doctor	daktari / tabibu	gitari	rigitari	mkanga	omutahwa
east	mashariki	kiumiriro	riumiriro	mshariki	ebulhwalhuba
flashlight	kurunzzi	tochi	tochi	toochi	akarabyo
flat	tambarare	muganano	mwaragano	andukulee	eribanda
fog	ukungu	mpundu	kibii	mauruuru	ekitwe
food	chakula	irio	irio	kyelya	ebyalya
frozen	lioganda	kuthita	kuganda	ifie mphiphi	erifukirira
fuel	mafuta[103]	maguta	maguta	—	—
gaiters	—	ngeta	ngeta	—	—
glacier	theluji	barabu	barabu	parafu	enzururu
gloves	grobe	ngrobe	—	kilofusi	ebyambalhu ebye byalha
go (as in, we go)	—	—	—	—	tughende ("tuwende")
goggles	miwani	machichio	machichio	mawanyi	amatalhatalha
goodbye	—	—	—	—	bukayage
good morning	—	—	—	—	wabukyire ("wabuchire")

ENGLISH	SWAHILI	MERU	KIKUYU	CHAGGA (MARANGU)	BAKONJO
good night	—	—	—	—	wasibere
guide	mwongozi	mutongoria	mutongoria	kaidi	omunyambara
hammer	nyundo	nyondo	nyondo	kiria	enyondo
harness	—	—	—	—	ekiharni
hat	—	—	—	—	esipio
headlamp	kurunzi ya kichwani	tochi ya kongo	tochi ya kongo	toochi ya mrwe	etalha
hello	—	—	—	—	kuthie ("cootie")
helmet	kofia ya chuma	nkobia	ngobia	kofia ya menya	yamba
help	saidia	gutethia	uteithio	tarama	endata
high	juu	iguru	iguru	wuye	akatwe
hill	kilima	karima	karima	kimsari	enzalha ("ensala")
hungry	—	—	—	—	ekiswa
hut	kibanda	kanyumba	thingira	kipanda	ebarafu
ice	barafu	mbarabu	barafu	parafu	embanzwo
ice ax	shoka ya barafu	ithanua ria mbrabu	ithanua ria mbrabu	soka la parafu	ekihutale
injury	jeraha	gukururua	gutihio	kidonda	—
jacket	kabuti	kabuti	kabuti	ipushiti	omuhamba
knife	kisu	gaciu	gahiu	kishu	erikundu
knot	kitanzi	gikundo	gikundo	itimbisho	endaghiriro
map	ramani	mabu	mabu	ramanyi	omubatsi
medicine	dawa	ndawa	ndawa	mri	obulhambo
mountain	mlima	kirima	kirima	msari	omusambi
mountaineer	mpadaji	mwitia wairima	muhaichi kirima	mruoyamsari	eyihi
no	hapana	gutiri	gutiri	ote	endata
north	kaskazini	ruguru	ruguru	kaskasinyi	—
pack	fungashsa	kubanga	kubanga	sanyia	enzira
pass	pita	gukuruka	kuhituka	ira	

English					
petrol	petroli	beteruri	beturo	petrolyi	esasi
photo	picha	mbicha	mbicha	picha	ekikanganio (ekisasani)
porter	mpagazi	makamati wamirigo	mukui mirigo	muiriamisiko	omukoli
rent	kodi	igoti	igoti	kodi	eripangisya
ridge	kiamba	gagaa kanini	tumu	—	omuramber
road	barabara	barabara	barabara	parapara	enguda
rock	mwamba	iga	ihiga	iwa	olhukuka
rockfall	mtelemro wa mawe	kwaruka kwa maiga	kiharuruko	mawe wayoloka	erikofu
rope	kamba	mukna	muknada	kiwowo	omuhuha
route	njia	njira	njira	njia	—
scree	mawe kidogo	mwambatiro	tumahiga tunini	ipeleshi	—
shovel	beleshi	giciko giatiri	giciko giatiri	—	—
ski	kiziwashiria kutekemka	kwirekiria mwimanoni	—	—	—
ski poles	viziti via kutelemka	tumititwa kwimana	muhuko wagukomera	—	eyisaho eyirikesamu
sleeping bag	mfarishi	mubuka yakumama	mukondoro	—	—
sleeping pad	ngondold	ithitho	—	—	—
snow	theluji	nkamia	barafu	parafu	—
socks	—	—	—	—	esokiso
south	kusini	ihiriro	itherero	kusinyi	—
stake, peg	vishikio vya hema	ikingi ziaigema	—	—	—
steep	mutelemko milali	mwinamo	haruruko	pichiny	embwe
stone	—	—	—	—	twimane
stop (group)	—	—	—	—	emana
stop (singular)	simama	rugama	rugama	tirima	—
stove	stofu	thitobu	thitobu	riko lya mafuraataa	—
straps	nyuji	ndigii	—	mikanda	—
stream	kijito	kamwera	karui	mfongo	omughende
summit	kilele	iguru	gathumbiri	—	endata

ENGLISH	SWAHILI	MERU	KIKUYU	CHAGGA (MARANGU)	BAKONJO
sunburn	kuchomwa na jua	kuja ni riva	kuhia ni riua	—	—
sunburn cream	dawa ya ngozi	ndawa ya ngothi	ndawa ua ngothi	mri wa muu	—
sunglasses	miwani ya jua	maitho ya riua	macicio ma riua	miwanyi ya muu	erighuliro lyebyalha
supermarket	supamaket	kathoko	thoko	iduka lying'anyi	obundu
tapioca					
tent	hema	kaema	hama	ihema	ehema
tent fly	kituniko cha hema	kiandavua			
thank you					wasingya
thirsty	kuwa na kiu	nyonta	kunyota	iyangaa	enyota
toilet	choo			choro	ekyoloni
trail	uchochoro	tujira twa mbiti	njira ya nyamu	kinjia	enzira
valley	bonde	kiolo	mukuri	pichi	omusya
village	kijiji	ituura	gichagi	kijiji	ekyalo
visa	viza	vija			
wait	ngoja	eterera	eterera	wera	lindaa
walk slowly					ghenda lyolho ("yenda yororo")
wall	ukuta	ruthingo	ruthungo	ukuta	ekidongo
water	maji	ruji	mai	mringa	amagetse
water bottle	chupa ya maji	cuba ya ruuji	cuba ya mai	chupa ya muringa	etsupa yamaghetse
weather	hali ya hewa	riera	riera	halyi ya hewa	obutuku
west	magharibi	muthiriro	ithuito	mangaribi	ebulengera lhuba
white man	mzungu				omujungu
white men	mzungus				abujungu
wind	upepo	rugo	ruhuho	upepo	omuyagha
yes	ndiyo	niu	iini	iyee	inga
zipper	zipu	nyororo	nyororo	sipu	—

Appendix H

ADDITIONAL READING

The following books are all recommended to further your understanding of East Africa, Kilimanjaro, Mount Meru, Mount Kenya, and the Rwenzoris.

Although most of these books won't be on the shelves at your local bookstore, there are ways of obtaining them. You can order many of the more common titles online, and if you're cheap, like me, used.

For the most difficult to find titles, check out the Henry S. Hall, Jr., Library at the American Alpine Club (AAC) in Golden, Colorado, or if you're in the United Kingdom, the Alpine Club (AC) Library in London, where most of the books listed below are available. Access is free at both libraries for club members, as well as (at the AAC library) for members of the Colorado Mountain Club, and (at the AC) for Fellows of the Royal Geographical Society (RGS). Nonmembers of the clubs can also use both libraries, but non-AC members and non-RGS members are required to make a small donation when they use the AC library (and be forewarned, seating is rather limited). Call before visiting either library, as hours are subject to change and unexpected closures sometimes occur. If you are a member of either the AAC or the AC, you can even have the books posted to you for two weeks at a time (you pay return postage).

Henry S. Hall, Jr., Library at the American Alpine Club
   710 Tenth Street, Suite 15, Golden CO 80401, USA
   Tel: +1-303-384-0112
   Fax: +1-303-384-0113
   Email: library@americanalpineclub.org
   www.americanalpineclub.org (click on "library")
   Hours: Tues and Thurs, noon–7:00 PM; Wed and Fri, 8:30 AM–4:30 PM
Alpine Club Library
   55/56 Charlotte Road, London EC2A 3QF, UK
   Tel: +44-20-7613-0745
   Email: admin@alpine-club.org.uk; library@alpine-club.org.uk
   www.alpine-club.org.uk/library
   Hours: Wed–Fri, 10:30 AM–5:00 PM (closed for lunch 1–2 PM, appointment required on Fri)

Allan, Iain, ed. *Guide to Mount Kenya and Kilimanjaro*. Nairobi: Mountain Club of Kenya, 1990. (PO Box 45741, Nairobi, Kenya; *www.mck.or.ke*) Historically, the best reference for technical mountaineers available.
Benuzzi, Felice. *No Picnic on Mount Kenya*. Layton, Utah: Gibbs Smith, 1989. Originally published in 1953. A classic account of an unusual ascent of

Point Lenana by three Italian prisoners of war in 1943. Benuzzi and his friends escaped from a British POW camp near Nanyuki to climb Mount Kenya, then escaped back into the camp after their ascent. Their route approximates the Burguret Route on the mountain.

Briggs, Philip. *Uganda*. 4th ed. Chalfont St. Peter, UK; Bradt, 2003. One of the few general travel guides dedicated entirely to Uganda (although expect more in the future) and a very well-done book.

De Filippi, Filippo. *Ruwenzori*. New York: E. P. Dutton & Company, 1908. One of the most fascinating books on East Africa ever written. De Filippi was the Duke of Abruzzi's chronicler during his long 1906 expedition in the Rwenzoris.

Finlay, Hugh, Geoff Crowther, and Mary Fitzpartick. *East Africa*. Footscray, Victoria: Lonely Planet, 2003. A general guide to East Africa and an excellent resource. Has good information on the towns of Moshi and Arusha, as well as traveling around Tanzania.

Fitzpatrick, Mary, Matthew Fletcher, and David Wenk. *Trekking in East Africa*. 3rd ed. Footscray, Victoria: Lonely Planet, 2003. Seemingly based on David Elses's excellent earlier versions, a well-written, comprehensive guide to trekking throughout East Africa. "Technical" routes are not included.

Lange, Harald. *Kilimanjaro: The White Roof of Africa*. Seattle: The Mountaineers Books, 1985. A large-format book that is part coffee-table glossy, part natural history, part anthropological dissertation. Out of print.

Mackinder, Halford. *The First Ascent of Mount Kenya*. Reprint, Athens: Ohio University Press, 1991. A diary-style record of Mackinder's first ascent of the peak in 1899.

Osmaston, Henry, and David Pasteur. *Guide to the Ruwenzori: The Mountains of the Moon*: Reading, UK: West Col Productions, 1972. A comprehensive, well-researched guide to the Rwenzoris by two of its most active pioneers. A new edition is expected out in 2006.

Pluth, David. *Uganda Rwenzori: A Range of Images*. Little Wolf Press, 1996. A nice, medium-format coffee-table book about the Rwenzoris.

Salkeld, Audrey. *Kilimanjaro: Mountain at the Crossroads*. Washington DC: National Geographic Books, 2002. A large-format book that is part coffee-table glossy, part natural history, part anthropological dissertation.

———. *World Mountaineering*. London: Mitchell Beazley, 1998. A collection of essays and factual information about mountains around the globe. Includes excellent sections of the Rwenzoris, Mount Kenya, and Kilimanjaro. Out of print but occasionally available used.

Shipton, Eric. *Upon That Mountain*. Reprint, Seattle: The Mountaineers Books, 1985. Includes an excellent account of Shipton's climbing activities in East Africa.

Stedman, Harry. *Kilimanjaro: A Trekking Guide to Africa's Highest Mountain*. Hindhead, UK: Trailblazer Publications, 2003/2004. One of the most extensive books covering only Kili. Has an excellent section on the cities/towns (Nairobi, Dar es Salaam, Arusha, and Moshi).

Swahili Phrase Book and Dictionary. Oxford, UK: Berlitz, 1995. (Peterley Road, Oxford, 0X4 2TX, England.) A good basic overview of the most important Swahili words and expressions.

Taylor, Rob. *The Breach*. New York: Coward, McCann & Geoghan, 1981. An excellent account of an early attempt on Kilimanjaro's Breach Wall.

Wielochowski, Andrew. *East Africa International Mountain Guide*. Reading, UK: West Col Productions, Reading, UK 1986. An extensive guidebook to *all* technical climbing in East Africa (Kilimanjaro, Mount Kenya, Rwenzoris), from small crags to the big peaks. Also includes caving in East Africa.

———. *Kilimanjaro Map and Guide*. Reading, UK: West Col Productions, 1990. Similar to Wielochowski and Savage's earlier *Mt. Kenya Map and Guide* (below), it includes a full-sized topographic map and a condensed technical mountaineering guide.

———. *Rwenzori Map and Guide*. Reading, UK: West Col Productions, 1990. This condensed technical mountaineering guide is a good starting reference for the Rwenzoris, but many of the trails marked in the southern portion of the map are either wildly out of place or don't exist altogether. However, for use around the main peaks, it's an excellent reference.

Wielochowski, Andrew, and Mark Savage. *Mt. Kenya Map and Guide*. Reading, UK: West Col Productions, 1990. This condensed technical mountaineering guide is generally regarded as having the best maps of Mount Kenya, including a full-sized topographic map.

Young, Isabelle. *Healthy Travel Africa*. Melbourne: Lonely Planet, 2000. A great, detailed resource for any African traveler by a qualified MD. Scarier reading than you might imagine!

ACKNOWLEDGMENTS

This book would not have been possible without help from many people.

In Uganda thanks to James Mbahimba; Peter Babughagle; Erik Baluku; Fred Bosco; John Babughagle; Morick Musenzera; Tobius Kule; Joash Kule; Saimon Bakamwegha; Elijah Baluku; Fred Bwambale; Sanairi Bwambale; Amos Mukongotsa; Corey Ander; Asanayire Bwambale; Peter Tsimitha; Stanley Mbotela, Nelson Bitswande; Girisoni Katwanga; Jackson Kighoma; Josiah Makwano; Roben Babughagle; Johnson Mbusa; Joshua Synantangia; and Kabau Uziah and Muhindo Kedress.

In Kenya, a huge thanks to Bongo Woodley, who went through the last edition and made hundreds of corrections. Thanks also to James Garrett, Geoff Tabin, Michael Wanjau, and Zakayo Leparie of Mount Kenya National Park; Alloyce Okello; Lawrence Gitonga; Mys Dyrekshun; Leonard Josphat; Frank N. Oepin; Ambrose Kirimi; Peter Short; Hughe Johnson; Willy Orwonty, Anthony Miriti Manene; Loyford Mutembei Mburia; I. B. Riggin; Daniel Mugendi Rufas; and Iain Allan.

In Tanzania thanks to Matthew Mombo and Miraji Mramba of Kilimanjaro National Park; Tom Masami of Arusha National Park; Darsie Culbeck; Sean Gaffney; Jacob Smith; Emmanuel Paul; Zainab and Roger Ansell; Omari Chambo; Marc Miwurtz, Filip Koverhult, Rump E. Bumpee; Mohammed Hemed; Frank Lee Psili, Allen Melickzedek Mremi; Sifuni Pallangyo; Dom Focker; Tom Masami; John Rafaeli; Hamadi Saidi; William and Michael Sandy; P. Zinapod; the late Sada Sherali; Count E. Siet; and Mohommed Ali Tenga. Desidere ("Desi") Munishi of Moshi straightened out much of the language in the glossary and added the Chagga terms.

Stateside, many people helped with either new route descriptions or corrections on existing ones, as well as photographs, including Bart O'Brien, Carey Hunt, Lindsay Griffin, Forchen Nife, Ian Howell, Doug Scott, Mark O'Keefe, Chaz Taminut, and John Temple. Additionally, thanks to Bridget Burke at the American Alpine Club's Henry S. Hall, Jr., Library and Yvonne Sibbald at the Alpine Club's library in London.

Thanks to my fellow adventurers: Ann, Zoe, and Mollie Burns; Benny Bach; Charlie French; Richard Handler; Mark Jenkins; Henry Osmaston; John Cleare; Bill Milayder; Miss Chore Cawling; Ray Wood; Rusty Bridges; the famed Welsh climbing twins, Jim and Reginald Perrin; Harry Kikstra; and Tristan Cooper. And thank you to my parents and parents-in-law—some of the finest luggage wranglers ever to have been seen patiently cruising Denver International Airport's confusing drop-off and pickup points: Kerry and Mary Burns and Bob and Sylvia Robertson.

NOTES

1. Official Kilimanjaro National Park (KINAPA) numbers for visitation as of early 2005 were "up to" 27,000.
2. Before my 2005 trip to East Africa, I attempted to offset my greenhouse gas emissions by cycling to work for four months, but I quit after I was nearly killed by a teenage SUV driver using a mobile phone. Instead, my family became, in May 2005, the first "family" entity to join the Chicago Climate Exchange (which trades credits for greenhouse gas emissions) so we could offset emissions from climbing trips and other travel.
3. Reinhold Messner reportedly commented that the Breach Wall was the hardest route he ever climbed. That said, recent emails I've received from Italian climbers indicate that these climbers have been working on other Breach Wall lines that look as hard or harder.
4. Most people I've met who've done Meru consider it more physically demanding than the main trekking routes on Kili.
5. These days, though, crampons are unnecessary on the standard route on Mount Baker.
6. The name Mediterranean comes from the Latin word *mediterraneus*, which translates as "inland" (*medius*, from "middle," plus *terra*, meaning "land" or "earth").
7. From the *History of Herodotus II*: "Let us leave these things, however, to their natural course, to continue as they are and have been from the beginning. With regard to the sources of the Nile, I have found no one among all those with whom I have conversed, whether Egyptians, Libyans, or Greeks, who professed to have any knowledge, except a single person. He was the scribe who kept the register of the sacred treasures of Minerva in the city of Sais, and he did not seem to me to be in earnest when he said that he knew them perfectly well. His story was as follows: 'Between Syene, a city of the Thebais, and Elephantine, there are' (he said) 'two hills with sharp conical tops; the name of the one is Crophi, of the other, Mophi. Midway between them are the fountains of the Nile, fountains which it is impossible to fathom. Half the water runs northward into Egypt, half to the south towards Ethiopia.' The fountains were known to be unfathomable, he declared, because Psammetichus, an Egyptian king, had made trial of them. He had caused a rope to be made, many thousand fathoms in length, and had sounded the fountain with it, but could find no bottom. By this the scribe gave me to understand, if there was any truth at all in what he said, that in this fountain there are certain strong eddies, and a regurgitation, owing to the force wherewith the water dashes against the mountains, and hence a Sounding-line cannot be got to reach the bottom of the spring." See *www.piney.com/Heredotus2.html*.
8. From Aristotle's *Meteorology*: "So, too, in Libya there flow from the Aethiopian mountains the Aegon and the Nyses; and from the so-called Silver Mountain the two greatest of named rivers, the river called Chremetes that flows into the outer ocean, and the main source of the Nile." See *http://classics.mit.edu/Aristotle/meteorology .mb.txt*.
9. Tyre was an ancient city in Lebanon, roughly 25 miles north of Acre.
10. Lest Ptolemy get all the attention, it's worth noting that Eratosthenes very nearly calculated the circumference of the earth (he estimated it at what historians believe translated to a value between 39,700 kilometers and 46,600 kilometers; the accepted circumference is around 40,008 kilometers). Meanwhile, Marinus's maps were the first in the Roman Empire to mention China.
11. Ibn Khordadbeh authored the mid-ninth century *Book about Roads and Kingdoms*. Al-Masudi was known as the "Herodotus of the Arabs" because he combined scientific geography, history, linguistics, religion, and other areas of scholarship in

his writings. His biggest effort was a thirty-volume history of the world, *Muruj adh-Dhahab.*

12. Some historians have postulated that the *Book of the Wonders of India* was the basis for the anonymously written *Sinbad the Sailor.*

13. See Harald Lange, *Kilimanjaro.* Considering Abulfida's first plural, then singular, reference to the *Mountain* of the Moon, I'd agree with Lange's assessment that he was describing Mount Kenya.

14. From *Suma de Geographia Que Trata de Todas Las Partidas Y Provincias Del Mundo* (The Complete Geography which Deals with All Parts and Provinces of the Earth), published in Seville in 1519.

15. Halford John Mackinder, *The First Ascent of Mount Kenya* (Athens: Ohio University Press, 1991).

16. Hans Meyer, *Across East African Glaciers: An Account of the First Ascent of Kilimanjaro* (London: G. Philip & Son, 1891).

17. The Slug Map's official (and imaginative) title was "Sketch of a Map from 1°N. to 15°S. Latitude and from 23° to 43°E."

18. One historian suggests it appeared in Augustus Petermann's *Geographische Mitteilungen* (Gotha, 1856) under the wearying title, "Eines Theils von Ost- u. Central-Afrika mit Angabe der wahrscheinlichen Lage u. Ausdehnung des Sees von Uniamesi, nebst Bezeichnung der Grenzen u. Wohnsitze der verschiedenen Vlker sowie der Caravanen-Strassen nach dem Innern, 1856."

19. Joseph Thomson, *Through Masai Land: A Journey of Exploration Among the Snowclad Volcanic Mountains and Strange Tribes of Eastern Equatorial Africa* (London: Frank Cass & Co., 1885).

20. Thomson, *Through Masai Land.*

21. Actually, two members of Stanley's expedition—T. H. Parke and A. J. M. Jephson—reported seeing the Rwenzori peaks about a month before Stanley saw them.

22. Moore's route up the Mobuku Valley followed that taken, in part, by the modern Bujuku–Mubuku Circuit trekking route.

23. On the approach march, the Duke of Abruzzi's Rwenzoris expedition stretched for 5 miles across the plain.

24. This is the reason that mountain massifs like Stanley and Speke have individual summits with names like Alexandra and Vittorio Emanuele.

25. Italians, Scandinavians, Germans, and Britons seem to be the most common visitors to Rwenzori National Park.

26. Dar seems to have a crime problem equivalent to that of other East African cities. One Canadian I heard about decided to go jogging in Dar in the afternoon. The hotel staff urged him not to; he insisted. He returned to his hotel several hours later completely naked. Muggers had stolen his wallet, his shoes, and all his clothing. But, for a Canadian, East African temperatures are pretty innocuous.

27. On the airport-to-Nairobi bus, one of the most frightening experiences of my life, I was crammed so tightly between people, I couldn't even move. Then hands—I couldn't tell whose (we were jammed so tight)—rummaged through all my pockets.

28. I recommend the Speke Hotel, a colonial-era hotel that was recently refurbished and has a delightful patio restaurant/cafe. We paid about $US100 a night (guides predating the refurbishment quote $US65 or so per night).

29. At *kchucknorris@yahoo.com.*

30. In 1997, the tax was US$20 in all three countries and caught some travelers unaware and short-changed. Ask when you arrive in case the departure tax has been reinstated.

31. Cell or mobile phones are the order of the day here. Yet it's easier to call East Africa directly than many other developing regions of the world. Try calling a hotel before you fly and making a reservation. It's easier than you might think.

32. In the first edition I suggested "overtip[ping] wildly," which is a bad idea—apologies to all. In some areas, the locals are getting used to this and can get aggressive about tips. During my most recent visit to East Africa, tourism workers in certain areas—notably the Arusha-Moshi strip—were very aggressive. Several came to me

immediately after service demanding a tip (a big one), something I hadn't seen on previous trips.

33. In Nairobi, Kenya, you might hear hear Sheng, a combination of English, Swahili, and native languages.

34. And if you can believe this, the cooks stole our sole leg of lamb for themselves.

35. For Konyagi, see *www.tdl.co.tz/Products/Gin/konyagi.htm*.

36. See *www.uganda-embassy.jp/e/business/waragi.htm*. Not ironically, this beverage is described on the website for Uganda's embassy in Japan. The beverage is remarkably like sake.

37. In the first edition I suggested that *changaa* was derived from vegetable scraps, which I remain adamant about.

38. Some of the world's worst cared-for wine, not surprisingly, is found in remote locations in East Africa.

39. Throughout this book I've used, primarily, U.S. dollars when discussing prices. When the amounts of money to be spent are especially small (for things like buses), I've used the local currency *and* U.S. denominations, as you'll likely pay with local currency. Bigger expenses, like entire mountain treks, are described in terms of U.S. dollars.

40. During a 2005 visit to Kasese, the Stanbic Bank wouldn't accept US$1 bills. When we went overbudget on another trip, we relied heavily on Western Union (and my wife back home) for additional cash. There are offices throughout East Africa if you get stuck.

41. Among my friends we have a saying: "There is no change in East Africa." I've learned that if you really start making a fuss (e.g., throwing a mild, controlled fit), they'll find some change somewhere.

42. Aside from Kili, I don't know if mobile phones work from other summits. Email me if you've called from them (*mountaincam@yahoo.com*).

43. I was nearly thrown in Tanzanian jail for videotaping my wife going through the Kenya–Tanzania border crossing. The Tanzania government official confiscated my videotape, but after a loud, lengthy haranguing, allowed me to keep my video camera.

44. I shot ASA 400 film nearly every day that I was in the Rwenzoris. ASA 200 film just wasn't fast enough much of the time.

45. On crowded buses I've even had hands reach up inside my well-tucked-in T-shirt for my money belt.

46. Because of cashflow problems, I've often exchanged money on the street; it hasn't been a problem for me (so far), but caution is advised. The exchange rates I've experienced—notably in Uganda—are generally better than at banks! There will likely be times when you simply have no choice other than to buy cash on the black market. I had to do this multiple times in Uganda, and was always taken into a legitimate business where the owner would walk to his shop door, look around at the street (presumably for cops), go back to a desk, then pull out a wad of cash and make the exchange. The so-called black marketeers were always honest, straightforward, offered decent exchange rates, and were miles easier to deal with than the banks.

47. About three of my friends are currently sponsoring East Africans so they can attend university.

48. During one trip up Mount Kenya, a friend and I bought US$250 worth of food at a small supermarket in a town near the base of the mountain. We piled all our chosen items onto the counter, and the store manager began totaling the purchases on a calculator. He didn't know I was keeping track and casually rang up fifteen candy bars when there were ten, two boxes of biscuits when there was one, and so on. He also piled items in such a way that he rang several things up twice. Keep track of your purchases if you want a sane price.

49. Several people I spoke to who'd experienced this phenomenon on Kili said their climbs ended up being more expensive than those offered by other outfitters.

50. During a trip up the Burguret Route on Mount Kenya in 1997, my climbing partner and I hired a well-known tour operator in Chogoria to organize seven porters and a cook for us and to pay our park entrance fees. While my partner and I, the cook, and

all the porters traveled to Nanyuki and began hiking up the mountain, the operator was supposed to travel around to the park's Naro Moru headquarters and pay the entrance and camping fees for two climbers for 18 days, our cook for 18 days, and the porters for 10 days.

After coming down from the mountain, I went over the fee system with Senior Park Warden Bongo Woodley and discovered that this operator had written into the park records only that two nonresidents of Kenya would be on the mountain for 3 days and had paid the park only about US$120. He had not paid any of the porters and cook's entrance fees and had pocketed the rest of the about US$560 we had given him for the park fees. My climbing partner and I had therefore spent 15 days, and the porters and cook all of their time, in the park illegally. The warden could easily have had us arrested but fortunately decided that a better option would be to bill the tour operator for the rest of the money owed.

51. I once did Kili with a Chicago man who'd paid US$2,500 for the same exact trip I paid US$600 for in Moshi.

52. This US$90–100 fee for multiple-entry visas is double what it was eight years ago, so expect commensurate rises in fees in the future.

53. In 2005, visas bought on arrival in Tanzania and Uganda were the same price as those bought at home.

54. Having been denied entry into Tahiti after a 10-hour flight once (Australia was protesting French nuclear testing in the South Pacific and American news media didn't cover it), I can't stress enough the importance of contacting East African embassies before you get on a plane.

55. I've met dozens of local people in East Africa who've had relatives die from malaria.

56. Despite the overwhelming Western aversion to any kind of medical treatment in East Africa, local healthcare can be very valuable. I came back from one East African trip severely ill, and no doctor at home could figure out what I had—it eventually went away. On another trip I got dysentery, and within a few minutes a Moshi technician had examined a stool sample and identified the bug I had. I was cured within hours.

57. I've always relied on a couple of drops of chlorine and a water purification tablet per liter when taking water from streams on Kili and Mount Kenya.

58. Arusha National Park literature doesn't mention the presence of hyenas. However, after I found the prints, which looked like giant dog prints, then quizzed one of the gun-toting park naturalists about them, he conceded they were hyena prints.

59. On my first trip up one Kili route I photographed what could only have been serval prints—right in the middle of the path.

60. During 15 days spent in the Rwenzoris, the most we saw were a few leopard tracks.

61. In a three-week trip through the range we saw several pairs of Rwenzori ducks.

62. As with safari-related deaths, East African officials are loathe to report or even mention them.

63. In 1999, one man died after falling from a rock rib near Barafu Hut while he was going to the toilet.

64. In nearly every situation, you give most of your gear (in a bag or big pack) to a porter, who carries it during the day. Each night, that bag is delivered to you so you can use the things in it, then in the morning, when you're ready to go, the porter picks it up from you and carries it again. A day pack, with things you'll want during the day's travel (sunglasses, a snack, camera, etc.), is highly recommended.

65. The list of outfitters is brief because researching outfitters should be done by the prospective client, regardless of the recommendations in *all* guidebooks. I've heard terrible stories about guidebook authors demanding free trips from *many* outfitters on Kili; if they don't get what they want, they go to another firm. Any list of outfitters is thus skewed. The companies I've had recommended to me (or that I've used, as listed) were recommended without the recommendees knowing I was putting this book together.

In 2005, a reputable operator told me of one guidebook publisher's authors demanding free ascents of Kili in return for a positive write-up in a forthcoming book. It is one of the biggest publishers on earth, and the story was a frightening tale. For the record, all my trips on East Africa's mountains were paid for at the rates any person can expect, with the exception of several nights' accommodation (visiting old friends) at the Zara Tanzania Adventures place in Moshi. And yes, I highly recommend Zara, have heard dozens of great reports from customers, and was not paid to recommend the company. I was not paid to recommend anyone or anything in this book.

66. And, to tell the truth, I've never, ever received a written response from KINAPA officials by mail, nor have I ever gotten through by phone, despite dozens of attempts!

67. I strongly encourage requesting female porters.

68. In February 2005, RMS employed seventy-four guides and "hundreds" of porters and guides from Nyakalengija.

69. I used a pair of Crocs on my last East Africa trip and hiked nearly to Meru's summit in them and they worked well. I wasn't paid to endorse the brand here, though.

70. A travel professional associated with a big airline told me they regularly "bump" luggage for other items, like medical supplies and blood, to later flights because the latter are much bigger money earners; an East African outfitter confirmed this story by relating the woes of many trekkers who've had footwear delayed.

71. In a customer survey quoted by Clyde Soles in *Rock & Ice Gear*, "8 percent felt their bags were much warmer than rated, 18 percent said they were somewhat warmer, 47 percent said the ratings were about right, 19 percent thought the bags were slightly overrated, and 8 percent considered the bags significantly colder than the ratings stated."

72. Sleeping in the huts is definitely a colder experience than sleeping in a tent, so take that into consideration if you bring a tent.

73. At first, you might think I was joking about the gum boots. Then, 2 days into the trek, you'll realize I wasn't. Porters will run down to Nyakalengija and back to bring you a pair when this occurs. I suggest you tip them well, or better yet, get used to gum boots early on.

74. The food has gotten much better in recent years.

75. They used to use burlap bags on other East African mountains but the practice seems to have stopped.

76. I would argue that hiking up Meru is harder than hiking up any route on Kili because the distances between overnight stops seem farther and the steepness seems greater.

77. In 1997, I did two huge traverses across the Kili massif with a large group, then—acclimatized—took a week "off" for a safari. I came back a week later for a third traverse across the massif and nearly everyone in the group—same exact people who were supposedly acclimatized—got very sick from altitude; only two of us reached Uhuru Peak.

78. A group of English women I met after Kili in 2005 had started taking ginkgo three months before going to altitude and reported good experiences, although they had never been to altitude before.

79. Experts debate the pathophysiolgy of HACE and HAPE. Some think the brain swells mainly because of fluid leaked by vessels in the brain and because of high pressure. As for the lungs, some believe that swelling results from high pressure and the shutdown of parts of the lungs' blood vessels, while others believe it results from a leaking of fluid due to high pressure.

80. I was criticized on numerous websites after the first edition of this book for recommending against Diamox use, and I still do (as a preparatory regime). Everything I've seen suggests Diamox is not a prophylactic—that is, it's not designed to be taken to acclimatize your body before you get to the mountain and begin an ascent. Diamox is a drug for high-altitude emergencies—when you have a serious problem. Getting in shape is a much better and safer regimen.

81. The nicest bathroom in Tanzania is located in the gate lounge, downstairs at KIA.

82. Check out the Java House near Gate 14.

83. We had Rwenzori Mountaineering Services pick us up at our Kampala hotel. There were three of us, plus a huge amount of gear; we paid US$200 each.

84. I was quoted US$1,000, but some of the literature I've seen says it's about US$200 to fly.

85. In 1997, I rented a car to circumnavigate Mount Kenya. Even parked on a busy roadside, with police stationed across the road, several people tried to steal parts as we ate at a roadside cafe just a few feet from the car.

86. A story related to me was that until the mid-1990s, the national parks had entry fees in shillings (e.g., Tsh20 per person per day). With the explosion of tourism in the 1990s, the park administrators in several East African nations simply crossed out the shillings symbol and replaced it with a U.S. dollar symbol.

87. These KINAPA visitation numbers came from a master-planning effort undertaken in the mid-1990s, whose lead author (Bart Young) I later inadvertently met in Colorado. Interestingly, total park visitors in the early 1990s were 36,000 (because the porters and guides added to the total).

88. Mgongo wa Tembo translates as "back of the elephant."

89. Near this rutted area of the Momella Route, after Mgongo wa Tembo, we saw hyena prints.

90. My companions and I were in extremely good shape for this day's climb— acclimatized and very fit after 2 weeks in the Rwenzoris—and it took us 2 hours to reach the top. Most parties will require at least double that.

91. My companions and I managed it in 1.5 hours.

92. The modern-day cousins of the Masai, the Samburu, still live in areas north of Mount Kenya.

93. Although it's hard to tell where the village of Nyakalengija ends, as there are huts scattered all over the place along this road.

94. We were told by other trekkers to purify the water from the Nyabitaba Hut cistern, but two people on my trip drank it without any ill effects.

95. We went on to Bigo Hut to shorten the number of hiking days, so we could climb peaks.

96. Animals in the Rwenzoris are too timid to take a person. The skull was likely the result of an accident or rebel fighting.

97. I recommend scheduling at least 2 nights at Kitandara Hut—it's that pretty.

98. "The path is so steep that you have to climb with hands and feet, clutching the few creeping plants and shrubs that grow within reach," according to Filippo de Fillipi, chronicler of the duke's 1906 expedition.

99. Our guide on a 2005 trip, Peter Babughagle, climbed this face in the mid-1970s. He was astonished that there was no sign of the ex-glacier.

100. This modern version of Stanley's Normal Route skirts the Elena Glacier by using the rock ribs to gain the East Stanley Glacier.

101. Our two guides hiked Baker's South Ridge Route in gumboots.

102. There are numerous variations in the Chagga dialect. These Chagga translations came from a Marangu resident and Kili guide.

103. *Mafuta* is a general Swahili word that means any kind of oil, including kerosene, petrol, lubricants, and ointments, while "fuel" is any source of heat energy and is broader than any Swahili word could describe.

INDEX

ABOUT THE AUTHOR

Born and raised in Australia, Cameron M. Burns received a bachelor's degree in environmental design from the University of Colorado and is currently doing graduate work in environmental management at Harvard. He has authored, coauthored, edited, and contributed to more than twenty books and thousands of magazine, newspaper, and journal articles. He has won twenty-eight national and regional awards for his writing, including the North American Association of Travel Journalists' 2002 Book of the Year award. His 2004 *Postcards from the Trailer Park: The Secret Lives of Climbers* was a finalist in the 2004 Banff Mountain Book Festival, and *World Mountaineering*, which Burns coauthored, won the festival's Grand Prize in 1998. He has climbed throughout North and South America, Asia, Europe, Australia, and Africa and has guided peaks and taught rock climbing in central Colorado. He has also done first ascents of nearly sixty virgin desert towers in the American Southwest. In 1997, he wanted to go climb a mountain; his wife wanted to watch wildlife—this book represents the resulting compromise. In 2005—as part of a greenhouse-gas offset effort for a trip to the Rwenzoris—his family became the first family entity to join the Chicago Climate Exchange. Burns recently started leading Kilimanjaro treks for Alaska Mountain Guides and his own firm (*www.zo-mo.com*), which offsets every client's greenhouse-gas emissions related to traveling to and from East Africa and within East Africa.

Cam Burns (Photo © Benny Bach)

ABOUT THE UIAA/TABLE OF DIFFICULTIES

UIAA

INTERNATIONAL GRADE COMPARISON CHART

UIAA	USA	GB	F	D	AUS
V−	5.5	4a	5a	V	13
V	5.6		5b		
V+	5.7	4b		VI	14
VI−	5.8	4c	5c	VIIa	15
VI	5.9	5a	6a	VIIb	16
VI+	5.10a		6a+	VIIc	
VII−	5.10b	5b	6b	VIIIa	17
VII	5.10c		6b+	VIIIb	18
VII+	5.10d	5c	6c	VIIIc	19
VIII−	5.11a		6c+	IXa	20
VIII−	5.11b	6a			21
VIII	5.11c		7a	IXb	22
VIII	5.11d	6b			23
VIII+	5.12a		7a+	IXc	24
IX−	5.12b		7b	Xa	25
IX−	5.12c	6c	7b+		26
IX	5.12d	7a	7c	Xb	27
IX+	5.13a		7c+	Xc	28
X−	5.13b		8a	XIa	29
X−	5.13c	7b	8a+		30
X	5.13d		8b	XIb	31
X+	5.14a		8b+		32
XI−	5.14b		8c		33
XI−	5.14c		8c+		34
XI	5.14d		9a		

The UIAA's Mountaineering Commission is concerned with the development of good practice and considers this book to be a useful reference document. The Commission has a range of "Model Standards" and gives approval to the leader/instructor training schemes of a large number of mountaineering federations. For more information visit *www.uiaa.ch.*

The UIAA encourages the inclusion of information in guidebooks that helps visitors from overseas to understand the most important information about local access, grades, and emergency procedures. The UIAA also encourages climbers and mountaineers to share knowledge and views on issues such as safety, ethics, and good practice in mountain sports. The UIAA is not responsible for, and accepts no liability for, the technical content or accuracy of the information in this guidebook. Climbing, hill walking, and mountaineering are activities with a danger of personal injury and death. Participants should be aware of, understand, and accept these risks and be responsible for their own actions and involvement.

THE MOUNTAINEERS, founded in 1906, is a nonprofit outdoor activity and conservation club, whose mission is "to explore, study, preserve, and enjoy the natural beauty of the outdoors...." Based in Seattle, Washington, the club is now the third-largest such organization in the United States, with seven branches throughout Washington State.

The Mountaineers sponsors both classes and year-round outdoor activities in the Pacific Northwest, which include hiking, mountain climbing, ski-touring, snowshoeing, bicycling, camping, kayaking, nature study, sailing, and adventure travel. The club's conservation division supports environmental causes through educational activities, sponsoring legislation, and presenting informational programs.

All club activities are led by skilled, experienced instructors, who are dedicated to promoting safe and responsible enjoyment and preservation of the outdoors.

If you would like to participate in these organized outdoor activities or the club's programs, consider a membership in The Mountaineers. For information and an application, write or call The Mountaineers, Club Headquarters, 300 Third Avenue West, Seattle, WA 98119; 206-284-6310. You can also visit the club's website at *www.mountaineers.org* or contact The Mountaineers via email at *clubmail@mountaineers.org*.

The Mountaineers Books, an active, nonprofit publishing program of the club, produces guidebooks, instructional texts, historical works, natural history guides, and works on environmental conservation. All books produced by The Mountaineers Books fulfill the club's mission.

Send or call for our catalog of more than 500 outdoor titles:

The Mountaineers Books
1001 SW Klickitat Way, Suite 201
Seattle, WA 98134
800-553-4453
mbooks@mountaineersbooks.org
www.mountaineersbooks.org

The Mountaineers Books is proud to be a corporate sponsor of The No Trace Center for Outdoor Ethics, whose mission is to promote and inspire responsible outdoor recreation through education, research, and partnerships. The Leave No Trace program is focused specifically on human-powered (nonmotorized) recreation.

Leave No Trace strives to educate visitors about the nature of their recreational impacts, as well as offer techniques to prevent and minimize such impacts. Leave No Trace is best understood as an educational and ethical program, not as a set of rules and regulations.

For more information, visit *www.LNT.org*, or call 800-332-4100.